THE CLASSIC DEITIES IN BACON

A STUDY IN MYTHOLOGICAL SYMBOLISM
(1933)

> Whatever the mystery might be, Francis Bacon tried to discover it. Herein are many symbols and what Bacon did with them. Contents: Symbols of Scientific Speculation: Coelum, Cupid, Pan, Proserpine, Proteus, Atalanta, Daedalus, Prometheus, Sphinx; Symbols of Worldly Wisdom: Orpheus, Perseus, Typhon, Cyclops, Pan, Pandora, Ulysses, Narcissus, Styx, and more!

The Enthroned Sun-God and His Twelve Powers

Charles W. Lemmi

ISBN 0-7661-0096-0

Kessinger Publishing's
Rare Mystical Reprints

THOUSANDS OF SCARCE BOOKS
ON THESE AND OTHER SUBJECTS:

Freemasonry * Akashic * Alchemy * Alternative Health * Ancient Civilizations * Anthroposophy * Astrology * Astronomy * Aura * Bible Study * Cabalah * Cartomancy * Chakras * Clairvoyance * Comparative Religions * Divination * Druids * Eastern Thought * Egyptology * Esoterism * Essenes * Etheric * ESP * Gnosticism * Great White Brotherhood * Hermetics * Kabalah * Karma * Knights Templar * Kundalini * Magic * Meditation * Mediumship * Mesmerism * Metaphysics * Mithraism * Mystery Schools * Mysticism * Mythology * Numerology * Occultism * Palmistry * Pantheism * Parapsychology * Philosophy * Prosperity * Psychokinesis * Psychology * Pyramids * Qabalah * Reincarnation * Rosicrucian * Sacred Geometry * Secret Rituals * Secret Societies * Spiritism * Symbolism * Tarot * Telepathy * Theosophy * Transcendentalism * Upanishads * Vedanta * Wisdom * Yoga * *Plus Much More!*

DOWNLOAD A FREE CATALOG AT:

www.kessinger.net

OR EMAIL US AT:

books@kessinger.net

The Classic Deities in Bacon
A Study in Mythological Symbolism

BY

CHARLES W. LEMMI, M. A.
Associate Professor of French and Italian at Goucher College

———

BALTIMORE
THE JOHNS HOPKINS PRESS
1933

COPYRIGHT 1933, THE JOHNS HOPKINS PRESS

PRINTED IN THE UNITED STATES OF AMERICA
BY J. H. FURST COMPANY, BALTIMORE, MARYLAND

TO THE MEMORY OF MY KIND AND INSPIRING MASTER

EDWIN GREENLAW

THIS ESSAY IS REVERENTLY DEDICATED

PREFACE

The following essay was written at the suggestion of Edwin Greenlaw, and if there is anything good in it the credit is chiefly due to him. Sceptical of Bacon's reputed originality as an interpreter of classical myths, Professor Greenlaw asked me to investigate, and the discussions which followed made the task a delight to me from beginning to end. It was his desire that I should undertake other inquiries of a similar nature, and I had hoped to dedicate to him something more ambitious than a monograph. I still hope to do so; but much remains to be done before I can adequately accomplish my purpose, and I have decided to publish without further delay what will perhaps re-appear in a more considerable work. In the meanwhile it is well that my views should be subjected to general criticism, for they are not those usually accepted. If they are correct, Bacon was heavily indebted to the mythographer Natalis Comes, not a little to the alchemists, and in a lesser degree to the Neo-Platonists, to Macrobius, and to others besides. Nor is this all. Notably in the case of the alchemists, the source of his exegesis points to that of the doctrines involved, and, if my conclusions are well founded, throws new light upon his scientific thought. I do not wish to imply that Bacon garnered interpretations and ideas uncritically. He selected those which he judged to be vehicles of truth. Indeed, every aspect of his mind and character is curiously illuminated by his treatment of classical mythology, and this essay is a study not only of the mythographer but also of the philosopher and the man.

I owe my warmest thanks to Professors Kemp Malone and Raymond D. Havens of the Johns Hopkins University for reading and criticizing the manuscript of this essay. Professor Charles W. E. Miller of the same university has given me of his learning and his time with boundless generosity. Dr. R. H. Heffner has greatly helped me through his editorial experience. To President David A. Robertson of Goucher College I owe the heartening encouragement which never fails any member of his faculty; to my colleagues Professors Alice F. Braunlich and Herman L Ebeling, kind and invaluable assistance of which I have availed myself not only on this occasion but a thousand times besides. Professor Ernest P. Kuhl is the same magician as of old to fire me with fresh enthusiasm. I should certainly be ungrateful if I brought my acknowledgments to a close at this point, for librarians and their staffs have been helpful courtesy itself. I owe my special thanks to Miss E. W. Falley of Goucher College and those who so ably assist her; to Dr. John French, Miss F. C. Thies, and Miss M. G. Thuman of the Johns Hopkins University Library; to Dr. L. H. Dielman, Mr. S. E. Lafferty, Mr. H. C. Kaufmann, and Mr. H. Fickus of the Peabody Public Library; to Dr. Frederick Harrison of the Library of Congress; to Mr. R. H. Haynes of Harvard College Library. I am greatly indebted, too, to Mrs. J. M. S. Waller, who has turned my scrawls into attractive typewritten sheets with a skill, judgment, and patience beyond all praise.

CHARLES W. LEMMI.

Goucher College.

CONTENTS

	PAGE
INTRODUCTION	1

PART I

SYMBOLS OF SCIENTIFIC SPECULATION	46
Cœlum	49
Cupid	55
Pan	61
Proserpine	74
Proteus	91
Deucalion, Ixion, and Ericthonius	98
Atalanta	104
Dædalus and Icarus	109
Æsculapius	118
Atlas and Scylla	122
Eolus and Hylas	124
Prometheus	128
Sphinx	141

PART II

SYMBOLS OF WORLDLY WISDOM	151
Orpheus	152
Perseus, Achelous, Diomedes, and Typhon	156
Metis, The Cyclops, Pan's Crook, and Pandora's Box	164
The Sister of The Giants, The Crown of Nemesis, and The Preference of Ulysses	173
Juno's Suitor, Endymion, Narcissus, and Styx	178
Actæon and Pentheus, Midas, Iambe, and Cassandra	187
Tithonus, Memnon, Silenus, and The Satyrs	192
The Sirens, Dionysus, and Nemesis	196
BIBLIOGRAPHY	215
INDEX	223

INTRODUCTION

When Francis Bacon wrote *De sapientia veterum* he once again approved himself an artist, for he transformed into an original thing of beauty a common and by no means artistic type of book. Treatises on classical mythology had a wide circulation during the Renaissance, and all profess to discover in the stories of the gods and goddesses the wisdom of the ancients. Few have any pretensions to literary excellence; they are student's companions or encyclopædias. Yet they make pleasant reading in their quaint way, and he who turns their yellowing pages gets many a glimpse of the thoughts, beliefs, and feelings of a far distant past.

It was in Italy and in the sixteenth century that the Renaissance produced the most widely known works on the classic deities. In 1548 appeared Giraldi's *Historia de diis gentium*, in 1551 Natale Conti's *Mythologiæ*, in 1556 Cartari's *Imagini degli dei degli antichi*. All ran through numerous editions before 1600. These books largely superseded Boccaccio's famous and in influential *De genealogiis deorum*, but they were far from causing it to be forgotten. Betussi's Italian translation, first published in 1547, was re-printed ten times in the next hundred years. Giraldi's history of the gods, also known as *De deis gentium libri sive syntagmata XVII*, is a thoroughgoing account of the deities, supported by copious references; but it gives relatively little space to interpretation. The purpose of Cartari's book is to describe and explain images of the gods,—statues, bas-reliefs, medals, coins, etc. It puts us in mind of Pausanias who, in fact, is very frequently cited. Everything described is interpreted, the names of Boccaccio, Macrobius, Servius, Capella, and indeed the whole gamut of mythographers recurring continually. The 1614 edition is enlarged with chapters on the Egyptian myths, which are interpreted according to Plutarch and to Giovanni Pierio Valeriano's *Hieroglyphica*, published at Basle in 1556. This edition is also illustrated, and we find many of these same engravings in late editions of Conti's *Mythologiæ*, a book so important as to deserve separate notice.

The Venetian humanist Natale Conti might have lived and died a translator, a not inelegant versifier in Greek and Latin, and a fair historian of his times;[1] but when he published his *Mythologiæ, sive explicationum fabularum,* he achieved something like a European reputation.[2] The book was published again in 1567; then, considerably enlarged, in 1581, both at Venice and at Frankfort. In 1583 came a Paris edition; the next year, another at Frankfort. In 1588 appeared a second edition at Paris; in 1596 there was another; in 1602 one was printed at Lyons, in 1605 still another at Paris. In 1616 and again in 1637 the treatise was published at Padua; in 1669 a Hanover edition came out. Meanwhile, in 1599, a French translation had appeared. It was re-published in 1604, 1607, 1611, 1612 and 1627. The reason is not far to seek. In the 1581 edition, with which the great popularity of this work began, the *Mythologiæ* is fully as learned as any of its competitors, pleasanter to read, and incomparably easier to use as a reference-book. Furthermore, it systematically interprets every myth it relates according to a multitude of authorities. The compact octavo of over seven hundred pages is provided with a list of authorities, an excellent index, and synopses of the interpretations divided into ethical and physical. In a general introduction, it gives an interesting account of rites, sacrifices, victims, lustrations, hymns, and prayers. The following chapters are preceded by pleasantly edifying disquisitions. A general conclusion sums up the teachings to be derived from the myths.

Addressing Giovan Battista Campeggi, Bishop of Majorca, to whom the book is dedicated, Conti sets forth his purpose, happily imparting a Ciceronian spaciousness to a syntax not too difficult for less accomplished readers:

Cum tantam esse perspicio cognitionis antiquarum fabularum utilitatem, Illustriss, atque optime Io. Baptista Campeggi, quas poetæ, veteresque sapientes suis scriptis inseruerunt, quantam nullo orationis genere complecti possem; admirabile quiddam profecto mihi videri solet, cur nullus ex antiquis scriptoribus ad hanc usque diem universam insignium fabularum explicationem susceperit. Atque id eo magis, quod universa philosophiæ præcepta sub his ipsis fabulis antiquitus continebantur: quippe cum non ita multis annis ante Aristotelis, et Platonis, et cæterorum philosophorum tempora, omnia philosophiæ dogmata non aperte sed obscure, sub quibusdam integumentis, traderentur.[3]

---

[1] Cf. Tiraboschi, *Storia della letteratura italiana,* VII. 3. 18.

[2] Cf. F. L. Schoell, *Mythologistes italiens et poètes élisabéthains,* in *Revue de littérature comparée,* 1924, fasc. 1.

[3] I. 1. 1.

Conti's purpose in writing his book, then, is to interpret the myths, to restore to them the recondite meanings which the ancients attached to them. It was from Egypt, continues our author, that the Greeks brought home the art of concealing philosophical doctrines from the multitude by embodying them in allegories which only the adept could understand. As time went on, however, these doctrines came to be generally known; then the myths, their original purpose forgotten, fell into disrepute with the cultured. But in the meanwhile they had become the religious beliefs of the vulgar. No wonder, therefore, that they were severely judged by the wise and good Fathers of the Church. Properly understood, however, the myths are of the greatest value, and indeed indispensable to whoever desires more than a superficial acquaintance with the poets. They explain the mysteries of nature and the loftiest conceptions of philosophy; they deter men from doing evil, and guide them and encourage them in the paths of virtue. Some, indeed, devised by foolish persons, do not teach profitable lessons; these will be passed by in silence. It is only the others that our mythographer has striven, with the aid of God, to elucidate.

It will be noticed that Conti is tender of religion and morality. He continues to be so in a notable manner throughout his treatise; and indeed we understand his feelings perfectly. The slightest possibility of his being supposed to regard Jove as a rival to Jehovah makes him almost forget the wisdom of the ancients and assume the tone of the Fathers. Thus in Book I, having given us a preliminary account of the pagan deities, he devotes the next chapter to proving that they, and especially Jupiter, were mere mortals. In the chapter which follows, he seeks to explain how it happened that immortality was ascribed to the gods. Jupiter, he tells us, was a powerful and ambitious prince who so imposed on the credulity of the multitude that after his death they came to regard him as a divine emanation, an embodiment of God's providence, or even as God himself. In the same way Neptune was identified with God's immanence in the waters, Juno with His presence in the air, etc. But all were mere men, and it was absurd to identify them with eternal things. Indeed, it is entirely unfitting that the splendors of Divine Providence should be contaminated with the names of mortals.[4] At this point we remember the fulminations of the Council of Trent against poets who dared to call God and His Saints by the names of heathen deities, and we understand why Conti carefully refrains from such dangerous interpretations as those of Legouais. The philosophers, concludes our author, seeing that the people could understand divine and abstruse things only in terms of earthly and material ones, sought to clothe some of their wisdom in fables. Here Conti seems inconsistent, for he has told us that the purpose of the myths was to conceal philosophic arcana from the multitude. He probably has in mind the Stoics; and after all is not really in contradiction with himself, for he has doubtless read in Strabo etc. that kings employed the poets and philosophers to teach their subjects morals. In any case, he rather neatly subscribes to patristic exegesis without sacrificing his theory that the myths are founts of wisdom.

Book II, which begins with the story of Jupiter, is full of Conti's pious determination to keep out of trouble. The introductory essay dwells emphatically and at length on the proposition that there can be but one God, and the account of Jove which follows is far from being a dispassionate rehearsal of what classic authors have to say on the subject. Our mythographer begins by saying that there were several Jupiters, that all were born on earth, that the ancients called all kings Joves. The dethronement and other misfortunes of Saturn provoke the narrator to stern reflections on the ruthlessness of ambitious men. Conti refuses to believe that Neptune and Pluto were given the sea and Hades as their portions, and, anticipating his commentary, agrees with Lactantius that they were subordinate princes who received vast domains by the western ocean and in the East respectively. For Jove was a great conqueror and law-giver, though so shamefully incontinent that no man's wife was safe from him. By some he was called the son of Æther and Day, who emerged in splendor from enveloping darkness. Aye, well may he have been said to have dwelt in darkness if he did not know that he owed all he had to God! All this patristic fervor in the narrative does not prevent Conti from repeating Stoic and other philosophic explanations in the commentary; but he makes it clear that these do not have his approval, and associates the conception of Jove as æther with the heresies of those who see

---

[4] I. 9. 14.

in the universe a fortuitous concourse of atoms: "those impure men whose nefarious ideas would subvert law, both human and divine!" Of course, what offends him in the Stoic view of Jove is the Stoic view of God, the two names being, despite his good intions, almost synonyms in his mind.

Saving Cupid and Venus, who again provoke him to dutiful wrath, Conti discusses the remaining deities in a much less patristic mood, and takes kindly enough to physical and other interpretations. Indeed, in his concluding essay, he declares that all the wisdom of the Greek philosophers was derived from the myths:

> For all that Aristotle, and divine, Plato before him, explained concerning nature's laws; all that Empedocles, or Parmenides, or Pythagoras brought to light; all, indeed, that other philosophers discovered about nature or morals: all this, it clearly appears, the ancient myth-makers had embodied in their fables, whence afterwards each derived wisdom according to his ability and his strength.[5]

In its general sense, this remarkable view was more or less conventional, and may in fact be regarded as fundamental to the theory of mythological symbolism; but Conti expresses it with unusual explicitness, and indeed carries it to its extreme consequence. At the end of his essay he states it again, and supports it with arguments:

> I maintain that such were the doctrines contained in the fables of the ancients, and that those who were afterwards called philosophers learned the beginnings of philosophy from these same fables. In my opinion, philosophy was nothing but the sense of these fables stripped of its fabulous wrappings. Since all philosophy was first brought to Greece from Egypt, what prevents our believing that the Greeks transmitted it from generation to generation in the form of myths? For indeed, when, in those early days, the Egyptian priests first began to speculate, they strove to keep their knowledge of sacred things to themselves, lest it should fall into the hands of the multitude; and to this end they invented signs, known as hieroglyphics, by means of which philosophical truths and sacred doctrines might be secretly expressed. In fact *hiera* means sacred things, and *glypho* means I carve. As for the Greek fables, this indeed is

---

[5] X. 671 Nam illa quae Aristoteles, et, ante illum, divinus Plato, de naturae opificio tradiderunt; quaeque vel Empedocles, vel Parmenides, vel Pythagoras, in medium protulerunt, aliique philosophi, aut quae de moribus singulorum, illa omnia fuisse patuit antiquarum fabularum artificum dogmata, e quibus tantum quisque hauserit quantum sui ingenii ferret facultas.

wonderful about them, that some admit of historical, physical, and ethical interpretation; others may be interpreted only physically, or only morally.⁶

Conti's defense of mythological symbolism is in some respects even more striking than Boccaccio's, and it may be safely asserted that it had a diffusion hardly less extensive. Professor Schoell is not mistaken when he says that in France and England, for example, "Natalis Comes" was the King of mythographers for almost a century.⁷

That much in the book I have been discussing reflects the author's fear of the Inquisition seems to me obvious; but it would certainly be rash to regard his entire exegetical apparatus as a piece of timorous hypocrisy. Having taken all necessary precautions, Conti ultimately stands by a conception of the myths which is not that professed by the Fathers. His gods are philosophical symbols, not diabolical travesties of sacred beings or, save where Jove is concerned, confused memories of bad kings. The authorities he cites most often are classic writers. We are justified in suspecting, at least, that the explanations of such men as Pausanias, Plutarch, Pliny, Cornutus, and Macrobius, appear to him to be worthy of much respect. The question is an interesting one because of its general bearing. Tasso allegorized his poem because he was afraid; but in all probability he wrote his *Messaggiero* because he really believed in the allegorizing of Marsilio Ficino. Indeed, he judged it wise to defend himself with a significant for-

---

⁶ *Ibid.*, 673; Ego sane, cum ista fuerint dogmata sub fabulis antiquorum contenta, illos qui postea philosophi nominati sunt philosophandi initia ab ipsis fabulis cepisse contenderim: neque aliud fuisse philosophiam quam fabularum sensa ab involucris exuvisque fabularum explicata. Nam cum ab Aegyptiis universa prope philosophia in Græciam primum fuisset deportata, quid prohibet illam per fabulas apud Græcos fuisse per manus traditam? Cum enim investigare philosophiam a principio Aegyptii sacerdotes priscis illis temporibus cæpissent, rerumque sacrarum cognitionem illi niterentur apud se retinere, ne traderetur in vulgus: dederunt operam ut aliquas notas invenirent, sub quibus sapientiæ præcepta, et arcana mysteria sacrorum continerentur, quas hieroglyphicas nominarunt. Sunt enim hiera sacra, at glypho sculpo. Illud vero admirabile fuit in Græcorum, fabulis, quod earum nonnullæ historicam, et physicam, et ethicam narrationem admittant, cum aliæ naturalem tantum, aliæ moralem solam contineant.

⁷ Cf. Bush, *Mythology and The Renaissance Tradition in English Poetry*, 31, 69, 89, 100, 241, 321. etc.

mula. Addressing Vincenzo Gonzaga, to whom the little book was dedicated, he assured him that while he philosophized as a Platonist he believed as a Christian. Again, nobody would accuse Giordano Bruno of being either timorous or retrogressive; yet, in *Lo spaccio della Bestia Trionfante* he interprets the gods much as the Stoics did. In the Italy which produced Fracastoro's *Naugerius,* some doubtless professed the allegorical theory of mythology without conviction and as a matter of expediency;[8] but we have no reason to believe that they constituted the majority. Still less are we justified in supposing that the rest of western Europe held emancipated views.

A shrewder critic than Michel Eyquem de Montaigne it would be hard to find; and in fact he does not believe that Homer's works are bottomless wells of wisdom:

Est il possible que Homère aye voulu dire tout ce qu'on luy faict dire: et qu'il se soit presté à tant et si diverses figures, que les théologiens, législateurs, capitaines, philosophes, toute sorte de gents qui traictent sciences, pour diversement et contrairement qu'ils les traictent, s'appuyent de luy, s'en rapportent à luy? maître général à touts offices, ouvrages, et artisans; général conseiller à toutes entreprises: quiconque a eu besoing d'oracles et de predictions, en y a trouvé pour son faict. Un personnage sçavant, et de mes amis, c'est merveille quels rencontres et combien admirables il y faict naistre, en faveur de nostre religion; et ne se peult ayséement despartir de cette opinion, que ce ne soit le desseing d'Homère; si luy est cet aucteur aussi familier qu' à homme de nostre siècle: et ce qu'il treuve en faveur de la nostre, plusieurs anciennement l'avoient trouvé en faveur des leurs.[9]

Here is a common sense not easily to be imposed upon; but what is the significance of this passage in regard to current opinion in Montaigne's day? Obviously, he does not refer to the ancients alone, but rather citicizes a belief which he finds held by those around him. He does not mention his learned friend as an eccentric; he brings him forward as an example. Nor is our author himself altogether in advance of his times.

In his essay on grief, Montaigne, speaking of the numbness and rigidity produced by extreme anguish, remarks:

---

[8] Cf. Toffanin, *Il Cinquecento,* 514; and Belloni, *Il poema epico e mitologico,* 357 seq.

[9] *Essais,* II. 12 (*Apologie de Raimond Sebond*).

> Voilà pourquoy les poètes feignent cette misérable mère
> Niobe, ayant perdu premièrement sept fils, et puis de
> suite autant de filles, surchargée de pertes, avoir
> esté en fin transmeue en rochier,
> > Diriguisse malis,
> pour exprimer cette morne, muette et sourde stupidité
> qui nous trainsit lorsque les accidents nous accablent,
> surpassants nostre portée.[10]

This is mythological exegesis, neither more nor less. The interpretation is that given by Cicero,[11] to whom Montaigne is indebted elsewhere in the essay and whose authority he probably accepts here. The shrewd Frenchman thinks vigorously, yet we find a passage in his book which says:

> Quand je me treuve désgousté de l'*Axioche* de Platon, comme d'un ouvrage sans force, en égard à un tel aucteur, mon iugement ne s'en croit pas: il n'est pas si sot de s'opposer à l'auctorité de tant d'aultres fameux iugements anciens, qu'il tient de ses régents et maistres, et avecques lesquels il est plus tost content de faillir; il s'en prend à soy, et se condamne, ou de s'arrester à l'escorce, ne pouvant pénétrer iusques au fonds, ou de regarder la chose par quelque fauls lustre. Il se contente de se garantir seulement du trouble et du désréglement: quant à sa foiblesse, il la recognoist, et advoue volontiers. Il pense donner iuste interprétation aux apparences que sa conception luy présente; mais elles sont imbécilles et imparfaictes. La pluspart des fables d'Esope ont plusieurs sens et intelligences: ceulx qui les mythologisent, en choisissent quelque visage qui quadre bien à la fable; mais pour la pluspart, ce n'est que le premier visage, et superficiel; il y en a d'aultres plus vifs, plus essentiels et plus internes, auxquels ils n'ont sçeu pénétrer.[12]

How mediæval a flavor have Montaigne's remarks about Æsop; how familiar is the readiness with which, despite his independence of judgment, he defers to the authority of those "fameux iugements anciens." Mythological symbolism in the Renaissance is sometimes spoken of as an aspect of the lingering Middle Ages, and in a measure it was. The reverence that in those earlier times had knelt at the feet of Aristotle now knelt at those of Plato; from the same portentous Bible of many meanings the people were instructed in the mysteries of their faith. Nor had the old mythographers and commentators been forgotten at the boundary-line between the centuries. Indeed, no such boundary-line existed.

---

[10] *Op. cit.*, I. 2.
[11] *Tusculanarum quaestionum*, III. 26.

Many a Renaissance writer cites Fulgentius or appropriates his moralizing interpretations.[13] To him is chiefly to be traced the symbolical Æneas whom we encounter in such embodiments as Ariosto's Ruggero [14] and Trissino's Narses.[15] Influential too was Pierre Berçuire, alias Petrus Berchorius. His version of the *Metamorphoses,* printed in 1484, 1493, and 1509,[16] scattered down the years a Christian exegesis [17] largely derived from Legouais' *Ovide moralisé.*[18] Rabelais dubbed him a "croque lardon" for his pains,[19] but others thought better of his commentary, which reached England and Spain.[20] A similar commentary, for which its author, Giovanni dei Buonsignori, was probably indebted to Dante's friend, Giovanni del Virgilio,[21] also reached England,[22] and served the purposes of various Italian translators of Ovid. Nor must we forget Nicholas Trivet, whose *In librum Boethii de Consolatione Philosophiæ* Henryson used; nor Bishop Federigo Frezzi;[23] nor, for that matter, Bishop Isidore of Seville. To these men is at least partly due the predicatorial tone which distinguishes much Renaissance exegesis from that of the classic age. There were others who had been less bent on edification: the Troubadours,[24] the twelfth-century Greek Euhemerist Tzetzes, Jean de Meun, Petrarch, and above all, Boccaccio.

Boccaccio's *De genealogiis Deorum* proved a tower of strength to the allegorical theory of poetry, and not only in the fourteenth

---

[13] Cf. Bush, *op. cit.*, 127, 233, 238, etc.

[14] Cf. Toffanin, *op. cit.*, 197; Rajna, *Le fonti dell 'Orlando Furioso*, 605.

[15] Cf. *L'Italia liberta dai Goti*, XXIV.

[16] Cf. *Œuvres de Francois Rabelais*, ed. by Lefranc, notes on Prologue.

[17] Cf. Morley, *English Writers*, III. 374.

[18] Cf. Petit de Julleville, *Histoire de la Langue et de la Littérature française*, I. 248, seq.

[19] *Gargantua et Pantagruel*, prologue.

[20] Cf. Bush, *op. cit.*, 33, 49, 67; Schevill, *Ovid and The Renaissance in Spain*, 229.

[21] Cf. Bush, *op. cit.*, 18.

[22] Cf. Bush, *op. cit.*, 49.

[23] For the influence of Frezzi's *Quadriregio* on Ariosto, cf. Rajna, *Le fonti dell' Orlando Furioso*, 175 seq.

[24] Cf. Rutherford, *The Troubadours*, 110 seq.; Mott, *The System of Courtly Love*, 7, 57; Graf, *Roma nella memoria e nelle imaginazioni del Medio Evo*, II. 385.

century but long afterwards.[25] Its vehement defence of the gods may be heard again in Laurence de Premierfait, in Lydgate, in Hawes, in Douglas; its interpretations can be more or less accurately identified in many a Renaissance author. The first printed edition appeared in 1472, and before the end of the century was followed by four more in Italy and a compendium in Germany. In 1511 two more editions appeared, one in Italy and one in France; in 1532 one was printed at Basle. A French translation of the first thirteen books was published at Paris in 1498, and republished in 1531.[26] All this has been often said before. What perhaps has received less attention is the sources of Boccaccio's exegesis. These are chiefly the following:[27] Cicero, Horace, Mela, Pliny, Solinus, Lactantius Placidus, Apuleius, the *Asclepius,* Martianus Capella, Boethius, Macrobius, Servius, Isidore, Rhabanus Maurus, the *Vita Sanctorum Barlaam Eremitae et Josaphat Indiæ Regis,* Orosius, Fulgentius, probably the third Vatican Mythographer, the Fathers, the mysterious Theodontius, the information he received from his learned friend Paolo Perugino, from his boorish guest Leontius Pilatus, and perhaps from Petrarch's quondam teacher Barlaam. The list is interesting because it suggests what sources were available at the beginning of the Renaissance. We notice that a good many of Boccaccio's authorities are classic or at least late classic writers. Here was something to appeal not only to the mediæval man but also to the humanist. That Boccaccio sincerely believed the myths to be veiled statements of truth cannot, I think, be doubted. How much stronger would his conviction have been had he been able to read the many works which the humanists were to discover.

As we turn the pages of *De genealogiis Deorum* we come upon the ultimately Stoic interpretation of Jove as the life-giving fiery Æther, Juno as the air, Neptune as the sea, Pan as nature; and we notice Boccaccio's protest against the notion that Jove is God. We also find the ultimately Neo-Platonic view that the deities stand for aspects of the sun, and the conception, familiar to us in Plut-

---

[25] Cf. the excellent introduction to Professor Osgood's *Boccaccio on Poetry.*

[26] Cf. Wilkins, *The Chicago MS. of the Genealogia Deorum,* 5 seq.

[27] Cf. Hortis, *Studi sulle opere latine del Boccaccio,* especially the chapter entitled *Degli autori consultati dal Boccaccio.*

arch, that they are demons. The old scholar respectfully names his great authorities much as we name the great physicists who are at loggerheads over the nature of the universe today. Often he explains a myth historically, citing Euhemerus and Ennius. Here he is indebted to the Fathers, and especially to Lactantius. The Fathers did no small service to the cause of the allegorical theory of mythology. They not only strengthened belief in it by declaring that the myths were travesties of sacred history, but they transmitted to the Middle Ages a large body of classical exegesis which might otherwise have remained unknown. Thus in Eusebius we find, besides a good summary of the ancient religions, abundant information on the interpretations of Plutarch and Prophyry.[28] In Augustine we may read an equally thoroughgoing account of Varro's *Antiquitatum rerum humanarum et divinarum;* and we may well ask ourselves what impression was produced by such a passage as the following on an age which believed in the Trinity, in star-dwelling angels, and in scholastic psychology:

And certainly the same Varro, in the book concerning the select gods, affirms that there are three grades of soul in universal nature. One pervades all the living parts of the body, and has not sensation, but only the power of life,—that principle which penetrates into the bones, nails, and hair. By this principle in the world trees are nourished, and grow without being possessed of sensation, and live in a manner peculiar to themselves. The second grade of soul is that in which there is sensation. This principle penetrates into the eyes, ears, nostrils, mouth, and the organs of sensation. The third grade of soul is the highest and is called mind, where intelligence has its throne. This grade of soul no mortal creatures except man are possessed of. Now this part of the soul of the world, Varro says, is called God, and in us is called Génius. And the stones and earth in the world, which we see, and which are not pervaded by the power of sensation, are, as it were, the bones and nails of God. Again, the sun, moon, and stars, which we perceive, and by which He perceives, are His organs of perception. Moreover, the æther is His mind; and by the virtue which is in it, which penetrates into the stars, it also makes them gods; and because it penetrates through them into the earth, it makes it the goddess Tellus, whence again it enters and permeates the sea and ocean, making them the god Neptune.[29]

After so striking an exposition, Augustine hardly crushes the Roman Stoic by declaring that stones are no more gods than bones are men. But let us return to Boccaccio.

---

[28] *Preparatio evangelica*, III. 1-2; III. 8-11.
[29] *De civitate Dei*, VII. 23.

To the more acrid views set forth in patristic literature Boccaccio devotes little space. These views we shall encounter frequently in the days of Catholic reaction, of Huguenot fervor, and of Puritan harshness. We shall find them in Du Bartas;[30] and in late editions of Conti's *Mythologiæ* we shall find appended to the treatise a patristic *Libellus* from which Sandys will paraphrase many a passage in his commentary on the *Metamorphoses* of Ovid. Boccaccio did not believe that the myths were works of evil, though, like Natale Conti, he looked askance at the Stoic God. As Comparetti pointed out,[31] the deities were inextricably identified with the phraseology and the ideals of poetry. No amount of churchly denunciation could make them appear repulsive; and when the Renaissance brought its ever-increasing enthusiasm and veneration for classic antiquity the gods of Greece and Rome did not certainly stand revealed as base and contemptible devices of Satan. The old scholar of Certaldo prefers to cite the Euhemeristic explanations of the Fathers. Occasionally, too, he mentions the Sibylline Oracles. About these and other writings produced at Alexandria in the early centuries of the Christian era it may be well to say a few words.

In that strange hotbed of mysticism and passion, Alexandria, were written the earliest extant specimens of the Sibylline Oracles,[32] often quoted by Renaissance exegesists inclined to see Christian symbolism in the myths. Outwardly imitations of Greek oracular poems, these compositions are savage attacks on the gods, heaped curses on the heathen, prophecies of the ruin of the Empire and the triumph of the Messiah. In the later oracles, which belong to the second and third centuries A. D., Christ appears. They are means of propaganda as well as vents of impotent rage, and a chaotic Hebrew-Christian mythology is often made their mouthpiece. According to some scholars, the polemic between Christians and Gentiles is reflected in another collection of poems also; I mean the eighty-eight Orphic Hymns [33] with allusions to which we become so familiar in Renaissance mythographers. Whether or not these really beautiful poems were the result of religious conflict; whether or not we are to see in them Neo-Platonic or earlier Neo-Pytha-

---

[30] Cf. especially the *Eden*.
[31] *Vergil in The Middle Ages*, XI. 163.
[32] Cf. Roscher, *Lexikon der Mythologie*, 790-813.
[33] Cf. *Ibid.*, 1058-1207; Lobeck, *Aglaophamus*, III.

gorean symbolism; whether they date chiefly from the third and fourth centuries A. D., or, in part at least, from very early times: all these are still matters of controversy. The fact remains that these invocations and praises of the deities clearly suggest, in several cases, physical interpretations of the deities themselves, and they were understood as allegories during the Renaissance. Thus Pan is obviously an embodiment of the universe; and Hera is one of the air, for, says the hymn:

> With sounding blasts of wind, the swelling sea
> And rolling rivers roar when shook by thee.

In Adonis we recognize the sun:

> Adonis ever flourishing and bright,
> At stated periods doomed to set and rise
> With splendid lamp, the glory of the skies.

Regarded by the Renaissance as of great antiquity, the Orphic Hymns seemed to make it certain that the myths were allegories. But let us not depart from Alexandria before considering another type of exegesis which largely originated there and which was as widely known in the Middle Ages and the Renaissance as that of the Sibyls. I mean the symbolism of the alchemists.

The Hermetic art: the words conjure up fifteen centuries of smoky groping and delusion, and remind us that here also blind deference to a name and a doctrine obstructed the way. To the last the alchemists clung to the half-mystic "Smaragdine laws" which they professed to have received from Hermes:[34] that same Hermes Trismegistos—the Egyptian Thoth or Mercury—at whose feet Asclepius and his friends so reverently sat. To him they attributed their doctrine that the first step towards transmutation was reduction to ultimate matter; to him their belief that a divine spirit informed and perfected men and metals alike. They recited the mystic hymn in the *Divine Poemander*,[35] a dialogue similar to *Asclepius;* Zosimus, Stephanus, and other early alchemists frequently cite supposed Hermetic writings as emanating more or less directly from the sacred inventor of their art.[36] Professor Berthelot thinks it possible that the priests of Hermes practiced the metal-

---

[34] Cf. Redgrove, *Alchemy Ancient and Modern*, 40 seq.

[35] Cf. M. Berthelot in *La grande Encyclopedie, sub Alchimie;* also the same work under *Hermes.* Cf. Redgrove, *op. cit.*, 40.

[36] *Ibid.*

lurgy of gold in Egypt,[37] but he shows that the "Hermetic philosophers" were indebted to various sources. They owed much to what the *Timæus* has to say about ultimate matter and the transmutation of the elements;[38] and in attributing the creation of individual metals to individual stars they probably reflected Eastern influence, for the belief certainly originated in Chaldea.[39] It was of long standing in Greece too, however. Pindar attributes the existence of gold to the sun; a commentator, writing in the Alexandrine Period, assigns silver to the moon, lead to Saturn, copper to Venus, etc.; a scholiast on Homer, earlier than the Christian era, calls Mars the star of iron.[40] It was largely a matter of associating gold with the golden sun, silver with the silvery moon, and so-forth, and may have sprung up independently in more than one country. In the Smaragdine Tablets the sun is probably a symbol of the One, and the moon of ultimate matter.[41] Such theory might not have formed a system; but the secret manufacture of false gold at Alexandria brought it to a head. About the third century A. D., a fraudulent practice became a mystic and religious one, and the gods were given a new task.[42]

The Renaissance believed in alchemy just as the Middle Ages did, and in magic, witchcraft, invisible demons, dreams, and astrology.[43] It was not a sudden awakening from superstition and mysticism. It remained faithful to a large body of mediæval writings and traditions, and even in Italy its thought was predominantly mediæval for at least a hundred years. Indeed, however broadened by a new familiarity with the classic authors, the Renaissance discovered in them the real or supposed confirmation of many of its beliefs. How far the fifteenth century was from discarding the allegorical interpretation of the classics appeared towards the end of it in the proceedings and publications, so to speak, of the Platonic Academy. It is significant that these proceedings and publications were part of an attempt at rationalism. Says Pro-

---

[37] *Ibid.*

[38] Cf. M. Berthelot, *Introduction à l'etude de la Chimie*, préface, IX.

[39] *Ibid.*, II. 74.

[40] *Ibid.*, 77.

[41] Cf. Redgrove, *op. cit.*, 42.

[42] E. von Meyer, *History of Chemistry*, Chap. II.

[43] Cf. Monnier, *Le Quattrocento*, I. 258; Burckhardt, *The Civilisation of The Renaissance in Italy*, VI. 4. 511, etc.

fessor Villari, discussing the glorification of pagan antiquity which had marked the century:

> Presently, however, the need is felt of discovering a foundation for life which shall be not revealed but rational, and which shall explain both pagan and Christian virtue, and remove the too visible contradiction between the two. Then begins more or less original work; it is begun by the Neoplatonists and by the Academy which they founded at Florence.[44]

After reading some of the publications I have referred to, one feels that an even better statement of the case is that made by Symonds:

> To philosophize and humanize the religious sentiments that had become the property of monks and pardonmongers; to establish a concordat between the Paganism that entranced the world, and the Catholic faith whereof the world was not yet weary; to satisfy the new-born sense of a divine and hitherto unapprehended mystery in heaven and earth; to dignify with a semblance of truth the dreams of magic and astrology that passed for science,—all this the men of the Renaissance passionately craved.[45]

As everybody knows, the leader in this attempt to reconcile Christianity and paganism was Marsilio Ficino, about whom Professor Villari remarks:

> The Neo-Platonic allegories which Gemistus Pletho and the other Greeks brought among us are the only means he knows of reconciling the various elements.[46]

The Christian-Neo-Platonic movement at Florence was as ambitious and as fanciful as alchemy, and it dreamed with the poetic enthusiasm of youth. In a sense it was the reaction of a new generation against the dry philologizing of the older humanists, most of whom were by now dead.[47] As Monnier says:

> Hé! qu' importent les diphtongues, less orthographies, Scipion, Cesar! C'est du christianisme, du platonisme de l'aristotelisme qu' il s'agit. Laissons une bonne fois les pures fadaises pour les nobles problèmes, les hautes idées, les intérêts suprèmes d'un univers trenscendantal.[48]

Yes indeed, Aristotle also was in question, for while Ficino sought to reconcile Plato with Christianity, Pico della Mirandola strove to reconcile Aristotle with Plato, both with Christianity, and all three with all systems of philosophy whatsoever! Alberti, Politian,

---

[44] *Niccolò Machiavelli*, I. 173.
[45] *The Renaissance in Italy*, II. 324.
[46] *Op. cit.*, I. 185.
[47] Monnier, *op. cit.*, II. 27.
[48] *Ibid.*, 81.

Ficino, Landino, Benivieni, Pico, Lorenzo himself: who does not envy these enthusiasts for their triumphant sense of discovering new worlds? And how many they discovered in that mystic glow of Platonic sunshine! Before their wondering eyes the *Æneid* revealed itself as a noble allegory of the pilgrimage of the soul to the lofty region of Ideas and of the Good; the *Divine Comedy* did the same.[49] And what magic is there in enthusiasm that, blind as it is, it so often finds treasure? The fantastic notion that Dante was a complete and profound Neo-Platonist greatly contributed to his re-instatement in the favor of the cultured, and, added to a similar conviction as to Petrarch, had much to do with the revival of Italian literature, long neglected and despised by the Latinists.

The Christian-Neo-Platonic movement was an orgy of allegorizing, and it turned most of the pagan gods into Neo-Platonic symbols. Of this fact there is abundant proof in Ficino's *Sopra lo Amore*,[50] in his *De Christiana religione*,[51] in Landino's *Disputationes Camaldulenses*,[52] and in Pico's *Apologia*.[53] About the first of these works, Monnier remarks that:

Le *Livre d'Amour* de Marsile soumet le *Symposion* de Platon à la torture d'une telle exégèse que la pensée lumineuse du maître de l'Academie y devient méconnaissable.

Monnier sees the chief reason for such fantastic exegesis in the fact that these men were poets rather than philosophers, and in a measure he is doubtless right; but as one reads Ficino's book another reason grows increasingly apparent. Cavalcanti, Landino, Marsupini, and the others who in turn expound the speeches in the Platonic dialogue, not only approach that dialogue through the Neo-Platonists, but also through the preconceptions of largely mediæval minds. For them Dionysus the Areopagite is as unquestionable an authority as Plato himself. And they believe implicitly in astrology, and in angelic regulators of the stars; and they are not far from regarding their emotions and impulses as conscious

---

[49] C. Trabalza, *La Critica letteraria*, 63.

[50] Monnier, *op. cit.*, II. 125; Villari, *op. cit.*, I. 180 seq.

[51] *Ibid.*, 107 seq.

[52] *Ibid.*, 126; Villari, *op. cit.*, I. 179; but see especially M. Y. Hughes, *Virgilian Allegory in The Faerie Queene*, in *P.M.L.A.* for September, 1929.

[53] Monnier, II. 125.

spirits. We are at once reminded of Dante's *Vita nuova* by this book which Ficino first wrote in Latin and then, "that the health-giving manna received by Diotima from heaven might be accessible to all" translated into most noble Italian. Indeed, towards the end of the book,[54] Ficino plainly acknowledges the nature of his Platonism, for he declares that all said by the speakers was anticipated by Dante's friend, Guido Cavalcanti. So little were these men able to free themselves from their mediæval thinking.

Astrology, patristic doctrine, and Platonism cooperate in reinstating the gods in heaven. Tommaso Benci is expounding the Platonic daemons:

> And the good ones, who watch over us, are by Dionysius the Areopagite called Angels, who rule over this lower world: which is not in contradiction with Plato's teaching. We may also, after the manner of Dionysius, call by the name of Angels, ministers of God, those spirits whom Plato calls gods, and souls of the spheres and of the stars. This is not contrary to Plato's doctrine: for it is clear that in the tenth book of his *Laws* he does not enclose those souls in the bodies of the spheres, as he encloses in their bodies the souls of terrestrial beings; but he declares them to be endowed with such excellence by supreme God, that they may at one and the same time enjoy Him and, without any effort or discomfort—such is the will of the Father—govern and move the spheres of the Universe; and in so doing, govern the things of earth. It follows, then, that between Plato and Dionysius there is a difference of words rather than of meaning.[55]

After this it is quite easy to understand the close of Carlo Marsupini's oration on the speeches of Agathon:

> Agathon is of the opinion that the arts were given to men, through Love, by the gods. Thus the art of ruling was bestowed by Jove; those of shooting, divining and healing, by Apollo; that of forging metals by Vulcan; the art of weaving, by Minerva; music by the Muses. Indeed, twelve deities have charge of the twelve signs of the zodiac: Pallas of the Ram, Venus of the Bull, Apollo of the Twins, Mercury of Cancer, Jove of Leo, Ceres of Virgo, Vulcan of Libra, Mars of Scorpio, Diana of Sagittarius, Vesta of Capricornus, Juno of Aquarius, Neptune of the Fish. By them we are granted all the arts: for those constellations infuse the ability to practice them in our bodies; and those Deities, in our souls. Thus Jove, through the constellation Leo, makes man fit to govern, that is to administrate worthily spiritual and earthly things; Apollo, through Gemini, gives us skill in shooting and in healing; Pallas, through Aries, bestows on us the art of weaving; and so with the others. And because they give us their gifts in a spirit of benign providence, we say that they give them

---

[54] Oration VII, chapter 1.   [55] Oration VI, chapter 3.

through Love. Besides this, we believe that the swift circling of the heavenly spheres gives rise to music, the eight spheres producing eight tones which blend in one perfect harmony. Therefore we call the nine musical sounds produced in heaven the nine Muses, because of their musical accord. Our souls were from the beginning endowed with the idea of this music; naturally enough, since they came from heaven. In them is this celestial harmony which they seek to imitate with various instruments. And this gift, like the others, was bestowed upon us through Love by Divine Providence. Therefore, my friends, let us love this god Love for his beauty, let us follow him because of his goodness, let us worship him in his blessedness, that in his clemency and generosity he may grant his beauty, his goodness, his blessedness to us.[56]

It will be observed that Love is ultimately God. Over against it, and abhorrent to it, stands love, in the ordinary acceptance of the word. It is the flesh, the Devil. Earthly love has nothing to do with the soul; it is a disease of the body. Ficino regards it much as Falstaff does the palsy:

One may get well of it in two ways; one is that of nature, the other that of art. The natural way is to let it wear off with time, and this it does as other diseases do. For the itching of the skin lasts as long as impurity remains in the blood or salty phlegm in the limbs. The blood clear again and the phlegm absorbed, the itching ceases and the disease departs.[57]

Earthly love is very catching, and one gets it through the eyes. In fact, we see in virtue of certain visual rays or spirits which are projected from the eyes. Now these rays emanate from the heart, and when they dart forth they bear with them a certain quantity of the spirit or essence of the blood. This essence may penetrate the eyes we gaze into, and descend into the heart of the person we gaze upon, and there condense into alien and perturbing blood. If it does, that person has a case of earthly love. The worst cases are those in which an elderly person catches it from a young one. Women have such a perverse power of projecting their blood in this way that according to Aristotle they have been known to stain a mirror. When one gazes into somebody's eyes and begins to feel indisposed, one may take various measures to nip the infection in the bud; but the best is not to gaze any more.[58] Ficino is not trying to be funny; he is telling us much what Dante does in the *Vita nuova*. Only in Dante's case it was not love but Love that made havoc among his spirits; and besides, Dante was a great poet.

---

[56] Oration V, chapter 13.
[57] Oration VII, chapter 11.
[58] Oration VII, chapters 4-12.

Introduction

If we turn to Landino's *Comento sopra la Comedia di Dante Alighieri Poeta Fiorentino,* we encounter the same sort of thinking. The *Divine Comedy,* the *Æneid,* and the *Odyssey* are three great allegories of the same Platonic doctrine which teaches how man may free himself from the dark forest and the stormy sea of the body and ascend to the contemplation of truth; and this Platonic doctrine proves at every turn to be the same as Christian doctrine, so that it may be freely illustrated from the Fathers or from Scripture. Truth, as Ficino has explained to us,[59] is spiritual or heavenly beauty, which in its turn is the beauty of God. Mary, Lucy, and Beatrice, who bring about Dante's rescue from the dark forest, are the three aspects of heavenly grace, of which the first, says Augustine, gives us the wish to turn our thoughts to heaven, the second gives us the power to do so, by directing us to the teachings of religion, and the third assures our success by revealing those teachings to us. "Nor should we disregard," continues Landino, "What the poets have said about the Graces, for any intelligent person will readily perceive that it does not differ much from what, here above, we have gathered from the true theologians."[60] And indeed, as he interprets the poets, it does not:

Hesiod writes in his Theogony that the Graces are three in number, nor does he depart from the truth. They are the daughters of Jove; which means nothing else but that from God alone proceed all graces.

He quotes Paul and David in support of this assertion, and having settled the matter concludes as follows:

Their names are Aglaie, Euphrosine, Thalia. Now in Greek *aglaos* means resplendent, and surely it is divine grace alone that illuminates our dark world; *Euphrosine* means happpiness, and indeed we owe our happiness to heavenly grace; *Thalia* means green and flourishing, and truly heavenly grace refreshes our souls and makes them bloom. The poets add that the two last are turned towards the first; and in fact on the splendor of it our souls depend for their joy and health.

A list of the individual interpretations to be found in the works of the Florentine Neo-Platonists would fill a book. In the *Comento,* Minos is explained as conscience,—sheer torment to the unredeemable sinner, who knows that he sins but can no longer extricate himself; Pluto represents greed of gold and is rightly placed over the

---

[59] Oration VI, chapter 18.   [60] Commentary on I. 2.

misers and spendthrifts; Medusa is absorption in earthly things, which turns the soul to stone. When he comes to the centaurs, Landino pauses to explain as Boccaccio does the story of their birth. In Ixion we are to see the man ambitious of royal power. He finds it to be an unsubstantial cloud, and his efforts to retain it bring forth in him the brute. In the *Disputationes Camaldulenses* Æneas is the soul; Venus, the upward yearning of the soul; Juno, earthly ambition; Troy, voluptuousness; Hades, the inner world of passion and temptation; Cerberus, with his three heads, the bodily need of food, drink, and sleep, which must be satisfied if the soul is to devote itself to contemplation, which is represented by Italy. In the *De Christiana religione,* Jupiter represents God; Pallas, the image of himself which God first created: the Intelligence, the second member of the Neo-Platonic triad. In *Sopra lo amore,* Coelus is God, and Saturn the Intelligence or collective angelic mind. Saturn is said to have castrated Coelus because the angelic mind represents a diminution of power as compared to God. Narcissus is the man who yearns after earthly beauty—the shadow—while his own soul—the substance—fades away within him. Thus we might go on indefinitely, always encountering the same habit of preconception which paralysed mediæval thinking.

It was under such conditions as I have sketched above that mythological exegesis passed into the second half of the Renaissance. Let us investigate its nature in that period a little further, choosing for the purpose a work significant in more ways than one. That Du Bartas discovered mythology to be an inseparable part of the poetic language of his time, and that he defended his use of it both by defining his gods as figures of speech and by explaining the myths patristically is well known.[61] Here we have the apologetic exegesis of religious fanaticism or fear. But the Frenchman's long-famous poem leads us to other aspects of contemporary thought. Du Bartas's commentators saw the matter somewhat differently, and going much further than he did, brought to bear on his allusions to the deities all the learning of the mythographers. Of the various commentaries composed on *La Semaine*,[62] let us consider one [63] which is of peculiar interest because it was translated into English

---

[61] Cf. Upham, *The French Influence in English Literature,* 147.
[62] Cf. H. Ashton, *Du Bartas en Angleterre,* 351 seq.
[63] It is that of Simon Goulart.

by Thomas Lodge. A glance at the list of authorities tells us that the author was a learned man. Let me enumerate some of the names it contains. Among the ancients we find Herodotus, Strabo, Diodorus Siculus, Plato, Plutarch, Pausanias, Lucretius, Cicero, Pliny, Plotinus, Macrobius, Servius, Boethius; among the mediæval writers, Fulgentius, Isidore, Orosius, Paulus Diaconus, Tzetzes, Albertus Magnus, Vincent of Beauvais, Petrarch, Boccaccio; among the authors of the Renaissance, Ficino, Pico della Mirandola, Pontano, Natale Conti; Cartari, Giraldi, Alciati, Pierius Valerianus, Paolo Giovio, Tasso, Porcacchi, Erasmus, Vives, Claude Mignault, Boiastuau. To these names may be added those of fourteen Fathers. There is no question, then, that Lodge was justified in calling the work *A Learned Summarie upon the Famous Poeme of William of Salust, Lord of Bartas*. Let us now see what sort of wisdom is contained in this book.

On Apollo, mentioned in the *Second Day,* we find a note rendered as follows by our translator: [64]

The Ancients have called divers effects of nature or of the starres, or of God himself, Gods. Moreover the Greek and Latine Poets have covered and clouded this naturall Philosophy with divers fables, so that by little and little the whole is converted into the horrible Idolatry of the Pagans. See beside Giraldus the fourth Booke of the *Mythologie* written in Latine by Noel de Comptes, these two having gathered all that a man can desire to reade touching this matter; to whom a man may adde Vincent Cartari, in his worke entituled *The Images of the Pagan Gods*, where in divers figures expressed by his discourse hee declareth, under the name of Apollo, the divers effects of the Sunne.[65]

It would appear, then, that our commentator accepts the allegorical theory of mythology. He makes this fact still clearer in a note on the *Fourth Day:*

It hath beene declared in another place that under the names of their gods the most ancient Grecians have hidden the most part of their naturall Philosophy.[66]

The esteem in which Conti is held may be inferred from the fact that he is cited thirteen times in the first two books. He is not regarded as an original interpreter, however. On Bacchus, in a note on the Second Day, the following is said:

He that would particularly know more of this, and to what end all the parts of the Fable of Bacchus (whom the Ancients esteeme to be the

---

[64] I am using the 1638 Edition.   [65] 54. 37.   [66] 181. 4.

inventor of Wine, and have called him Give-joy, Care-driver, and such other Titles) let him reade the third chapter of the 5 Booke of the *Mythologie* of Noel de Comtes, the 8 Booke of the *History of the Pagan Gods* of Lilius Giraldus, and Cartari *Of The Images Of The Gods:* for these have for the most part collected all that which the Ancients have written thereupon.[67]

Our scholar does not, of course, refer exclusively to the treatises. Discussing the winds, he cites Aristotle, Pliny, Seneca, and Plutarch;[68] and he quotes Tully on Pluto:

Cicero, in his 2 Booke *De natura deorum* discovereth the sence of Plutoes Fable. "Terrena (saith he) vis omnis atque natura Diti patri dicata est; qui dives, ut apud Graecos Πλούτων, quia et recidant omnia in terras et oriantur e terris."[69]

Again in regard to the Griffin, mentioned in the *Fifth Day:*

Belon, in his Preface upon the second booke of *The Nature of Birds*, reputeth all that to be fabulous which is spoken of the Griffons. The Poet hath followed the common opinion, described by Ælian in the fourth booke of *De animalibus*, Chapter 27.[70]

Here is will be noticed that belief as to the existence of griffins was still a "common opinion," which one of the leading naturalists of the day took seriously enough to refute. It was probably a matter of common opinion, too, that the Sirens represented courtezans. At least, no authority is given for the statement that

under this fiction they have represented the nature of Harlots, to which the Poet seemeth to have some Relation, making mention of the inchanting Charmes of these deceitful Syrens.[71]

Our commentator is also familiar with Giovanni Pierio Valeriano's *Hieroglyphica:*

Sithence this John Pierius hath made a most ample Commentary wherein whatsoever a man can desire as touching the portrait[72] of Memphis or Egypt, which are their hieroglyphicks, is represented and expounded particularly.[73]

---

[67] 61. 54.

[68] 64. 58.

[69] 75. 77. This, of course, is said by Balbus the Stoic. It will be noticed that the opinion is attributed to Cicero himself.

[70] 236. 36.

[71] 128, 72.

[72] By *portrait* more was once meant than at present.

[73] 14. 32.

Introduction

We are now acquainted with the wisdom of the *Learned Summarie* in the field of mythology; but, by way of refreshing our minds further as to the spirit of the age, let us benefit by its teachings in other fields. We have noticed that Vincent of Beauvais is included in the list of authorities. Was he not, however, quite out of keeping with the enlightenment of the times? Here is a note on the *Second Day*:

Vincent, in his Historiall Mirror, Booke 23, Chapter 148, and in his 24 Booke, Chapter 97, makes mention of Raines of Wheate, Barley, Pulse, and of little fishes in divers places. Some certaine yeers past, in a quarter of Almaine, there rained a great quantitie of Wheate, fit for the nourishment of man's body in time of Famine, wherewith an infinite number of Peasants were relieved and comforted. A friend of mine brought for remembrance-sake halfe a pound thereof, and gave me a little quantitie thereof, about a Horne-full.[74]

Our author has also heard of its raining frogs, but here he must correct tradition:

as touching Frogges, they seeme to fall with the Raine, which I have seene happen in the greatest heate of the day; but they fall not from the ayre but are generated in a small moment of time of grasse and thicke drops of Raine falling upon the dust over-heated by the Sunne. We must coniecture, then, that this is effected by a rainy moisture and a terrestriall heate, proper for generation. Besides, in such a part of the earth as is fat, and furthereth the same very much, wee have seene Rats and other such Vermine engendered of putrifaction. Garcæus, in his *Meteorologie*, speaking of prodigious Raines, thinketh that these Frogges are formed in the Aire (being sometimes wholly formed, sometimes halfe) of thick vapours raised from Pooles or other boggy places.[75]

It is to be feared that Garcæus was not as keen-sighted as our observer, and that he allowed Ovid and Diodorus to mislead him.

Sixteenth-century France did not see the gods or anything else with modern eyes. Just like the rest of Renaissance Europe, it still clung to authority, and confused knowledge with belief to an extent which we frequently under-estimate. Often an old interpretation of a myth appeared reasonable and convincing in the light of a still unquestioned superstition. In our commentary certain tales about Diana and Juno are readily enough reconciled with the supposed facts:

---

[74] 89. 107.   [75] 61. 55.

Iuno and Diana are taken for the Moone by Cicero in the 2 Booke of *De natura deorum*: " Iunonem Lucinam in pariendo invocant, quae eadem Diana omnivaga dicitur." Under this fiction hath been hidden the naturalle cause; that is, that according to the estate of the Moone womens labours are more easie or more difficult. But superstitious ignorance hath overthrowne all.[76]

These considerations lead to the following, in which another current belief, the supposed exhaustion of nature, is included:

Although the Earth (groning under the burthen of the corruption and malice of mankinde) seemeth to be weary of increase, as a woman that is broken by bearing many children: yet see wee dayly that Gods blessing shineth, and sheweth itselfe in the fruitfulnesse thereof.

The mermaids have by no means been relegated to the province of fancy; they have become " sea-women " or " fishes," the two conceptions abiding quite amicably together:

As touching the fishes that have resemblance of men and women, in the *Theater of Cities*, in the description of Harlem, we reade that in the yeere 1403 there was fisht out of the Lake of Harlem in Holland a Sea-woman which had been driven thither by a spring-tide, which being brought into the towne, suffered her selfe to be clothed and fed with bread, milk, and other meates: moreover she learned to spinne, and performe other pretty offices of women. She kneeled downe before the Crucifix, and obeyed her Mistrisse, never spake, but all the rest of her life remained dumbe, and lived thus many yeeres.[77]

Our author gives us another sample of his mentality in a note on Copernicus. Commenting on the Fourth Day, he tells us that Du Bartas has not deigned to do more than mention this man who so obviously discredits himself, and adds:

To prevent the absurdities which he preferreth, hee setteth down that it is more convenient that the earth should have motion.[78]

Here piety and perhaps prudence enter into the matter to a certain extent, but neither explains our commentator's imperviousness to the conception of scientific " convenience." How general this attitude was I need hardly recall. Bruno's experience in England will be remembered, and Butler's sneer at Galileo in *Hudibras* reminds us that the old mentality died hard. That the religious reaction of the later Renaissance did much to keep it alive is of course clear. It was chiefly pious zeal that made our commentator

[76] 127. 61.   [77] 231. 3.   [78] 162. 5.

concur so heartily with Du Bartas in calling Democritus "a meere mad man," [79] and caused him to close his remarks on the philospher with a reference to

his false and detestable opinion which suverteth the Article and pure doctrine of the Creation.

It was doubtless religious zeal, too, that warmed him to admiration for his poet's theory of earthquakes:

Our Author, raising himselfe as farre as the true cause of these agitations, and writing like a Christian, showeth that mens mis-demeanors draw on the wrath of God, who, by the trembling of the earth, threatneth the dwellers thereupon to exterminate them utterly; and when as at any time some few of them are thus terrified (as divers Histories doe testifie) they that survive, though remote farre off from them, are seriously admonished to examine their consciences narrowly.[80]

Lodge's translation of *La Semaine,* from which I have been quoting, was published in 1625 and again in 1638. The seventeenth century, then, did not scoff at the beliefs of the sixteenth. Between 1626 and 1700 appeared eight editions of George Sandys's Ovid, all but the first of which are furnished with an exhaustive exegetical commentary introduced to the reader as follows:

Since it should be the principall end in publishing of Books, to informe the understanding, direct the will, and temper the affections; in this second Edidtion [81] of my Translation, I have attempted (with what succcesse I submit to the Reader) to collect out of sundry authors the Philosophicall sense of these fables of Ovid; if I may call them his, when most of them are more ancient than any extant Author, or perhaps then Letters themselves; before which, as they expressed their Conceptions in Hieroglyphicks, so did their Philosophie and Divinitie under Fables and Parables: a way not un-trod by the sacred Pen-men; as by the prudent Lawgivers, in their reducing of the old World to civilitie, leaving behind a deeper impression, then can be made by the livelesse precepts of Philosophie. Plato in his imaginary Commonwealth ordaineth, that Mothers and Nurses should season the tender mindes of their children with these instructive fables, wherein the wisdome of the Ancients was involved: [82] some under Allegories expressing the wonderful works of nature: Some

---

[79] 12. 5.

[80] 123. 3.

[81] I am quoting from the fourth.

[82] If this reference is to *Republic,* II 377 seq., it is hardly a felicitous one. The allusion to the "wisdome of the Ancients" recalls *Theatetus,* 180, which may have suggested a title to Bacon.

administring comfort in calamitie; others expelling the terrors and perturbations of the minde; Some inflaming by noble examples with an honest emulation, and leading, as it were, by the hand to the Temple of Honour and Vertue. For the Poet not onely renders things as they are; but what are not, as if they were or rather as they should be; agreeable to the high affections of the Soule, and more conducing to magnanimitie; juster than either men or Fortune, in the exalting of Vertue and suppressing of Vice, by shewing the beautie of the one and the deformitie of the other, pursued by the divine Vengeance by inbred terrors, and infernall torments. For apparent it is, that they among the Heathen preserved that trueth of the immortalitie of the Soule: and therefore Epicurus, who maintained the contrary, dehorted his Scholars from the Reading of Poetry. In the Mythologie I have rather followed (as fuller of delight and more usefull) the varietie of mens severall conceptions, where they are not over-strained, then curiously examined their exact proprietie; which is to be born-with in Fables and Allegories, so as the principall parts of application resemble the ground-work.

The passage quoted above is hardly a model of punctuation, and the statement that poetry describes what is not as if it were, and indeed as it should be, might conceivably be misunderstood; nevertheless, it is very interesting. Here we have the Italian-Aristotelian criticism now current in England; and beside it, the Horatian doctrine and the poetic view of Scripture. Here too we have the allegorical theory of poetry. In his readiness to sit at the feet of whoever can enlighten him as to the meaning of the classical myths, our commentator is not peculiar, for most of the exegesists are equally ready; but presently he does something much more unusual, for he names his authorities. Just before the commentary on Book I, there occurs the following notice:

Although I conceived at first that it would seeme a vain ostentation in me (who am onely a lover of learning) to stuffe the Margent with Quotations: yet upon second thoughts, lest it should be objected how I make that my owne which I doe but borrow, and prove ungratefull to the lenders; I hold it not amisse in this empty Page, (so left by the oversight of the Printer) to mention those principall Authors out of whom I have compiled these commentaries. The first place is due to diverse of the Greeks, and most of the Latine Poets, together with their Expositors. I am much indebted to Plato, the poeticall Philosopher: not a little to Palaphates, Apollidorus, Aratus, Strabo, Diodorus, Pausanias, Plutarch, and Lucian: among the Romanes chiefly, to Cicero, Higinus, Pliny, and Macrobius. Neither have I been sparingly supplied by those ancient Fathers, Lactantius, Eusebius, St. Augustine, and Fulgentius. Of moderne writers, I have received the greatest light from Geraldus, Pontanus, Ficinus, Vives, Comes, Scaliger, Sabinus, Pierius, and the Crowne of the latter, the Viscount of St. Albans: assisted, though less constantly, by other authors, almost of all Ages and Arguments. Having beene true to my first purpose, in making choice for the most part of those interpretations, which either bear the stampe of Antiquitie, or receive estimation from the honour of the Author.

In the pages which follow we encounter the names of Seneca, Servius, Mantuan, Erasmus, and Alciati as well as those enumerated above: and also that of Orpheus, to whom the Orphic hymns are unquestioningly attributed. Plato, we notice, is credited with having interpreted more than one fabulous tale; as in the commentary on Book IX, where we read:

Plato delivers Hydra for a Sophister whose confutation begat more wrangling. Therefore to cut off a head from Hydra is to take away one inconveniency that more may succeed, like sutes in law, which begin where they end and continually multiply.

Occasionally Sandys discusses the interpretations he repeats; once or twice he challenges them.

That the expounding of the gods in the Renaissance was not merely a mediæval survival, Sandys's list of authorities would be sufficient to prove. Classical literature is fairly saturated with mythological exegesis, and it was conceived to be even more so than it is. The Greek tragedians, Plato, Aristotle, Lucretius,—all are cited as interpreters of the poets; everything in *De natura deorum* is accepted with an "ut Cicero ait"; Empedocles and Democritus are made expounders of Homer on doubtful grounds.[83] Furthermore, a number of spurious works of a more or less exegetical nature are still confidently attributed to Aristotle, Seneca, and so-forth. Again, the Orphic hymns, as we have seen, are believed to be the work of Orpheus, the most ancient of the poets. But even if all the names I have mentioned were omitted, the remainder would appear impressively numerous. The doctrines and interpretations of classic antiquity flowed down to the Renaissance in two veritable floods, the historical and the more strictly allegorical, of which the second, in its turn, composed two main streams, the Stoic and the Platonic. It may be well to recall a few of the more important names involved.

---

[83] Cf. Hersman, *Studies in Greek Allegorical Interpretation*, I. 7, 13; and Decharme, *La critique des traditions religieuses chez les Grecs*, I. 2. 60. But see also Gomperz, *Greek Thinkers*, III. 3. 380.

Through the Fathers the Renaissance was familiar with the historical exegesis of Euhemerus and Ennius. It found more historical interpretations in Herodotus, Thucydides, Strabo, Polybius, Diodorus Siculus, Lucian, and Palœphatus. The last two were especially popular. To Lucian, if the essay *Of Astrology* be accepted as his—and it was so accepted throughout the Renaissance—we owe the oft-repeated statement that Icarus was really a young astrologer who strayed from the path of reason and truth and fell into a bottomless ocean of opinions. Palæphatus made many things clear. He told how Acteon, an Arcadian, so neglected his fields for the pleasures of the chase that at last he was eaten up, as it were, by the expense of his hounds. He explained that Dædalus fled from Crete not on wings but in the first sailing-ship, his invention. Briareus, he declared, was no giant with one hundred arms; he stood for the inhabitants of a town in Macedonia who joined with those of Mount Olympus in a war against the Titans. The abridgement of his book, entitled *Concerning Incredible Tales*, probably furnished Orosius with the material for most of his abusive exegesis, and seems to have been known generally in the Middle Ages. It may well have been the tale of Acteon, read in the abridgement or in Fulgentius, that suggested to Petrarch the comparison between his tormenting passions and the Arcadian's hounds,[84]—a comparison repeated by many English poets.[85]

To Augustine, as we have seen, the Renaissance owed its knowledge of Varro's *Antiquitatum rerum humanarum et divinarum*; but it presently came into possession of a far better account of the Stoic gods: the *Allegoriæ Homericæ* of Heraclitus.[86] Here, after a vigorous defence of Homer against Plato's accusations, we have interpretations of all the deities. Zeus is the Stoic æther. Hera is the air, and she is called white-armed because the air is often white with mist. Athene is reason, wherefore she checks Achilles in his hasty wrath [87] and appears to Telemachus when that young man has reached years of discretion.[88] Proteus is a symbol of the

---

[84] *Canzoniere*, Canzone I, beginning: "Nel dolce tempo della prima etade," stanza 8.
[85] Cf. Bush, *op. cit.*, 71.
[86] This book, of course, was originally in Greek.
[87] Cf. *Iliad*, I. 190.
[88] Cf. *Odyssey*, I.

universe, which passing from its initial state of shapeless uniformity, assumed the variety we know in it today. We notice that Empedocles is cited in support of the view that Ares and Aphrodite represent universal attraction and repulsion. Hermes stands for persuasive eloquence; and in fact it is with his aid that Ulysses induces Calypso to let him go on his way.[89] More widely known than the *Allegoriæ* was the *De natura deorum* which Lucius Annæus Cornutus composed for the benefit of his son. Many a familiar interpretation does the student of the Renaissance find in this book. Zeus, the soul of the universe, is said to have suspended Hera from heaven with two anvils attached to her feet because Hera symbolizes the air, which occupies a position between the creative fire of heaven on the one hand and the two masses of earth and the ocean on the other. Zeus is also said to have dethroned Chronos and cast him down to Tartarus; for Chronos represents mutability or time, whose operations, after the creation of the universe, were restricted to the lower region of the earth. Pan is an image of the universe, and to him are attributed panic fears; for the sounds of nature, proceeding from cave or forest, often stampede flocks and herds. Thus we might go on indefinitely; but let us glance, instead, at the *Dissertationes* of Maximus Tyrius, despised of Gosson. The philosopher and the poet, says Maximus, expound the same doctrines. The presence of these in poetry, he adds, will appear clearly enough if for Zeus we substitute the mind or soul of the universe, for Poseidon the aspect of it which permeates land and sea, for Athene its wisdom, and so forth. We might now go on to Martianus Capella, but enough, perhaps, has been said about the Stoics.

Fundamentally Platonic, despite its characteristic syncretism, is Plutarch's beautiful essay, *Isis and Osiris*. Platonic too, in all probability,[90] is Apuleius's *Metamorphoses*, long famous as the *Golden Ass*, with its charming episode of Cupid and Psyche, so uncouthly mediævalized by Fulgentius.[91] It would be pleasant to discuss these works; but we must hurry on to the Neo-Platonists, for they are many. Plotinus, Prophyry, Iamblichus, Proclus,

---

[89] Cf. *Odyssey*, V. 112.
[90] Cf. Whittaker, *Macrobius*, 3; and Haight, *Apuleius and His Influence*, 52.
[91] *Mythologicon*, III. 6.

Julian, Macrobius, Boethius: it would certainly be a task to treat of them all in detail. About some of them a word will suffice; for *De consolatione philosophiæ* is too well known to require comment, Iamblichus is reflected in his pupil Julian, and as for Proclus it will be enough to recall that his commentary on Plato's *Republic* expands to an apologetic essay of considerable length when it comes to the famous criticism of the myths. These are declared to be allegories, and as such they are interpreted. About Plotinus, Porphyry, Julian, and Macrobius, it may be well to say a little more, as their interpretations illustrate different aspects of a complicated and perhaps not entirely familiar type of exegesis.

The interpretations of which Plotinus's *Enneads* are full do not delight us as Plato's myths do. They are often congested rather than dense with meaning, and the nervous vigor of the philosopher's style rarely stops for leisurely elucidation. As we read we understand why the master's fame was greatly enhanced by his brilliant and charming disciple Porphyry. Plotinus's metaphysics is ultimately psychological.[92] Just as intuition provokes in the mind an effort at logical conception, so in his system Intelligence, or the self-conscious essence of all things, produces the imitative effort of universal creative reason or Soul. This effort Plotinus identifies with Eros or heavenly Love, and the Soul he identified with Celestial Venus.[93] Eros is the activity of Venus. Eros is also, as Plato says, the child of Abundance and Want, for the Soul, which derives from the overflowing abundance of the universal Intelligence, is impelled to make its imitative effort by lack of identity with its source.[94] The creative activity of the Soul conceives the sensible world, which in its turn is prompted to physical reproduction. There is, then, as Plato teaches, an Earthly Venus and there is an Earthly Love.[95] Human souls, in a way involved in matter, yet continuous with the one Soul, may be misled into mere procreation or other material making, the impulse to approximate the ideal through imitation degenerating into delight in the image for itself. Prometheus symbolizes the soul thus beclouded.[96] According to Plotinus's version of the myth, he makes Pandora out of clay and becomes completely absorbed in his task. Presently he is chained

---

[92] Cf. Whittaker, *op. cit.*, 53.
[93] Plotinus, *op. cit.*, III. 5. 2.
[94] *Ibid.*, 9.
[95] *Ibid.*, 3.
[96] IV. 3. 14.

to the mountain, or matter. He is set free by Hercules or the soul in a state of virtue. It will be noticed that Prometheus is not entirely freed from matter but only from an excessive attachment to it. In fact Hercules represents the soul guided by the practical virtues, which protect it from excess without, however, leading it to that exclusive contemplation of the spiritual which alone liberates. It is for this reason that Homer declares Hercules to be in heaven but his shade to be in Hades.[97] The merely moral soul is still half a denizen of earth, and has but imperfectly identified itself with its great original.[98] Thus Plotinus uses the myths, which, he remarks,[99] serve to analyze the conceptions of philosophy, embodying and presenting separately their elements and aspects. Let us now see how Porphyry uses them.

Porphyry's *De antro nympharum* is a pretty bit of allegorizing and incidentally a good example of the syncretism of the times. In it the philosopher expounds that cave,

> Cool and delightsome, sacred to th' access
> Of Nymphs whose surnames are the Naiades,

near which the Phæacians leave the travel-worn Ulysses wrapped in forgetful sleep. It would be hard to forgive Porphyry if he were to make an uncouth disturbance in this quiet nook; but he does not. The cave is that sleep of the spiritual known as the sensible world. Says Plato:

Behold men as if dwelling in a subterraneous cavern, and in a den-like habitation, whose entrance is expanded to the admission of the light.

And do not the Persians, mystically signifying the descent of the soul into sublunary regions, introduce the neophyte into a cave? Did not Zoroaster consecrate to Mithra, he the maker of the world, symbols of ever-formless, changing matter, that yet is so hospitable to form. Yes, here is water, the female principle;[100] and here are amphoræ, symbols of life-giving Bacchus. The Naiades are spirits, are souls. They enter here into enclosing matter, and weave the rosy rayment of fair bodies; and the bees, that bring them the sweet intoxication of their honey, make them forget. The cave has

---

[97] Odyssey, Xi.
[98] I. 1. 12. Cf. VI. 5. 7. See also Whittaker, 96.
[99] III. 5. 10.
[100] This symbolism is prorbably of Stoic origin.

two entrances, one opening to the north, the other southward; one open to mortals, the other to immortals. So it is with the sensible universe. Into it, as Plato tells us, souls enter by the northern gate of Cancer, pausing presently to drink of the Cup of earthly forgetting. But one day they remember, they are awakened, and rising on viewless wings to the far gate of Capricorn, they vanish into its flooding light. Above the cave there grows a silvery olive-tree. It too has a meaning. It is a symbol of the divine wisdom that presides over all. No, Porphyry does not disturb Ulysses. Rather, he weaves a charming dream above his sleeping head.

The Emperor Julian, who sacrificed oxen for the good of Hellenism and worshipped the Neo-Platonic entities in the gods, was more deeply tinged with Eastern beliefs than Porphyry. Indeed the school of Iamblichus marks a certain degeneration in Neo-Platonic doctrine. The Syrian philosopher, seeking to elaborate and perfect Plotinus's system, multiplied states of being, and so identified them with the popular deities as to turn a religious philosophy into a philosophical religion.[101] A craving for continuity seems to have possessed Iamblichus; intermediate stages of emanation unfold at every step. Doubtless he associated with these conceptions thoughts of Mithra, the mediator between God and man; Mithra who, manifested in the sun, intervened between men and the harshness of darkness and cold. Certain it is that Julian attributes to him his doctrine of Helios,[102] a trinity consisting of the sun in its three manifestations of heavenly body, creative reason, and transcendental spirit. The luminary is conceived of as a physical embodiment thanks to which universal reason descends into the sensible world without ceasing to exist outside of time and space. It is a deputy to the extent of being an alter ego. In the same way the rational sun incarnates in reason the transcendental spirit, and the transcendental sun incarnates the One. Each brings to a focus in itself the emanation of the sphere above and creates with it its own sphere. This trinity is identified with Mithra,[103] especially in its second person; but in a less devout way it is, by hook or by crook, made to comprehend most of the other deities also. To it Julian offers his thanks, his praise, his pleading desire

---

[101] Cf. Zeller, *A Historical Outline of Greek Philosophy*, Section 3.
[102] Julian, *Hymn to King Helios*, 146. A.
[103] *Ibid.*, 1 B.

to be with it, his prayers,—such prayers as Christians offer to a personal God. Who does not remember poor Hypatia clinging in an agony of tears and supplication to Pallas's marble knees?

We have now come to one of the great store-houses of Renaissance symbolism: Macrobius's *Saturnalia*. This little book is an early example of those pleasant dialogues after the manner of Plato's which were so popular in the humanistic centuries. It tells us how certain Roman noblemen and scholars met several times at each other's houses during the festival of the Saturnalia, and how, banqueting together, they engaged in conversation on the history of the festival, the origin of the myth of Saturn, the beginnings, indeed, of Roman mythology in general; then, one subject leading to another, how they discussed the art and learning of Virgil; and when the coming in of dessert turned their thoughts to nuts and fruit, how they talked about the names and varieties of these. Indeed, it was pleasant and learned table-talk, and it ranged far and wide, touching now on old Roman customs, now on the psychology of the senses, now on optics. It dwelt longest on Virgil, and we seem to hear Eusebius brilliantly comparing the poet's beauties with those of nature, or the general murmur of assent and admiration which follows when the great Mantuan is declared to have been not less an orator than a poet. Much, however, was said about the myths; and as we listen to this part of the conversation we become aware that Praetextatus, who is leading it, is a Neo-Platonist. His views are not unlike Julian's;[104] yet they are simpler, they smack of Stoicism, they are more Roman. Of their transcendental aspect we get only glimpses. When Avienus asks his fellow banqueter to explain why the sun is worshipped under different names, Praetextatus hints at ultimate and recondite reasons but immediately goes on to speak of the visible luminary as controlling, in various ways and under various names, all earthly matters.[105] By the gods, he contends, the poets intended aspects and activities of the sun. In other terms, he refers his interpretations to the third or physical embodiment of Helios.

That Apollo is a name of the sun, Praetextatus proves etymologically by the epithets applied to the god.[106] He is the Darter

---

[104] For Macrobius's sources, cf. Whittaker, *Macrobius*, 18.
[105] *Saturnalia*, I. 17.
[106] *Ibid.*

of Rays, the Composed of Fire, the Encircler. He is also called the Slayer; for, explains Praetextatus, evidently thinking of the Stoics, the sun is the cause of pestilence and death as well as of growth and life.[107] Æsculapius is the sun considered in its healthgiving powers; and in fact, says Praetextatus, repeating what Julian has asserted before him, some call Apollo his father.[108] Hercules is the sun as giver of strength. Minerva "as Porphyry says," is that power of the sun by which it infuses reason into human minds;[109] wherefore it was rightly enough reported that she was born of Jove's head, Jove standing for the aether from which the sun derives its source. We note the metaphysical implication and pass on. Mercury is the swift sun, that sweeps up into the sky and puts out the stars just as the god closed the eyes of Argus.[110] He is called Powerful of Mind, and is sometimes represented by a block of wood with a head on it, because the sun is the mind of the world.[111]. Here again we notice the implication. The sun is the visible embodiment of Helios, or, in Stoic terms, of Zeus, *anima mundi*. Praetextatus is not, therefore, inconsistent, when he identifies Isis[112] or Venus with the earth. This last he does in one of his most delightful interpretations.[113] Venus blooms and glows with happiness while her bright love Adonis is with her. But alas, he is taken from her every year. The shaggy boar Winter, which loves dampness and mud and wintry acorns rattling down in the forest, attacks him. Then his vital warmth and brightness fade away, and he sinks down to Proserpine; for so the Phoenicians call that hemisphere which is remote from us. How wretched now is Venus! Her head is covered with a mournful veil of clouds, her desolate face appears in the bare fields, the springs, which are Earth's eyes, pour forth her tears. The long months of her widowhood drag by. At last they are over. At last Adonis is with her again. "Tunc est Venus laeta, et pluchra virent arva segetibus, prata herbis, arbores foliis."

Bound with the *Saturnalia* one usually finds another little work by Macrobius, the *Commentarium in somnium Scipionis*. It is a philosophical commentary on the sixth book of Cicero's *Republic*, in which the younger Scipio dreams that he ascends to heaven,

---

[107] *Ibid.*
[108] I. 20.
[109] I. 19.
[110] *Ibid.*
[111] *Ibid.*
[112] I. 20.
[113] I. 21.

where the spirits of some of his ancestors explain to him in Platonic terms the nature of the future life and the rewards of the patriot. Macrobius, defending the propriety of introducing fiction into philosophical writings, is led to speak of myths, and justifies the use of these also provided that they are not of a scandalous nature. Within these limits the ancients did well to veil their wisdom in allegories:

because they knew that to blurt out all would be disregardful of Nature, who, even as she conceals herself from the vulgar under physical appearances, so also desires that her mysteries should be handled by the wise under the cloak of allegory.[114]

Proceeding now to interpret Scipio's dream Neo-Platonically, he presently has occasion to explain the elder Scipio's assertion that what men call life is death. Of course he does so *con amore*. What but the body is the grave of the soul? What but the body is lightless, hollow Hades?[115] And the infernal streams,—are they not the violent and unhappy impulses of our darkened spirits? Phlegethon may well represent the burning rush of anger or desire within us, Styx the submerging deeps of hatred, Cocytus the grief that makes us dissolve in tears. The so-called living are familiar enough with the torments of Hades. The man who ignores what he has in his greediness for more is a Tantalus; he who trusts to luck and is spun around by circumstances, an Ixion; he who wears himself out with profitless ambitions pushes boulders up-hill which will roll back on him. Another fruitful interpretation in the *Commentarium* is that of Jupiter's golden chain. Of course it is explained as symbolizing the series of Neo-Platonic emanations through which the material world is united to the One.[116]

Perhaps the most learned of those Roman banqueters was Honoratus Maurus Servius. His famous commentaries on Virgil are richly erudite, and with scholarly eclecticism interpret the mythological allusions now according to Pythagoras, now to the Orphics, now to the Stoics, the Epicureans, the Platonists, or the Neo-Platonists. Occasionally, there is a historical interpretation, perhaps from Ennius. Servius thought it likely enough, I take it, that the myths were allegories; else how account for such a note as the following:

[114] I. 2.   [115] I. 10.   [116] I. 14.

According to the fable the daughters of Atlas were nymphs and had a garden in which grew golden apples sacred to Venus. These Hercules, by command of Eurystheus, carried off, after killing the dragon that watched over them. The truth of the matter is that the nymphs were noble maidens whom Hercules robbed of their flocks after murdering their shepherd. It was feigned that he stole apples because in Greek sheep are called μῆλα.[117]

On the other hand, here is his comment on Virgil's relating the myth of Deucalion and Pyrrha in the sixth Eclogue:

A question arises at this point; for abandoning prudent explanations as to the beginning of the world, he abruptly passed to fables. We believe that he did so either in compliance with the practice of the Epicureans, who always mingle pleasure with serious matters; or in order to delight boys with marvelous tales. For fables were invented to give pleasure, as he himself teaches in the *Georgics*.[118]

The conclusion would seem to be that while Servius himself more or less accepts the myths as allegories, he does not regard Virgil as doing so; and in this he is probably right. In his attitude towards the old religion as such he reflects the times; only the country-folk take it literally. Judging by the commentaries, his philosophic views lean to Stoicism and Pythagorism, much as the poet's did in his later years; but apparently he is more inclined than Virgil was to accept the Stoic doctrine of the gods.

Roughly speaking, one may say that Servius brings the minor beings of the old mythology to earth, and dissipates the major ones into aether or emanation. The many-headed hydra was a troublesome lake—" and indeed hydra has reference to water "—which was no sooner dammed up in one place than it overflowed in another. Hercules drained it.[119] Scylla, he learns from Sallustius, is a rock. The waves bark and yell around it, which might account for the tale of dogs and wolves; but as a matter of fact the waters are infested by sea-monsters.[120] As for the Sirens,[121] the truth is that they were courtezans who lured the passer-by to financial shipwreck. Ulysses would have nothing to do with them, and they died. Presumably they died of starvation. Ulysses was not kind old Johnson. Phorcus is supposed to have been a son of Neptune:

---

[117] *Commentarius in Virgilii Aeneidos*, IV. 484.
[118] *Com. in Virgil. Bucol.*, VI. 41.
[119] *Com. in Virgil, Aeneid*, VI. 287.
[120] *Ibid.*, III. 420.
[121] *Ibid.*, V. 864.

Varro, however, says that he was a king of Sardinia who, in a naval engagement with King Atlas, was sent to the bottom with most of his fleet,—wherefore his allies pretended that he had become a sea-god.[122]

The Gorgons, according to the poet Serenus, were maidens of such powerful charms that the young men who saw them became quite torpid, as if they had been petrified.[123] The sea-skimming wings of Daedalus were sails, declares Servius; Virgil did well when he cautiously said " ut fama est." And Daedalus had his reasons for " flying from Minos' scepter ":

Nam Taurus notarius Minois fuit, quem Pasiphae amavit, cum quo in domo Daedali concubuit; et quia geminos peperit, unum de Minoe et alium de Tauro, enixa esse Minotaurum dicitur.[124]

Conti challenges this explanation and with delicious gravity argues it out of court.

Professor Glover has pointed out [125] that for Virgil the gods are not even " those manifestations of the supreme divinity, which the Neo-Platonists later on held them to be." Servius, it seems to me, is ready enough to understand the old deities in this way provided that proof be forthcoming. One must keep an open mind; " many things have been said about the rule of the gods." He too, I think, is " filled with the though of the divine life pervading all things; " and that he heartily dislikes extreme materialism is fairly evident. A vigorous refutation of the Epicureans, " qui stulte Solem de atomis dicunt constare," [127] might be taken as indicating Neo-Platonic leanings. He expresses himself rather positively, too, when he says:

Sed constat, secundum Porphyrii librum quem *Solem* appellavit, triplicem esse Apollini potestatem; et eundem esse Solem apud superos, Liberum patrem in terris, Appollinem apud inferos.[128]

Macrobius, who was also indebted to Porphyry's book, gives the sun different names according as it is in our hemisphere or the other.[129] This, I think, is what Servius means to do when he speaks of Liber and Apollo. Sol is the sun as regulator of the other heavenly bodies. The three *potestates* alluded to are the

---

[122] *Ibid.*, V. 824.
[123] *Ibid.*, VI. 289.
[124] *Ibid.*, VI. 14.
[125] T. R. Glover, *Virgil*, 301.
[126] *Com. in Virgil Aen.*, VI. 264.
[127] *Ibid.*, IV. 584.
[128] *Com. in Virgil. Bucol.*, V. 66.
[129] *Saturn.*, I. 18. 8-10.

ruling of the stars, the giving of life, and the inflicting of disease and death. This last prerogative Servius attributes to Apollo, not impossibly thinking of the winter sun which, like dead Adonis, goes down *ad inferos* and leaves the world striken and lifeless. Here, then, we have an example of Servius's Neo-Platonism. Elsewhere,[130] he identifies the gods with Zeus according to the Stoics. Much more picturesquely, he embodies earth the devourer in Cerberus;[131] or portrays earth the creator and shelterer in the Great Mother,[132] crowned with walled cities; or shows us universal nature in a splendid portrait of Pan.[133] his horns towering to heaven, his face red with the vital fire of life, a mottled hide, vast as the starry sky, flung about his body above those forest-covered crags his shaggy legs.

Let us now turn back in time and space and consider one more authority often cited by Renaissance mythographers. It will not be unfitting to discuss his interpretations at this point, for like Servius he was something of an eclectic. As Plutarch is a type of the advanced religious thinker, so Pausanias, in his attitude towards religion, is probably representative of the average Greek in the second century A. D. He does not question the existence of Zeus, and he believes that gods and dæmons intervene in human affairs;[135] but as for the myths, he is inclined to regard them as allegories:

Such of the Greeks as were formerly reckoned wise designedly concealed their wisdom in enigmas; and I conjecture that what I have just now related concerning Saturn contains something of the wisdom of the Greeks. We should consider things relative to divine concerns in this manner.[136]

It is noticeable, however, that Pausanias, like Hecataeus and Herodotus, seems chary of meddling with the legends of the major deities. Most of his interpretations have to do with heroes and monsters. Thus he explains Orpheus[137] as a poet of great authority who exerted himself in the cause of religion and civilization. He agrees with Hecatæus that Cerberus was a cavern-dwelling serpent called the dog of Pluto because of its deadly bite.[138] " With-

---

[130] *Com. in Virgil. Georg.*, I. 5.
[131] *Com. in Virgil. Æeneid*, VI. 395.
[132] *Ibid.*, III. 113.
[133] *Com. in Virgil, Bucol.*, II. 31.
[134] *Description of Greece*, I. 40.
[135] VIII. 10.
[136] VIII. 8.
[137] IX. 30.
[138] III. 25.

out attending to fable," he repeats the story that Medusa was an African queen who, defending her country against the army of Perseus, "was slain in the night by strategem." [139] At Ægium he accepts, though remarking testily that it is "no more Phœnician than Greek," an interpretation of Æsculapius given him by a Sidonian:

> Æsculapius, he said, is the air, which is equally subservient to the health of man and of all animals. Apollo is the sun, and is very properly denominated the father of Æsculapius because the sun, harmonizing the seasons by his course, gives salubrity to the air.[140]

Elsewhere he sees a temple of Aphrodite the Black; whereupon, dreary soul, he comments on the amorousness of night in a way to make Juliet turn in her grave with indignation.[141] A certain plebean matter-of-factness leads him to identify the glamorous with the ordinary. The Stymphalides are nothing more than fierce Arabian birds somewhat like cranes;[142] he has seen a dead Triton;[143] certain seamen have given him a detailed account of a band of Satyrs by which they were attacked on an island off the coast of Africa.[144]

Greek and Roman expounders of the myths have engaged our attention for a considerable time, and the fact is significant of their number and importance. Some of those discussed were known to the Middle Ages, but the rest brought a new increment to mythological exegesis in the Renaissance. All must have made a strong impression on an age which worshipped antiquity. The Stoics presented with new force and precision their cosmic Olympus and such great ethical symbols as Hercules and Ulysses;[145] the Platonists made men familiar with their Helios, their Eros, their heavenly and earthly Venus; the historical exegesists appeared the clearer and the more interesting in the light of a growing knowledge of ancient history. The names of most of them triumphed in the mythographer's list of authorities. All were worthy of much respect. The long-established tradition of manifold exegesis made all acceptable. All might be right. Characteristic of the general attitude is the title of Sabinus's widely-read commentary on Ovid:

---

[139] II. 21.
[140] VII. 23.
[141] VIII. 6.
[142] VIII. 22.
[143] IX. 21.
[144] I. 23.
[145] Cf. Zeller, *Stoics, Epicureans, and Sceptics*.

Fabularum Ovidii interpretatio, ethica, physica, et historica. Small wonder that Conti waxes eloquent; the ancients themselves have been assuring him of the truth. And be it noted that these ancient authors are as eloquent on the subject as Conti is. They not only interpret the gods but again and again set forth the doctrine that the myths are allegories. We have heard Pausanias; let us hear some others.

In his *De antro nympharum,* Porphyry says as follows:

It must not, however, be thought that interpretations of this kind are forced, and nothing more than the conjectures of ingenious men. When we consider the great wisdom of antiquity, and how much Homer excelled in intellectual prudence and in an accurate knowledge of every virtue, it must not be denied that he has obscurely indicated the images of things of a more divine nature in the fiction of a fable. It would not have been possible to devise the whole of this explanation if the figment had not originally been applied to the expression of certain established truths.

He begins his essay with another argument:

Hence, since this narration is full of such obscurities, it can neither be a fiction casually devised for the purpose of procuring delight, nor an exposition of history; but something allegorical must be indidcated in it by the poet.

We are reminded of Julian, who says:

Whenever myths on sacred subjects are incongruous in thought, by that very fact they cry aloud, as it were, and summon us not to believe them literally but to study and track down their hidden meaning.[146]

Here we are reminded of Proclus:

It likewise appears to me, that whatever is tragical, and unnatural, in poetic fictions, excites the hearers to the investigation of the truth, attracts them to recondite knowledge, and does not suffer them to rest satisfied with superficial conceptions, but compels them to penetrate into the fables, to explore the obscure intention of their authors, and survey what natures and powers they intend to signify to posterity by such mystical symbols.

Since, therefore, fables of this kind excite those of a naturally more excellent disposition to a desire of the concealed doctrine which they contain, and to an investigation of the truth established in the adyta through their apparent absurdity, but prevent the profane from busying themselves about things which it is not lawful for them to touch, are they not eminently adapted to the gods themselves, of whose nature they are the interpreters?[147]

---

[146] *To the Cynic Heracleios,* 222. D.
[147] Commentary on Plato's *Republic.*

Thus I might go on indefinitely, quoting Maximus Tyrius, Heraclitus, Cornutus, Pliny, Strabo, etc.; but enough has been said to illustrate the teachings of at least a large number of the ancients.

Let us now conclude. What may we infer from the evidence which has passed before our eyes in the preceding pages? What did the Renaissance really think of the classic myths? There can be little doubt, it seems to me, that, taken as a whole, the Renaissance believed the myths to be allegories or at least vehicles of something deeper than their apparent meaning. The Renaissance believed many strange things. From the confines of a half-undiscovered world many strange tales were brought to it. It still judged largely by hearsay; it still clung to tradition and authority. From the ancients it received such teachings as we have seen above. Some, doubtless, were wholly sceptical; and we should probably have more evidence of their scepticism had not religious considerations interfered. Some were willing to accept the theory within the bounds of common sense. Some accepted one aspect of it,— like Sir Thomas Browne, who warns us against the fantastic allegories of the Greeks and bids us pin our faith to Palæphàtus.[148] Many more were of two minds on the subject; they were not quite sure one way or the other. Of these last, in my opinion, was Francis Bacon.

The preface to *De sapientia veterum* is a curious document. Much like Spenser's cantos on Mutability and his episode of the Garden of Adonis, it shows us a Renaissance mind sifting classical opinion in an effort to form a judgment. Bacon tells us that he is quite aware of the pitfalls in the path of the allegorist. Like Montaigne, he has no doubt that many, in recent and ancient times, have twisted the fables of the poets " to gain the sanction and reverence of antiquity for doctrines and inventions of their own "; he knows " that Chrysippus long ago, interpreting the oldest poets after the manner of an interpreter of dreams, made them out to be Stoics." Here we pause, for Bacon has taken his unfavorable view of Chrysippus bodily and in a curiously unquestioning way from Cicero. In *De natura deorum,* Velleius the Epicurean, attacking Stoic mythology, says:

Chrysippus, who is looked upon as the most subtle interpreter of the dreams of the Stoics, has mustered up a numerous band of unknown gods

---

[148] *Enquiry into Vulgar Errors*, I. 6.

... He endeavors to accommodate the fables of Orpheus, Musaus, Hesiod, and Homer ... in order that the most ancient poets, who never dreamed of these things, may seem to have been Stoics.[149]

Bacon also knows, he tells us that:

The Alchemists more absurdly still have discovered in the pleasant and sportive fictions of the transformation of bodies, allusion to experiments of the furnace.

We shall presently see that our philosopher was not so disdainful of the Alchemists and their symbolism as he appears to be here.

Despite all the reasons for scepticism Bacon knows, he propends to the allegorical theory. "I cannot change my mind," says he:

For in the first place to let the follies and license of a few detract from the honour of parables in general is not to be allowed; being indeed a boldness savouring of profanity; seeing that religion delights in such veils and shadows, and to take them away would be almost to interdict all communion between divinity and humanity. But passing that and speaking of human wisdom only, I do certainly for my own part (I freely and candidly confess) incline to this opinion,—that beneath no small number of the fables of the ancient poets there lay from the very beginning a mystery and an allegory.

Again we pause, for we recognize the famous doctrine of the poetic nature of Scripture which, spread far and wide by Legouais, Petrarch, and Boccaccio, marked the revolt of the later Middle Ages against ecclesiastic disapproval of poetry. I need hardly recall that it was often advanced during the Renaissance despite the protests of Savonarola.[150] Bacon accepts the doctrine without question, and elsewhere alludes to it almost in Petrarch's words when he speaks of "Parables, which are a divine poesy."[151] It is constantly borne in on us that notwithstanding a deceptive spontaneity of expression most of Bacon's thinking is erudite rather than original. He is a man of his time. The very completeness with which he appropriates the ideas of others, and especially of the great men of the past, is characteristic of it. But let us pass on to other reasons which he adduces for looking favorably on the allegorical theory of mythology.

Continuing his discussion, Bacon points out how closely the

---

[149] I. 15.

[150] Cf. Spingarn, *A History of Literary Criticism in The Renaissance*, I. 14 seq.

[151] VIII. 409.

episodes of mythology and the names of the deities [152] are seen to fit certain interpretations. Nor is this all, for presently we read:

> But there is yet another sign, and one of no small value, that these fables contain a hidden and involved meaning; which is, that some of them are so absurd and stupid upon the face of the narrative taken by itself, that they may be said to give notice from afar and cry out that there is a parable below. For a fable that is probable may be thought to have been composed merely for pleasure, in imitation of history. But when a story is told which could never have entered a man's head either to conceive or relate on its own account, we must presume that it had some further reach.

Are we not strangely reminded of Julian and Porphyry? And now comes one more reason. Probably implying his belief in a golden age of perfection, Bacon adduces as an argument of capital importance the fact that the myths are far more ancient than Hesiod or Homer. Whatever superficial alterations the poets may have made in them, their antiquity gives them a special significance:

> for so they must be regarded as neither being the inventions nor belonging to the age of the poets themselves, but as sacred relics and light airs breathing out of better times, that were caught from the traditions of more ancient nations and so received into the flutes annd trumpets of the Greeks.[153]

Such are Bacon's reasons for inclining to the allegorical theory of mythology. But at this point another theory rises before his mind.

Gosson's tirade in the *School of Abuse* implies, of course, that Maximus Tyrius forced allegorical meanings on Homer's poetry. Vives explicitly declares that not the ancient poets but later writers (including, we notice, Landino) attributed philosophical meanings to the stories of the gods.[154] Bacon is probably answering criticism of this kind and conceding something to it when he says:

> Nevertheless, if any one be determined to believe that the allegorical meaning of the fable was in no case original and genuine, but that always the fable was first and the allegory put in after, I will not press that

---

[152] Etymology was, of course, the master key of Stoic exegesis. Cf. Zeller, *op. cit.*

[153] Petrarch, and Boccaccio after him, advance the theory that poetry was invented as a sacred language of praise and prayer when men "began to feel sure that there really is some higher power that controls our destinies." Cf. Petrarch, Epistolae de rebus familiaribus, X. 4; and Boccaccio, *op. cit.*, XIV, 232.

[154] *De causis corruptarum artium*, II.

point; but allowing him to use that gravity of judgment (of the dull and leaden order though it be) which he affects, I will attack him, if indeed he be worth the pains, in another manner upon a fresh ground. Parables have been used in two ways, and (which is strange) for contrary purposes. For they serve to disguise and veil the meaning and they serve also to clear and throw light upon it.

His answer to the critics is, then, the following. Even granting that the myths were not originally intended as allegories, we may still believe that in relatively primitive times they were used as such by wise men who saw their value as vehicles of instruction,

the understandings of men being then rude and impatient of all subtleties that did not address themselve to the sense,—indeed scarcely capable of them. For as hieroglyphics came before letters, so parables came before arguments.

Says Natale Conti:

At quia viderent sapientes animos multitudinis apertis rationibus ad eruditionem non posse adduci, horum figmentorum suavitate illos ad se allexerunt, quae sola causo fuit, cur tot postea fabulae sint inventae.[155]

We have already heard what Conti has to say about hierogylphics.

What Bacon's inclination was, amid arguments for and against the allegorical theory of mythology, we have seen; but ultimately his common sense told him that he did not really know:

Upon the whole I conclude with this: the wisdom of the primitive ages was either great or lucky; great, if they knew what they were doing and invented the figure to shadow the meaning; lucky, if without meaning or intending it they fell upon matter which gives occasion to such worthy contemplations.

Such, I believe, was his final judgment. In *The Advancement of Learning* he had written:

I do rather think that the fable was first, and the exposition devised, than that the moral was first, and thereupon the fable framed. For I find it was an ancient vanity in Chrysippus, that troubled himself with great contention to fasten the assertions of the Stoics upon the fictions of the ancient poets. But yet that all the fables and fictions of the poets were but pleasure and not figure, I interpose no opinion.[156]

In *De augmentis scientiarum* he wrote:

Now whether any mystic meaning be concealed beneath the fables of the ancient poets is a matter of some doubt. For my own part I must confess

---

[155] I. 9. 14.   [156] VI. 206.

that I am inclined to think that a mystery is involved in no small number of them.[157]

What the mystery might be Bacon tried to discover; for, as a brilliant student of the Renaissance [158] once remarked, the great Chancellor was strong for experimental investigation and yet not averse to taking a short-cut if the ancients really had one to offer him. Like his contemporaries, our mythographer turned for guidance to the most accredited expounders of such mysteries; like them, as we shall see, he accepted Natale Conti as the leading light on the subject. Bacon was a man of his time. Indeed, he had a distinctly mediæval turn of mind. Yet there has long existed a disposition to regard him as a modern thinker. It has been said about the allegorical theory of poetry that " The death-knell of this mode of interpreting literature was sounded by Bacon "[159]—surely a rash assertion, disproved by Sandys's list of authorities. More recently it has been said of his mythological exegesis that " a good deal of it seems to be original." [160] I hope to show in the following pages that even this cautious estimate goes too far.

---

[157] VIII. 443.
[158] I refer to Professor Greenlaw.
[159] Spingarn, *op. cit.*, III. 276.
[160] Bush, *op. cit.*, 241.

PART I

SYMBOLS OF SCIENTIFIC SPECULATION

In nothing is Bacon more delightful as a writer than in his copious allusions to classical mythology. The myths of Greece and Rome are so familiar to him that they become almost a new, vivid language on his lips, whence they flow in a profusion of apt similes and striking metaphors, or in less obvious comparisons to which he deftly gives point and meaning as he goes, or again in complete allegories which embody whole trains of thought in picturesque and memorable images. Indeed, as we turn the pages of *De sapientia veterum* we are almost ready to believe, as he would have us, that the myths themselves are his subject, and that from them really emerge the ingenious or sagacious ideas which he wishes to convey to us. In a measure, Bacon doubtless believed this himself; for he was at least of two minds as to the actual existence of a golden age whose wisdom the poets had turned to mystery and song. Certain it is that in these pages he appears to us more than ever as the eager inquirer after truth, and as we follow in his steps we feel with a pleasant excitement that we are sharing in his discoveries.

So disarmingly spontaneous are Bacon's interpretations of mythology that scholars have generally accepted them as entirely original.[1] In doing so, however, they have, perhaps, been hasty. The tendency to adopt and adapt so characteristic of the Renaissance is by no means unnoticeable in the *Essays;* and we have no sooner begun the introduction to *De sapientia veterum* than we are reminded of Cicero by a remark about Chrysippus and of Julian by a reflection on the significant absurdity of certain myths.[2] Indeed, it would have required no small effort to expound the gods in an entirely new way. Pausanias, Plutarch, Lucian, Cornutus, Servius,

---

[1] See, for example, *The Works of Francis Bacon*, edited by Spedding, Ellis and Heath, XXI. 407. I may here add that all allusions to Bacon's works in this and the following chapter are to be referred to this edition.

[2] Cf. *De natura deorum*, I. 15; and Julian's essay *To The Cynic Heracleios*, 222. D. Since this monograph was written, Professor D. Bush has furnished me with another *a priori* argument. Cf. his excellent *Mythology and The Renaissance Tradition in English Poetry*, 241.

Macrobius, Fulgentius, to mention but a few, were familiar to educated men; so were the Neo-Platonists and the Fathers. The treatises of Giraldi, Cartari, Sabinus, counted many readers; the *Mythologiæ* of Natalis Comes was famous. Numerous emblem-books might also be mentioned. Nor must we forget the strange writings of the alchemists who, extremely active and copiously productive of books throughout the seventeenth century, often used the classic myths for their pseudo-scientific symbolism. Under these circumstances it becomes of interest to investigate Bacon's possible sources, all the more so as the inquiry involves the origin of some of his ideas. I have made such an investigation and will endeavor to show that while all Bacon's interpretations bear the mark of his creative fancy, and while some are practically original, most are, in varying degrees, adaptations of others which preceded them.

Nobody has denied, I take it, that some of Bacon's mythological symbolism was conventional in his time. Even if no special literature had existed, it would have been natural, in an age saturated with classical learning, that classical mythology should be drawn upon for metaphor, and simile, and painted emblem. Therefore, when Bacon refers to "the works of Bacchus and Ceres,"[3] or to those of Dædalus and Vulcan,[4] or when he says that Henry VII wisely sowed Hydra's teeth,[5] he is following a common practice and would probably have been understood even without the brief elucidations which he gives in passing. James I, we may be sure, did not miss the compliment when he was referred to as laboring with the laws, which he had in his head " as Jupiter had Pallas."[6] The reader at large was not mystified by the exhortation to princes and divines that they should damn and send to Hell, "as by their Mercury rod,"[7] violent religious intolerance; nor did he fail to see the point of the comment, in regard to conflagrations considered as cataclysms, that "Phaeton's car went but a day."[8] Even we moderns understand the remark, on Solomon's regarding all novelty as oblivion, that "the river of Lethe runneth as well above ground as below."[9] These are but a few examples of what were probably current figures of speech. I think it safe to believe that in a gen-

---

[3] VIII. 118.   [4] *Ibid.*, 401.   [5] XI. 145.
[6] Spedding, *Francis Bacon and His Times*, I. 641.
[7] XII. 91.   [8] XII. 274.   [9] *Ibid.*, 273.

eral way Pan was a familiar symbol of nature, Prometheus of the progressive leader and reformer, Paris, in his famous decision, of the man who flings away wealth and wisdom for love. Not only do all three interpretations occur in both Comes's [10] and Boccaccio's works,[11] but the first and second are to be found in Alciati's *Emblematum flumen,* and the third in Thynne's *Emblemes and Epigrames.* So, too, in a general way, Tantalus was commonly understood as a symbol of money-greed, the Sirens were held up as a warning to the voluptuous, Scylla and Charybdis as one to the intemperate and rash.

It will be noticed that Bacon applies the myth of the dragon's teeth in his own way. Anybody would have understood him to mean the raising of soldiers, but not necessarily "for the service of this Kingdom." So too, Mercury's task of leading departed spirits to Hades is extended to the conducting of opinions and tendencies. The famous frontispiece of the *Instauratio magna,* with its ship sailing triumphantly between the Columns of Hercules, doubtless told the beholder that here was promised an excursion into the unknown; but the ship sailed in defiance as well as in high hopes: "For how long," demands Bacon,[12] "Shall we let a few received authors stand up like Hercules' columns, beyond which there shall be no sailing or discovery in science?" No symbol was commoner in a moral sense than that of Scylla and Charybdis; Bacon skillfully refreshes it by making it enjoin moderation on scientific thinking. Even commoner was the symbolism of Tantalus; but we shall presently see how deftly it is made to express the dull palate and stupidly grabbing hands of primitive rapacity in general. Indeed, a subtle gift of transmutation is natural to the man; but for that very reason we must beware lest we come to regard it as exclusively his own. In warning the scientists to forsake Minerva and the Muses "as barren virgins,"[13] he seems to enliven a hackneyed figure with a characteristic quirk; yet Minerva suggests the following comment to Boccaccio: "As

---

[10] Natalis Comes, *Mythologiæ sive Explicationis Fabularum,* V. 6; IV. 6; VI. 23. I have used the 1581 Venice edition.

[11] Boccaccio, *De genealogiis deorum,* I, sub. *De Pane;* IV, sub *De Prometheo;* VI, sub *De Paride.*

[12] VIII. 396. See also VI. 419.

[13] VIII. 401.

for temporal matters, she is barren, for the fruit of wisdom are eternal." [14] The quirk is there, but we may doubt whether it amounts to more than a clever reversal of judgment.

While Bacon's short interpretations are frequently conventional, his elaborate ones are not; and it is here that the question of sources becomes especially interesting. In discussing these passages and essays, I shall begin with those which are most clearly adaptations, and in a measure I shall group them according to sources; but I shall do so subordinately to my purpose of keeping those of similar subject together, for the question is one of content as well as form. Thus I shall first consider the interpretations of a scientific nature; then such as are more an expression of worldly wisdom than of purely scientific doctrine.

Cœlum [15]

According to the poets, Cœlum, the most ancient of the gods, was dethroned and castrated by his son Saturn, a monster who devoured his own children. One of these, Jupiter, having escaped the fate of the others, served his father as his grandfather had been served, and cast him into Tartarus. His præcisa membra he threw into the sea, where they generated Venus. In the early part of his reign Jupiter had to sustain two wars: one against the Titans, whom he defeated with the assistance of the Sun; and another against the giants, whom he also defeated.

Bacon interprets the myth briefly related above as symbolizing "the origin of things"; that is, the early history of the universe and especially of the world. Cœlum, he explains, is "the concave or circumference which encloses all matter"; Saturn is "matter itself"; both may be said to have been castrated because neither the extent of the universe nor the totality of matter is capable of increase. The reign of Saturn he explains as a period of "frequent dissolutions and short durations" in which "the agitations and motions of matter" produced "mere attempts at worlds." It was followed, he tells us, "by that other, which proceeds by Venus, and belongs to a state in which, concord being powerful and predominant, change proceeds part by part only, the total fabric re-

---

[14] *Op. cit.*, II, sub. *De Minerva*.
[15] XIII. 113.

maining entire and undisturbed." As for the state of things which had characterized the reign of Saturn, it was relegated to a place:

midway between the lowest parts of heaven and the innermost parts of the earth: in which middle region perturbation and fragility and mortality or corruption have their chief operation.

Twice, however, the safety of the world was endangered; once by heavenly commotions, and once "by convulsions in the lower regions, by inundations, tempests, winds." Nor were these the last perils to be apprehended, for "the world might yet relapse into its former confusion."

Bacon compares his interpretation to the cosmogony of Democritus, but the two differ considerably. Democritus no more believed in an enclosing heaven than Lucretius did; nor did he postulate the relative stability of the heavenly bodies, as we must understand Bacon to do since he relegates fragility and corruption to the earth. According to Democritus, aggregation and dissolution go on throughout the universe; and they have been doing so from eternity, for they are not peculiar to an initial period. Again, when Bacon talks of concord he is using the language not of Democritus but of Empedocles. His enclosing sky, too, recalls Empedocles, and his period of tentative creation reminds one of that philosopher's account of the first appearance of living creatures. It is noticeable that in discussing change "part by part" (by which I take him to mean non-cosmic change),[16] he says that it "proceeds by Venus": almost as if he had in mind the sexual reproduction which according to Empedocles followed spontaneous generation. On the other hand, his departures from Empedoclean cosmology are apparent; and in banishing corruption from the stars and relegating it to a sublunary region, he is at one with Aristotle.

From what has been said above, it appears that in Bacon's interpretation of the myth of Cœlum we have a curious cosmological eclecticism largely based on Empedocles. Is this odd system original with Bacon himself? The following table will conclusively prove, I think, that it is not.

---

[16] By the stability of "the total fabric," Bacon doubtless means the integrity of the organized universe in that of its parts. This he conceives of as having remained intact; for the mutability made peculiar to the earth has not, so far, proved radical. Yet, he tells us, our world has been severely shaken. Indeed, the heavens themselves have suffered great convulsions, and the universal world may yet succumb.

Bacon	Natalis Comes
By Cœlum is meant the concave or circumference which encloses all matter.	It was called Cœlum because it is concave, which among the Greeks is expressed by χοιλου.[17]
By Saturn is meant matter itself; which, inasmuch as the sum total of matter remains always the same, and the absolute quantum of nature suffers neither increase or diminution, is said to have deprived its parents of all power of generation.	Cœlum was castrated, as I interpret the myth, because there are but one upper air and one universe; nor can any time suffer another upper air or another universe to be created, because it consists of universal matter.[18] As the universe is one and not several, and as it cannot be several, it was rightly said that Cœlum was castrated by his son. . . . There is but one heaven and there is but one time, for the latter is produced by the motion of the former; both are said to have been castrated because there cannot be more of them than there are.[19]
Now the agitations and motions of matter produced at first imperfect and ill compacted structures of things that would not hold together, —mere attempts at worlds. Afterwards in the process of time a fabric was turned out which could keep its form. Of these two divisions of time, the first is meant by the reign of Saturn; who by reason of the frequent dissolutions and short durations of things in his time, was called the devourer of his children; the second, by the reign of Jupiter, who put an end to those continual and transitory changes,[20] and thrust	It was feigned that Saturn devoured and then vomited his children, and that on this account he was driven from his kingdom, because it was believed that the upper air was exempt from corruption and unaffected by the assaults of time, which, therefore it expelled and hurled down from its kingdom. Thus then, as I was saying, it was signified that the elements were corrupted, while the fifth element, which is called ονοια, remained by its nature eternal.[21] The place of the elements was called Tartarus, almost απο των ταραχωμ because of

---

[17] X, sub *De Saturno*.

[18] My translation is literal, the original being: " neque ullum tempus patietur posse aliud cœlum procreari, cum ex universa constet materia." Comes does not identify Saturn with matter; but he seems to, and may thus have suggested the idea to Bacon.

[19] II. 3. 87.

[20] Cf. VIII. where, comparing self-perpetuating with discontinuous, phenomena, Bacon says:

them into Tartarus,—that is to say, the place of perturbation; which place seems to be midway between the lowest parts of heaven and the innermost parts of the earth: in which middle region perturbation and fragility and mortality or corruption have their chief operation.

But as soon as this mode of generation ceased, it was immediately succeeded by that other which proceeds from Venus, and belongs to a state in which, concord being powerful and predominant, change proceeds part by part only, the total fabric remaining entire and undisturbed.

the perturbations of which it is full.[22]

The power of time, however, was brought to an end in the kingdom of Jove because after God created the elements Saturn wrought such havoc with them that he was expelled from heaven.[23]

Jupiter's parents [24] signify that God next created all things, for the elements are related to Jove.[25] Next is signified their mutual creation and corruption according to parts, since the total mass is eternal and the heavenly bodies are not susceptible of corruption and since change is more frequent in the vicinity of the earth.[26]

That the Titans leagued with

The motions therefore of assimilation and excitation I call motions of the generation of Jupiter, because the generation continues; but this, the motion of the generation of Saturn, because the birth is immediately devoured and absorbed.

[21] Here Comes is practically quoting Aristotle in *De coelo*, I. 2. The fifth element, is, of course, that of which the heavenly bodies, as distinct from the earth, are supposed by Aristotle to be constituted.

[22] X, sub *De Saturno*.

[23] X, sub *De Iove*. I believe that Bacon's idea of tentative creation was suggested to him by Empedocles, and also, perhaps, by Democritus and Lucretius; but Saturn's destructiveness implies a period of "frequent dissolutions."

[24] Saturn and Earth.

[25] Comes interprets Jove as the ether, or upper air; but he repeatedly implies (what Vergil, whom he quotes, asserts) that the ether is a creative force. For example, in II. 1:

It is related that Jupiter was fed by bees because the elements mutually procreate each other without the intervention of sex, and, as I have said, they are favored by the ether.

Of course, the procreation referred to here is the production of vapor by water, rain by vapor, and so forth. Bacon, then, may have found here a suggestion for his comprehensive change proceeding from Venus under the rule of Jupiter.

[26] X, sub *De Iove*. See also II. 1, where it is said that God next made the elements.

Saturn (on condition that he would slay his children) means nothing more than that, as Empedocles declared, friendship and discord are the two powerful causes of natural phenomena.[27]

For the sake of greater clearness, it may be as well to give a summary of Comes's interpretation which, it will be noticed (as it doubtless was, with approval, by Bacon), brings the gods into the Christian fold. God, then, first created the heavens, or Cœlum, from whose motion arose time, or Saturn. Both Cœlum and Saturn were said to be castrated because neither may reproduce itself. God next created the elements, of which the ether, or pervading principle of life and reproduction, is represented by Jupiter. The ether and the heavenly bodies, exclusive of the earth, were created eternal; therefore, Saturn or time was said to have been cast out from among them. The earth, instead, was made the seat of mortality; therefore, it was thought of as in the power of Time. On earth, the forces of disgregation seem leagued against those of union, even as Empedocles observed; therefore, the Titans were imagined to be in league with Saturn against Jove.

Natalis Comes, with his "as I interpret the myth," is almost as disarming as Bacon; nevertheless, and indeed in the very passage I refer to, he is probably elaborating on a famous predecessor. What is more to our purpose, there is good reason to believe that in a measure Bacon is directly indebted to the same man. The following from Macrobius[28] will, I think, make this clear:

As for Saturn, indeed, the physicists have done as much to make his story credible as the mythologists to deprive it of credibility. It is said that he castrated his father Cœlum, whose præcisa membra, flung into the sea, generated Venus, called Αψροδινη because of the foam which, coalescing, produced her. By this[29] it was meant to signify that while chaos lasted, time did not exist; for time arises from the revolution of the sky. Thence Time arose; and from the same source[30] is supposed to have sprung κρονος who, as we have said, is χρονος. As soon as the sky had come into

---

[27] II. 1. 71.

[28] *Saturnaliorum*, I. 8. 6-9.

[29] By the statement that Saturn was the son of Cœlum.

[30] The Romans identified the Cronos of the Greeks with Saturn, but Mocrobius seems to feel a distinction. The fact does not affect his interpretation of Saturn's castrating Cœlum.

existence, there poured from it the seed of all things to be created, and the fundamental elements which were to complete the universe were brought forth by them. When the universe was finished in all its parts and members, Time, we may truly say, put an end to heaven's scattering seed for the procreation of the elements; and these were now fully procreated. The faculty of generating and to all eternity reproducing animals from moisture was transferred to Venus, so that animals should multiply gradually by the union of male and female.

Here we have change "that proceeds by Venus" as Empedocles understood it. It seems to me very probable that Bacon had this passage in mind. Partly influenced by Comes, partly following what, as we shall see, was his common practice, he generalized and elevated, retaining, however (and this too is characteristic of him), the picturesquely concrete figure of Venus.

I think it probable that Bacon was at least in a measure indebted to Macrobius for his region of fragility and mortality "midway between the lowest parts of heaven and the innermost parts of the earth." The idea of a sublunary region of mutability is Aristotelian, but Macrobius dwells on it at length and expresses it in terms more nearly approaching Bacon's:

And they declared that the unchanging part of the universe extended from the sphere called απλανης to the beginning of the lunar globe; the changeable, from the moon to the earth. Souls were said to enjoy immortality while they remained in the changeless region, but to become subject to death when they descended into the other; therefore, the space between the moon and the earth was called the region of the dead, and the moon itself the boundary between the dead and the living.[31]

Again, explaining the passage "ex quibus erat ea minima quæ ultima a cœlo" etc.:

Truly, the orbits of the stars are greater than that of the sun, since what contains is greater than what is contained, and since it is the order of the planets for the upper to circle around the lower. Therefore, he said that the sphere of the moon, which is the last in heaven and the nearest to the earth, is the smallest.[32]

And about the earth:

The physicists called the upper hemisphere of the earth, which we inhabit, by the name of Venus; the lower, by that of Proserpine.[33]

---

[31] *Comm. in somn. Scip.*, I. 11. 6-7.
[32] *Op. cit.*, I. 16. 12-13.
[33] *Saturnaliorum*, I. 21. 1-3.

Bacon's allusion to cataclysmic disturbances on earth remains to be accounted for. It reminds one of certain lines in *De rerum natura*.[34] The resemblance between the two passages will appear in the following table.

Bacon	Lucretius
For first there followed notable commotions in the heavenly regions; which however, by the power of the sun predominating in those regions, were so composed that the world survived and kept its state; afterwards in like manner followed convulsions in the lower regions, by inundations, tempests, winds, earthquakes of more universal character than any we now have; and when these likewise were subdued and dispersed, things settled into a more durable state of consent and harmonious operation.	Fire gained the mastery and licked and burnt up many things, when the headstrong might of the horses of the sun dashed from the course and hurried Phaethon through the whole sky and over all lands. But the almighty father, stirred then to fierce wrath, with a sudden thunderstroke dashed Phaethon down from his horses to earth, and the sun meeting him as he fell caught from him the ever-burning lamp of the world and got in hand the scattered steeds and yoked them shaking all over; then guided them on their proper course and gave fresh life to all things. . . . Water too of yore gathered itself and began to get the mastery, as the story goes, when it whelmed many cities of men; and then when all that force that had gathered itself up out of the infinite, by some means or other was turned aside and withdrew, the rains were stayed and the rivers abated their fury.

Cupid.[35]

In *De sapientia veterum* and, more extensively, in *De principiis atque originibus*, Bacon treats of the elder Cupid, as he calls him, or Eros. In Hesiod this being stands for love,—the principle uniting and ordering the universe. In the Orphic poems, Eros is the progenitor of Gods and men, from whom all other beings derive their existence. As for his own origin, he comes out of an egg into which Chaos has formed itself. According to Aristophanes, Chaos lays the egg; then, uniting with Eros, produces birds, gods, and

---

[34] V. 396-405; 411-415. [35] X. 343; XIII. 122.

men. Eros is represented as a winged boy much like the traditional Cupid. Bacon might have found a discussion of both in Plato; but, as has been well said, "it is more probable that his account of the distinction between them comes from some later writer." [36]

Bacon interprets Eros as the atom, informed with its energy: at once the ultimate foundation of all bodies and the ultimate source of all energies, including those of procreation. Eros, he says, is "matter itself, and its energy and nature; in short, the fundamental principle of all things." [37] And again:

This love I understand to be the appetite or instinct of primal matter; or to speak more plainly, the natural motion of the atom; which is indeed the original and unique force that constitutes and fashions all things out of matter.[38]

And further, in regard to the younger Cupid:

And yet there remains a certain conformity between him and the elder Cupid. For Venus excites the general appetite of conjunction and procreation; Cupid, her son, applies the appetite to an individual object. . . . Now the general disposition depends upon causes near at hand, the particular sympathy upon principles more deep and fatal, and as if derived from that ancient Cupid, who is the source of all exquisite sympathy.[39]

Bacon regards the atom as the ultimate cause of the physical and biological universe. Beyond it is God, whom it is not for the scientists to investigate. How the atom causes physical phenomena, what it is in its present nature: this, science may seek to learn, though with little hope of success.[40] But the manner of its creation is a divine mystery: the ancients rightly asserted that Eros had no parents.[41] Nevertheless, Bacon interprets Chaos, from which Eros was born, and tells us that it embodies:

some description of the state of things as it was before the work of the six days, wherein distinct mention is made of earth and water, which are the names of forms; but yet in the whole the mass was still unformed.[42]

---

[36] V. 272 See, however, *Symposion*, 181, which Bacon doubtless read.
[37] X, 344.   [38] XIII. 122.
[39] XIII. 125. By "the particular sympathy" I take Bacon to mean love as distinct from mere animal desire. This passion attaches itself to an individual object in virtue of a feeling which it shares with domestic affection and love of friends; in short, with something far more comprehensive and subtle than lust.
[40] XIII. 123.   [41] X. 345.   [42] X. 353.

It would seem, then, that Chaos was matter qua matter; not to be identified with earth or water. But what else is the atom? Bacon himself assers that atoms:

are neither like sparks of fire, nor drops of water, nor bubbles of air, nor grains of dust, nor particles of spirit or ether.[43]

Surely he is not trifling with us by informing us that the atom arose out of itself.

A few lines above the passage just quoted, there occurs another which may shed some light on the question. Strenuously denying that matter could ever have existed *in posse*, in the scholastic sense, Bacon says:

Now that the first matter has some form is demonstrated in the fable by making Cupid a person: Yet so that matter as a whole, or the mass of matter, was once without form; for Chaos is without form, Cupid is a person. And this agrees well with Holy Writ; for it is not written that God in the beginning created matter, but that he created the heaven and the earth.

If any single thing were needed to convince one that Bacon was largely mediæval in his thinking,[44] this extraordinary passage would suffice. He wishes to prove that ultimate matter had from the start an intrinsic reality; that every atom of it was such a reality, quite independent of intellectual abstraction. He goes about it cumbered with what here seems to be a genuine belief in the significance of the myth, and furthermore, with two considerations of authority: Holy Writ, and, as I shall show in a moment, the *Mythologiæ*. The result is that his reason plays him false in a typically mediæval way, and he declares that the first matter was intrinsically real, yet in the aggregate was not so because it did not take such forms as air or earth. In other words, he passes directly from the atom to its aggregations as if the two were identical. That there was confusion in his mind as to the precise aspect of Chaos which he meant to discuss is seen in a still earlier passage [45] in which he says: "Itaque Chaos . . . massam sive congregationem materiæ inconditam significabat": *inconditam,* disorderly, confused. Here

---

[43] X. 347.

[44] I owe my thanks to Professor Edwin Greenlaw for making what have proved to be most illuminating remarks to this effect.

[45] V. 290.

there is no question of intrinsic reality. Bacon is not thinking, here, of the atom itself, but of the atom as that building material by the orderly arrangement of which are made air, earth, water: the "elements." Chaos was the assembly of the elements in solution. Bacon, however, intended to discuss not the elements but the ultimate matter of which they are composed.

One has only to turn to the *Mythologiæ* to feel convinced that here lies the principal cause of the slip noted above. Says Comes:

> By saying that Cupid was the eldest of the gods the poets may be perceived to have meant that, as Empedocles conceived, all things, at first confused together, were separated by the alternate action of concord and discord; for by themselves, without these, they could have produced nothing.[46]

As in the case of Cœlum, Bacon has temporarily slipped from atomism into the philosophy of elements of Empedocles; and once again under the influence of Natalis Comes. Here a question arises. According to Empedocles, the universe did not pass once for all from chaos to order, but had from eternity alternated between the two, according as the force of concord or that of discord predominated. Comes, instead, implies the occurrence of a single, initial period of chaos, during which neither of the two forces was operative. Bacon obviously implies something closely similar. Does he mean us to understand that when God created the heavens and the earth He simultaneously endowed matter with energy? If he does he has gone a step beyond the atom, and his interpretation of Chaos is a curious and genuinely significant application of the philosophy of Empedocles to theology and to atomic philosophy.

The passages discussed above are not the only indications that Bacon was influenced by Comes in his treatment of the myth of Cupid. The following table will make this apparent:

Bacon	Natalis Comes [47]
Another younger Cupid, the son of Venus, is also spoken of, to whom the attributes of the elder are transferred (in quem attributa antiquio-	However, several Cupids existed. To one, Venus's son, almost all the things said about Love have been transferred (omnia prope quæ de

[46] IV. 14. 271.
[47] IV. 14. 266.

Symbols of Scientific Speculation

ris transferuntur) and many added of his own.[48]

Amore dicta sunt transferuntur).

Thales asserted water to be the principle of things.[49] . . . But by far the greatest error is that they set up for a principle that which is corruptible and mortal; for they do no less when they introduce such a principle as forsakes and lays aside its nature in compositions. "For when a thing shifts and changes, that which it was dies."[50]

Thus Thales declared water to be the ultimate principle of all things (Thales aquam rerum omnium principium posuit), which certainly is well adapted to generation; yet nothing may be procreated by it alone without this agent, whether it is called concord, or the female or the male principle, or warmth: that is to say, divine energy which brings things forth.

For Venus excites the general appetite of conjunction and procreation; Cupid, her son, applies the appetite to an individual object. From Venus, therefore, comes the general disposition, from Cupid the more exact sympathy.[51]

Others thought him the son of Venus because Venus, as I have said, is the desire of procreation in the things of nature, which arises from the symmetry of bodies and the qualities of the air. As for his fabulous procreation by Wealth and Want—parents so different from each other—it may be applied to these same matters; though still better to morals. For as avarice is as often the result of lack as of abundance, so Cupid, because of the violent desire of individuals may be

---

[48] X. 343. This in *De principiis atque originibus*. In the corresponding passage in *De sapientia veterum*, the last four words are altered, but the part paralleled by the *Mythologiæ* is repeated unchanged, as though by heart:

There was also another Love, the youngest of all the gods, the son of Venus, to whom the attributes of the elder are transferred, and whom in a way they suit.

[49] X. 355. The paragraph continues, giving Thales' arguments; then it goes on to Anaximenes and his arguments in favor of air; then to Heraclitus and his theory as to fire. Each hypothesis is criticised and found wanting.

[50] *Ibid.*, 264. The quotation is from Lucretius, III. 518; but the passage quoted from could not have served Bacon as the source of what he says. It doubtless occurred to him because he was thinking of Comes's "diviner principle"; for Lucretius implies the unchangeable nature of such an informing spirit in denying that the human soul, which he declares to be susceptible of change, is immortal.

[51] XIII. 125.

For the summary law of nature, that impulse of desire impressed by God upon the primary particles of matter which makes them come together, and which by repetition and multiplication produces all the variety of nature,[53] . . .	transferred in meaning from his application to universal nature.[52]
	As I was saying, Cupid, according to the ancients, was nothing else than what Empedocles felt it to be: the energy of similar things urging them to join and coalesce; or to put it better, the Divine Mind which induces these impulses in nature.
His last attribute is archery: meaning that this virtue is such that it acts at distance: for all operation at a distance is like shooting an arrow. Now whoever maintains the theory of the atom and the vacuum (even though he suppose the vacuum not to be collected by itself but intermingled through space), necessarily implies the action of the virtue of the atom at a distance.[54]	Arrows were attributed to him because of the torments endured by lovers; or better, because of the admirable quickness of the Divine Mind, which goes forth to, and most penetratingly enters into, all things (quae per omnia transfunditur et acuissime penetrat).
Now this Cupid is truly an egg hatched by Nox; for all the knowledge of him which is to be had proceeds by exclusions and negatives: and proof made by exclusion is a kind of ignorance, and as it were night, with regard to the thing included.[55]	The above mentioned plagues[56] are said to have been born of her because ignorance and malignity, which are the night of the mind, are the parents and nurses of all the calamities which afflict humanity.[57]

There remain to be accounted for a few interpretations in which Bacon was not anticipated by Comes.[58] They regard Cupid's indi-

---

[52] In other words, even as the term *avarice* may be applied not only to the vice of a class but to the singular parsimony of the penurious individual, so the symbol Cupid may stand not only for a force of nature but also for its intense manifestation in individual men.

[53] XIII. 123. Let it be remembered that, according to Bacon, Cupid symbolizes this "summary law" in the atom.

[54] XIII. 125.

[55] X. 347.

[56] Deceit, fraud, envy, strife, obstinacy, etc.

[57] III. 12: interpretation of Nox. 153.

[58] Owing to considerations of space, I have omitted what seems to me fairly convincing evidence of Bacon's indebtedness to Comes for the order of his topics in *De principiis atque originibus*. For the first couple of

vidual reality, his age, his blindness, and his nakedness. I think it probable that Lucretius suggested them. In attributing to the atom (symbolized by Cupid) individual reality, Bacon is in part expressing his opposition to the conception of potential matter; but he is also reiterating Lucretius's contention [59] that the atom is not an arbitrary portion of matter to be subdivided at pleasure. And Lucretius's atom remains unchanged forever in the eternal minuteness which Bacon symbolizes by Cupid's eternal childhood.[60] As for his comparing the blindness of Cupid to the undiscriminating force of inter-atomic attraction,[61] it is perhaps significant that Lucretius applies the word *blind* to the atom,[62] though in the sense of invisible, and that Bacon quotes the passage.[63] Finally there is the interpretation of Cupid's nakedness: the absence of sensible physical qualities in the atom.[64] Lucretius, asserting this same absence of sensible qualities, says that ultimate matter is "nullo velata colore," [65] "Orba colore," [66] "spoliata colore." [67] Now H. S. J. Munro, in his translation of *De rerum natura,* renders these phrases by "clothed with no color," "denuded of color," and "stripped of color." May not the same expressions have been suggested to Bacon? It will be noticed that he applies the word *velum* to matter as defined by the Ionian physicists.[68]

Pan.[69]

As a symbol of nature, Pan dates at least as far back as the early Stoics, and Bacon's interpretation is largely a compilation from several of those which preceded it. These resemble each other in a measure, and to some extent are derived from each other; yet they differ sufficiently for it to be possible to trace Bacon's individual sources with a fair degree of accuracy.

"Orpheus" merely invokes Pan as the embodiment of the uni-

---

pages that essay follows the *Mythologiæ* closely, and despite copious digressions thereafter, it is still possible to trace the sequence of Comes's topics. In other words, I think it probable that *De principiis atque originibus* is an expansion of Comes's chapter on Cupid.

[59] I. 218. seq.
[60] XIII. 124.
[61] XIII. 125.
[62] I. 780.
[63] X. 347.
[64] XIII. 124.
[65] II. 797.
[66] II. 838.
[67] II. 842.
[68] II. 300.
[69] XIII. 92; VIII. 444.

verse,[70] and the classic authors in general do not go into details. For anything approaching Bacon's minute symbolism we must turn to later writers. Servius,[71] followed by Isidore of Seville [72] and by Albricus Philosophus,[73] explains Pan's horns as symbolizing the sun and moon, his ruddy face as standing for the ether or heaven of fire, his leopard skin cloak and his pipes as symbols of the star-dotted sky and the harmony of the spheres. In his shaggy legs he sees an allusion to the forest-covered earth, in his crook the badge of his rule. Rabanus Maurus,[74] while obviously following Isidore in the main, adds that Pan's hoofs are meant to suggest the solidity of the earth, and extends the symbolism of the furry legs to the living creatures with which the earth is covered. Bacon was doubtless familiar with Servius and probably with the others, but the interpretations of these authors are meager as compared with his. He could find more and better elsewhere.

Macrobius [75] interprets Pan as the sun, which, however, he regards as the creator of life, the energy permeating all bodies, the regulator and ruler of all things in nature. According to him, Pan's horns and his long beard stand for the sun's rays, which descend from heaven to earth; his goat's hoofs are an allusion to the sun itself which whether at dawn or sunset, is seen among the mountains as goats are. Pan's crook represents the sun's ruling power. His pipes "reveal order in the unequal breathing of the air; for the winds, in which is no regularity, derive their substance from the sun." Echo, "Pan's love and delight," is identified with the harmony of the spheres, "for she must be the friend of him who is almost the moderator of the spheres to whose motion she owes her being." Anyone familiar with *De sapientia veterum* will at once be struck by Macrobius's interpretation of Pan's beard and by his mention of the mountain-climbing habits of the goat. Now Bacon might have found the first of these details repeated, with due acknowledgment, by Boccaccio; but the second he found neither in Boccaccio nor in Natalis Comes, though the latter contributed the

---

[70] Cf. hymns.
[71] *Comm. in Virgil. Bucol. II. 31.*
[72] *Etymologiæ*, VIII. 11.
[73] *De deor. imagin.*, sub *Pane*.
[74] *De Universo*, XV. 6.
[75] *Saturnaliorum*, I. 21. 7-11; 22. 10-35.

difference between his interpretation and Macrobius's. The following table will make Bacon's two-fold indebtedness clear:

Bacon	Macrobius	Natalis Comes
There is also a very ingenious allegory involved in that attribute of the goat's feet, which has reference to the motion upwards of terrestrial bodies towards the regions of air and sky; for the goat is a climbing animal and loves to hang from rocks and hang to the sides of precipices: a tendency which is also exhibited in a wonderful manner by substanstances that belong properly to the lower world, witness clouds and meteors.[78]	Therefore for his extremities were chosen the feet of an animal which, though it is a terresterial animal, yet always seeks the heights while feeding: even as the sun which, whether it pours down its rays from above or gathers them back to itself, is seen in the mountains.[76]	His goat's feet have been interpreted as symbolizing sudden subterranean disturbances; or by others as standing for the stability of the earth and the shifting of the clouds in heaven.[77]

Bacon picturesquely elaborates Macrobius's interpretation of Pan's beard;[79] but the god's horns, which he conceives of as converging heavenward till they meet,[80] he explains as symbolizing that gathering of individuals into species, species into genera, and genera into more comprehensive groups, which suggest the assembling of all nature into a single unit mysteriously responsive to a single and divine law. In *De sapientia veterum*,[81] Bacon gives us no clue as to the source of his interpretation; but in *De augmentis scientiarum* [82] he does, for he adds:

---

[76] I. 22.   [78] XIII. 97.
[77] V. 6. 302.   [79] XIII. 96.

[80] Here again he may be indebted to Macrobius who, in *Sat.* I. 17, tells us that the Hieropolitani represent the sun with a pointed beard and a tall cap on his head (eminente super caput calatho), which last they understand as a symbol of the ether, of which they believe the sun to be composed. The cap, then, reaches up to the creative source.

[81] XIII. 95.

[82] VIII. 449. See also VIII, 478, where Bacon interprets the chain and Jupiter's words about it, in the sense that "it were a vain labor to

64   *The Classic Deities in Bacon*

And hence the famous chain of Homer (that is, the chain of natural causes) was said to be fastened to the foot of Jupiter's throne; and we see that no one has handled metaphysics and the eternal and immovable in nature, and withdrawn his mind for awhile from the variable succession of things, without falling at once on Natural Theology; so easy and so near a passage is it from the top of the pyramid to matters divine.

Now in Macrobius [83] there occurs the following passage which, especially in view of the fact that Pan's horns are interpreted as emanations of divinity, accounts for Bacon's interpretation clearly enough: [84]

From God pure mind emanated, from pure mind arose vital energy, and this orders and permeates all things. Thus the one light illuminates the universe and appears in every part of it, as one face in many mirrors; for all things follow each other in a continuous sequence, descending in order to the bottom, and from God to the last dregs of things there exists an unbroken connection which binds every part to every other. This is Homer's golden chain which Jove, it is related, ordered to be suspended from heaven to earth.

It would seem, then, that Bacon was chiefly indebted to Macrobius for his interpretation of Pan's horns, beard, and hoofs. It is not unreasonable to suspect, too, that he owed him something for his explanation of the god's hairy body, in which he sees an "allusion to the rays which all objects emit; for rays are like the hairs or bristles of nature." [85] Finally, it is not improbable that at least in a measure Bacon's interpretation of Pan's pipes comes from the same source. It will be remembered that in the pipes of unequal length and different tones Macrobius sees law governing the winds: that is, law in seeming lawlessness; harmony in discord. Now Bacon interprets the pipes as follows: [86]

The pipe compact of seven reeds evidently indicates that harmony and

---

attempt to adapt the heavenly mysteries of religion to our reason," and that we had better "raise our own minds to the adorable throne of heavenly truth." In this sense the symbolism of the chain was probably conventional. See Cesare Ripa's *Inconologia*, where this emblem appears.

[83] *Comm. in somm. Scip.* I. 14. 23-34.

[84] It should be borne in mind, however, that even the scientific interpretation of the chain was probably well known. It occurs in Sir John Davies' *God's Eternal Law*, in an alchemistical *Aurea catena Homeri*, and elsewhere. See J. Timbs, *Curiosities of Science, Second Series*, 33

[85] XIII. 95.

[86] XIII. 97.

consent of things, that concord mixed with discord, which results from the motions of the seven planets.

It will be noticed that Bacon is thinking less of fabulous cosmic music than of actual cosmic law, and that he also is impressed with the element of discord involved. Presently, shifting his symbolism from Pan to Apollo, he expresses the idea again: [87]

For it seems there are two kinds of harmony and music; one of divine providence, the other of human reason; and to the human judgment, and the ears as it were of mortals, the government of the world and nature, and the more secret judgments of God, sound somewhat harsh and untunable.

Whatever the influence of Macrobius in the matter of Pan's pipes, it seems probable that Boccaccio also contributed to Bacon's interpretation.[88] Explaining the nymph Syringa, who, pursued by Pan, was turned into the reeds of which the god made his instrument, Boccaccio says: [89]

We might see in Syringa the music of the spheres . . . or instead, considering that the heavens exert their influence on all things, the works of nature, moving with such harmonious order to their ends that, as it were, they make music for us not inferior to that of the best singers.

That Bacon's interpretation of Pan was influenced by *De genealogiis deorum* appears clearly, I think, in that part of it dealing with the Fates. As far as I know, Boccaccio is the only writer before Bacon, who associates the Fates with Pan as symbolizing the forces of nature. Like Bacon, he first discusses the Fates as three; then Fate as one. Like him he paraphrases a certain passage in Cicero; and he approaches a verbal parallel of what Bacon says immediately afterwards. The most conclusive of these resemblances appears in the table below:

Bacon	*Boccaccio*
To the nature of things, the Fates or destinies of things are truly represented as sisters. For natural	As for the Fates, born at the same birth, and given as ministers to their brother, I believe them to have

---

[87] XIII. 100.

[88] Boccaccio's influence may extend to what is said of Pan's hairiness; for in *Gen. deor.* I, sub *Pane*, he attributes to Macrobius the interpretation of Pan's leopard skin as "the beauties which embellish the earth and which are derived from the light of the sun."

[89] *Gen. deor.* I, sub *Pane*.

causes are the chain which draws after it the births and durations and deaths of all things; their fallings and risings, their labours and felicities: — in short, all the fates that can befall them.[90]

been imagined in order that we might understand Nature to have been assigned the task of creating, nourishing, and rearing all things.[91]

Boccaccio's paraphrase [92] practically amounts to a translation, and Bacon doubtless knew his Cicero as well as Boccaccio did. The fact remains, however, that both writers lead up to the Ciceronian lines in much the same way, and that Bacon's phrasing presently recalls that of *De genealogiis deorum* in an earlier but analogous passage. In all likelihood Bacon was as familiar with the one source as with the other. I therefore give Boccaccio's paraphrase as including both.

Bacon

But if Fate be taken in a wider acceptation, so as to signify every event of any kind, and not the more noble only, yet in this sense too it excellently answers to the universal frame of things; seeing that there is nothing in the order of nature so small as to be without a cause, nor again anything so great but it depends on something else; so that the fabric of nature contains in her own lap and bosom every event whatever, both small and great, and develops them in due season by a fixed law. Therefore, no wonder that the Parcæ are represented as sisters of Pan, and certainly legitimate.[93]

Boccaccio

Cicero, in his book called *De divinatione*, writes thus about Fate: "I call Fate that which the Greeks call marmedinis; that is to say, order, chief of causes, cause of itself; and this is the eternal truth, which has abounded from all time. This being so, nothing will ever occur of which nature does not have the cause within itself. Therefore it is clear that Fate is not what it is superficially understood to be, but that it must be understood philosophically as the eternal cause of things, which underlies what was, what is, or shall be." [94]

And they called him Pana, from Pan, which means *the whole*. By this they meant that all things whatsoever, which are in the lap of Nature, are definitely the sum of things, whence Nature is the all.[95]

---

[90] XIII. 95.
[91] I. sub *De Demogorgone*.
[92] Cf. *De divin.* I, 5.
[93] VIII. 448.
[94] I, sub *Clotho, Lachesis et Atropos*.
[95] sub *De Pane*.

Boccaccio and Cicero are not the only sources of Bacon's interpretation of the Fates. The following table will show, I think, that Comes also contributed. It will further show (at least, so I believe) that the *Mythologiæ* had a considerable influence on Bacon's treatment of Pan in general.

Bacon	Natalis Comes
In addition to this the ancients feigned that Pan lived always in the open air, but the Fates in a huge subterranean cave, whence they suddenly flew to men with exceeding swiftness; because nature and the face of the universe is open and visible, whereas the fates of individuals are secret and rapid.[96]	They were said to live in a certain cave because the judgements of God are secret; nor do his punishments fly at once to wicked men, but when the opportune time for the vengeance of God arrives.[97]
Now it is Pan, that is the nature of things, that reduces these separate individuals to such various conditions; insomuch that the chain of nature and the thread of the Fates are (so far as individuals are concerned) the same thing.[98]	The Fates were said to draw the threads from the distaff for those about to be born (threads which determined the fortunes of these babes) because the philosophers believed that the fortunes, habits, actions, and vital energy of infants were from the first determined by the state of the air when they began to breathe.[99]
About his origin there are and can be but two opinions for Nature is either the offspring of Mercury,— that is the Divine Word (an opinion which the Scriptures establish beyond question, and which was entertained by all the more divine philosophers); or else of the seeds of things mixed and confused together.[100] For they who derive all things from a single principle either take that principle to be God, or if they hold it to be a material prin-	Pan was said to be the son of Mercury because Mercury is the Divine Power or Will, as we have said, which brings all things about, and Pan, or the totality of simple natural bodies, is governed by the Divine Will. . . . As for his having been generated by Penelope and all her suitors, the idea is abhorrent to nature, because. . . . But as Pan embraces all the natural bodies, and so his name signifies, he is said to have been generated by all that

[96] VIII. 448.　　[97] III. 6. 138.　　[98] VIII. 448.　　[99] III. 6. 137.

[100] This recalls Lucretius more than Comes. Cf. *De rer. nat.* V. with its description of primeval matter as "a strange stormy crisis and medley, gathered together out of first beginnings of every kind." I think it probable that Bacon had both sources in mind.

ciple, assert it to be though actually one yet potentially many; so that all difference of opinion on this point is reducible to one or other of these two heads,— the world is sprung either from Mercury, or from all the suitors.[101]

exist; that is to say, to consist of all.[102]

Again, the body of Nature is most truly described as biform; on account of the difference between the bodies of the upper and lower world. For the upper or heavenly bodies, are for their beauty and the equability and constancy of their motion, as well as for the influence they have upon earth and all that belongs to it, fitly represented under the human figure: but the others, by reason of their perturbations and irregular motions, and because they are under the influence of the celestial bodies, may be content with the figure of a brute.

Pan is the totality of natural bodies, as his name signifies, in which the divine is joined to the human (*sic*). This was expressed by the upper part of his body which was conceived of as beautiful and god-like, while the lower part was uncouth, as are the lower natural bodies, which constitute an hypostasis in nature.[104]

The scarf or mantle of Pan is very ingeniously feigned to be made of a panther's skin; on account of the spots scattered all over it. For the heavens are spotted with stars, the sea with islands, the earth with flowers; and even particular objects are generally variegated on the surface, which is as it were their mantle or scarf.[105]

Some have said that he wore not a hare-skin but a panther-skin (*pardalis pelle*), which some have compared to the stars, others to the earth; for the earth brings forth a multitude of animals and plants, and exhibits a wonderful variety of mountains, rivers, and seas.[106]

Pan is likewise especially called president of mountains.[107]

Nor did they regard him as other than the sun who called him president of mountains.[108]

---

[101] XIII. 94.
[102] V. 6. 301.
[103] XIII. 96.
[104] X. sub *De Pane*.
[105] XIII. 97.
[106] V. 6. In extending the comparison to the sea Comes is closer to Bacon than his predecessors; but the difference is slight enough. Bacon's observation of particular objects is probably original.
[107] XIII. 98.
[108] V. 6. Comes implies a source, but I have not found it.

With regard to the audacity of Pan in challenging Cupid to fight, it refers to this,— that matter is not without a certain inclination and appetite to dissolve the world and fall back into the ancient chaos; but that the overswaying concord of things (which is represented by Cupid or Love) restrains its will and effort in that direction and reduces it to order.[109]	It is said that he had a fight with Cupid. He was beaten by him because, as we have said, love and discord are regarded as the foundations of nature. Love provokes matter to multiplication, and stimulates procreation in all its forms; therefore it is said to be conquered by the maker in the struggle.[110]
As for the tale that the discovery of Ceres[111] was reserved for this god, and that while he was hunting, and denied to the rest of the gods though diligently and especially engaged in seeking her, it contains a very true and very wise admonition, which is, not to look for the invention of things useful for life and civilization from abstract philosophies, which are as it were the greater gods, even though they devote all their strength to the purpose; but only from Pan, that is from sagacious experience and the universal knowledge of nature; which oftentimes, by a kind of chance, and while engaged as it were in hunting, stumbles upon such discoveries.[112]	She was discovered to Jove by Pan, because the seed which have dropped lie hidden for some days till they strike root; but presently Pan (that is, nature herself, full of numberless seed) reveals them to Jove; for by natural necessity, and because of nature's warmth, the green things begin to sprout.[113]

Pan was attended not only by the Fates but also by the nymphs, and the fact is stated with significant similarity of expression by Bacon and Comes. Says Bacon:[114]

---

[109] XIII. 99.

[110] V. 6. 302.

[111] Ceres had hidden in distress because of the abduction of Proserpine.

[112] XIII. 100.

[113] V. 14. This passage is rather a suggestion than a source; yet the suggestion is quite distinct. Nature herself presently reveals her secrets, exhibiting them, as it were, to the sky above. Bacon elaborated, generalized, drew the inference. I am the more inclined to regard the passage as significant because a few lines above it there occurs, and in connection with Ceres, an *aliquid utile humanæ vitæ* which pretty closely parallels Bacon's *things useful for life and civilization.*

[114] VIII. 445.

He was regarded as the leader and commander of the Nymphs, who were always wont to dance and frisk around him.

With this compare Natalis Comes:[115]

Pan himself, since he embraces all things, was called the leader and prince of the nymphs.

Bacon, however, adds an interpretation for which, as applied to Pan and the nymphs, I can find no source. It goes as follows:[116]

Pan delights in the nymphs, that is, in spirits; for the spirits of living creatures are the delight of the world. And with reason is he styled their leader, for each of them follows its own nature as a guide, round which after their own fashion they leap and frisk in endless variety and constant motion. And therefore one of the moderns has ingeniously referred all the powers of the soul to motion.

The origin of this passage is to be found, I believe, in the account of the Muses given by Natalis Comes.[117] Comes quotes Hesiod on the Muses surrounding Apollo, "who stands in the midst," and "the energy of whose mind moves all the Muses," and comments as follows:

For Zezes has left it written that the Muses are nothing but knowledge and *those mental faculties which grasp it.*

Again, he identifies the Muses with the informing spirits of the planets which, as he explains at length, produce the various types of mind, and in their circling before the throne of God are as the Muses dancing around the altar of Jove.

Bacon regards it as confirming his interpretation of Pan that the god is not reported to have had many amours:[118]

For the world enjoys itself and in itself all things that are. Now he that is in love wants something, and where there is abundance of everything want can have no place.

The ultimate source of this conception is doubtless Plato, who, in his account of the creation, says:[119]

and he made the universe a circle moving in a circle, one and solitary, yet by reason of its excellence able to converse with itself, and needing no other friendship or acquaintance.

---

[115] V. 6. 302.
[116] VIII. 453.
[117] VII. 15. 512.
[118] XIII. 101.
[119] *The Dialogues of Plato*, trans. by B. Jowett, III. 453.

It must not be forgotten, however, that the *Timaeus* had a profound influence on the Fathers of the Church. Thus Thomas Aquinas:[120]

Love is of two kinds: the love of concupiscence and the love of friendship. But God cannot love irrational creatures with the love of concupiscence, for He lacks nothing external to himself.

and Dionysius the Areopagite:[121]

For in all things, from the beginning and forever, Divine Love desires itself, moving as in an eternal circle, from goodness, in goodness, to goodness; proceeding in unchanging change, ever the same, ever according to the same; proceeding ever, and ever remaining.

Bacon's interpretation does not ignore Pan's wife, Echo; or even his less legitimate love, Syringa. In fact, he continues:[122]

The world therefore can have no loves, nor any want (being content with itself) unless it be of discourse. Such is the nymph Echo, or if it be of the more exact and measured kind, Syringa. And it is excellently provided that of all discourses or voices Echo alone should be chosen for the world's wife. For that is in fact the true philosophy which echoes most faithfully the voice of the world itself, and is written as it were from the world's own dictation; being indeed nothing else than the image and reflection of it, which it only repeats and echoes, but adds nothing of its own.

Bacon is still in agreement with Plato, but with subtle differences. As in the case of Pan and Ceres, he has drawn a lesson from his text, and he has picturesquely embodied in concrete images the world's converse with itself. In this last, however, he is not original. Broccaccio leads up to his interpretation of Syringa as the harmony of nature in the following words:

What the ancients wished to signify when they said that Pan was conquered by love will not, I suppose, prove hard to understand. Just as soon as God created nature, it began to operate; and taking delight in its operations, it began to love them. Thus, moved by delight, it subjected itself to love.

Behind Boccaccio's interpretation, and doubtless not unknown to Bacon, are, I believe, the speculations of the churchmen: of Thomas Aquinas, for example, who says:[123]

God does not desire Himself alone, but other things also. . . . Indeed, in nature, beings have an inclination not merely to acquire what they lack

---

[120] *Summa Theol.*, I. 20. 2.
[121] *De Divinis Nominibus*, IV. 14.
[122] XIII. 101.
[123] *Summa Theol.*, I. 19. 2.

and enjoy what they have, but also to communicate what they have to others, within the limits of possibility. Therefore we see every agent, in proportion to its perfection, creating in its own image. And if this is true of every agent it must be even more so of the Divine Will, which in fact communicates its goodness to the external world in its own image as far as is possible. In short, God desires Himself as an end and the external world as a means.

Again, Dionysius, discussing the world as an image of God, calls it an echo: [124]

As in vision an image is a certain approximation which in a manner conveys to us its original; so in hearing, an echo (resonantia) is an approximation of the speaking voice, from which, indeed, it is as it were reflected. Think therefore of the beauty and grace of God as giving forth an echo (echus), so to speak, from the absolute and the occult, in which approximation it is granted to God's creatures to grasp the absolute itself.

Having discussed Pan's wife, Bacon passes on to his progeny, which, he tells us, should be regarded as non-existent, reports to the contrary being later additions to the myth. He interprets Pan's childlessness as follows: [125]

That the world has no issue, is another allusion to the sufficiency and perfection of it in itself. Generation goes on among the parts of the world, but how can the world generate, when no body exists out of itself?

Like the preceding allusion to the world's sufficiency, this passage is ultimately of Platonic origin, and like the other may be referred to the *Timaeus*: [126]

His intention was, in the first place, that the animal should be as far as possible a perfect whole and of perfect parts: secondly, that it should be one, leaving no remnants out of which another such world might be created: and also that it should be free from old age and unaffected by disease.

Here again, however, Thomas Aquinas reminds us [127] that Bacon probably had more sources than one:

According to Dionysius, in *De Divinis Nominibus*, IV, love draws the lover out of himself and in a manner conveys him into the beloved object. But it is not possible to conceive of God as existing outside of Himself, therefore it would seem impossible to conceive of Him as loving any but Himself.

---

[124] *De Coelesti Hierarchia*, II. 25.
[125] XIII. 101.
[126] Dialogues, *ed. cit.*, III. 452.
[127] *Summa Theol.*, I. 20. 2.

It is in refutation of this view of the Areopagite that Thomas formulates the doctrine of God's love of His creatures as means which I have quoted above.

We do not need to go further than Vergil to find the source of Bacon's statement that Pan was aptly called the god of hunters because all life is a pursuit.[128] The passage in the *Bucolics* which he quotes in part expresses the same idea:[129]

The grim lioness goes after the wolf, the wolf, for his part, after the goat, the playful goat after the flowering lucern, Corydon after you, Alexis,—each is drawn by his peculiar pleasure.

So, too, the assertion that Pan was rightly considered the god of country-folk, because these are closer to nature than city-dwellers,[130] is implicit, especially if the suggested disapproval of the town-folk be considered, in such Vergilian passages as the following:[131]

Yet not the less blessed is he who has won the friendship of the rural gods, Pan and old Silvanus, and the sisterhood of nymphs. He is not moved by honors that the people confer, or the purple of empire. . . .

Indeed, the happy closeness of the country-man to nature was a favorite theme throughout the Renaissance and may be regarded as a literary convention. Conventional, too, was the identification of "Panic terror" with the instinct of self-preservation, though it harmonizes admirably with the truly philosophical tone of Bacon's noble essay.

In discussing the myth of Coelum, Bacon, as we have seen, takes into consideration the fact of corruption regarded as physical decay, and accounts for it according to classical philosophy. In the present essay he considers the phenomenon in its wider aspect of evil, and in a manner interestingly characteristic of the Renaissance blends in his explanation of it classical philosophy and Christian doctrine. His vehicle is the myth that Pan was born of Jupiter and Hybris or contumele.[132] Orthodoxly enough, he identifies the sin of Adam with contumele against God,[133] and, duly attributing to it "death and all our woes," interprets as follows:[134]

---

[128] XIII. 98.
[129] *Eclogues*, II. 63.
[130] XIII. 98.
[131] *Georgics*, II. 493.
[132] See Apollonius, *Library*, I. 4. 1.
[133] *Numbers*, XXVII. 14; John, XII, 43.
[134] VIII. 447.

From the third story of Pan's origin, it would seem as if the Greeks, either by intercourse with the Egyptians or otherwise, had heard something of the Hebrew mysteries. For it relates to the state of the world, not at its very birth, but after the fall of Adam; exposed and made subject to death and corruption. For that state was and is the offspring of God and Sin (or Contumely). For the sin of Adam, when he wished to "become like God," was a kind of contumely. Therefore the threefold account of the birth of Pan may be allowed as true, if rightly distinguished with respect to facts and times. For this Pan (as we now view and understand him) is the offspring of the Divine Word, through the medium of confused matter (which itself however was the work of God), and with the help of Sin, and by Sin Corruption, entering in.

The interpretation is predominantly a Christian one; yet, as far as I know, the doctrine that God achieved the creation with the help of sin has not been advanced by any Christian theologian. Saint Augustine and Thomas Aquinas may be said to imply some such idea, for both regard sin as necessary to the harmonious completeness of God's work;[135] but both are obviously indebted to the *Timæus,* and it is Plato's God who deliberately creates mortal and corruptible beings with the help of a coöperating agency.[136] I think it probable, therefore, that Bacon also has the *Timæus* in mind.

Proserpine.[137]

Few myths are more famous than that of Proserpine, carried away to Hell, while gathering flowers, by Pluto; long sought, torch in hand, by her mother Ceres; and at last, though the pomegranate seed which she had eaten prevented her complete release, yet granted leave by Jove to return to earth six months every year. The usual interpretation of this myth, which Bacon might have found in Cicero[138] and elsewhere, is that Proserine symbolizes the seed of all plants, and that her yearly return stands for the sprouting of all green things. Bacon, however, offers an explanation of his own,—one of the most peculiar and interesting in his repertory. Let him speak for himself:

The fable relates, as I take it, to Nature, and explains the source of that rich and fruitful supply of active power subsisting in the under world, from which all the growths of our upper world spring, and into which they

---

[135] St. Aug., *De civ. Dei,* XI. 18; Thom. Aquin. *Sum. Theol.*, II. 2, 47. 1 and II 2. 48. 2.
[136] Jowett's Plato, III. 460.
[137] XIII. 163.
[138] *De nat. deor.*, II. 26.

again return and are resolved. By Proserpine the ancients signified that ethereal spirit which, having been separated by violence from the upper globe, is enclosed and imprisoned beneath the earth (which earth is represented by Pluto), as was well expressed by those lines:

> Whether that the Earth yet fresh, and from the deeps
> Of heaven new-sundered, did some seeds retain,
> Some sparks and motions of its kindred sky.

We have here, then, a symbol not merely of the forces of vegetation but of all the creative energies of the earth. Of this Bacon leaves us no doubt when further on in the essay he discusses " the spirit which is contained in metals and minerals."[139] These energies are one in essence and, as we presently learn, quite distinct from the matter they give life to. Proserpine is well named the queen of the subterranean world,[140]

for the spirit does in fact govern and manage everything in those regions, without the help of Pluto, who remains stupid and unconscious.

Indeed, the creative power would escape to the upper regions and leave the world a dead mass behind it; but it is nourished and thus detained, even as Proserpine was.[141]

The peculiar Hylozoism set forth above is of exceptional interest because of its importance in Bacon's philosophy. The essay on Proserpine is in fact an allegory of his theory of spirits. In his *Sylva sylvarum* he tells us so himself:[142]

For spirits are nothing else but a natural body, rarified to a proportion, and included in the tangible parts of bodies, as in an integument. And they be no less differing one from the other than the dense or tangible parts; and they are in all tangible bodies whatsoever, more or less; and they are never (almost) at rest; and from them and their motions principally proceed arefactions, colloquation, concoction, maturation, putrefaction, vivification, and most of the effects of nature; for, as we have figured them in our *Sapientia veterum*, in the fable of Proserpina, you shall in the infernal regiment hear little doings of Pluto, but most of Proserpina: for tangible parts in bodies are stupid things; and the spirits do (in effect) all.

Bacon implies the same identification in much else he says about the spirits, and in some of these passages throws further light on his interpretation of Proserpine. Thus in *Historia vitæ et mortis.*:[143]

---

[139] XIII. 166. [141] XIII. 166. [143] X. 156.
[140] XIII. 165. [142] IV. 219.

No known body in the upper parts of the earth is without a spirit, whether it proceed by attenuation and concoction from the heat of the heavenly bodies, or by some other way. . . . Now the grosser parts of bodies, being of a sluggish and not every movable nature, would last for a long time, if this spirit did not disturb, agitate and undermine them, and prey upon the moisture of the body, and whatever else it can turn into fresh spirit; after which both the pre-existing and the newly formed spirit gradually escape together.

The spirits prey on matter, but by their expansion create bodies out of it: [144]

Generation or vivification is likewise the combined work of the spirit and the grosser parts, but in a very different manner. For the spirit is entirely detained, but swells and moves locally; and the grosser parts are not dissolved, but follow the motion of the spirit, which as it were inflates and thrusts them out into various figures.

Whence did Bacon derive the curious doctrine embodied in the essay on Proserpine? The lines which he quotes occur in Ovid's account of the first appearance of man,[145] and the ideas expressed in them are mentioned by Lucretius [146] in an obvious allusion to Empedocles's theory of the first appearance of living beings in general. His "ethereal spirit," too, which he describes as "enclosed and imprisoned beneath the earth," answers more or less to Empedocles's imprisoned fire or ether, whose yearning to its native upper regions, whence it was forcibly divorced, pushed to the surface animals and plants.[147] Again, Heraclitus's vital fire "feeds on vapors which rise from the damp." [148] All this comes to mind as we read Bacon's essay and his other discussions of his theory, and doubtless he is indebted to it to some extent; but it does not account satisfactorily for his doctrine. Bacon speaks of spirits as well as of a spirit, and he traces their origin to the stars. It has been remarked that Paracelsus does likewise,[149] and I believe this obser-

---

[144] *Ibid.*, 158.

[145] I. 80-85.

[146] V. 906-908.

[147] Gomperz, *Greek Thinkers*, I. 237.

[148] *Ibid.*, 65.

[149] III. 319, where, also, it is recalled that the idea of a vital spirit permeating animals and plants "seems to be coeval with the first origin of speculative physiology," and it is stated that Bacon "was one of those by whom this idea was extended from organised to inorganic bodies." I believe this last statement to be without solid foundation.

vation to be the key to the whole question, provided that we extend it to the alchemists in general. Paracelsus's "smoke-souls," [150] which coagulate into the things of earth, but would ultimately be resolved into the universal cosmic spirit were they not nourished by the stars, are at most a modification of the spirits described in all Hermetic writings, and I think I can show that it is to these writings that Bacon is chiefly indebted. Indeed, one is irresistibly reminded of the alchemists in reading the essay on Proserpine. Bacon uses their language throughout. Proserpine is surely the " anima mundi" which they again and again represent as a florid and prolific mother.[151]

Let us compare Bacon's utterances in our essay with those of the alchemists. As for his general conception, let us compare it with the following: [152]

> The quickening power of the earth produces all things that grow forth from it, and he who says that the earth has no life makes a statement which is flatly contradicted by the most ordinary facts. For what is dead cannot produce life and growth, seeing that it is devoid of the quickening spirit. This spirit is the life and soul that dwell in the earth, and are nourished by heavenly and sidereal influences. For all herbs, trees, and roots, and all metals and minerals, receive their growth and nutriment from the spirit of the earth, which is the spirit of life. This spirit is itself fed by the stars, and is thereby rendered capable of imparting nutriment to all things that grow, and of nursing them as a mother does her child while it is yet in the womb. The minerals are hidden in the womb of the earth and nourished by her with the spirit which she receives from above.
>
> Thus the power of growth that I speak of is not imparted by the earth but by the life-giving spirit that is in it. If the earth were deserted by this spirit, it would be dead, and no longer able to afford nourishment to anything.

The correspondence is not perfect; yet here we have the influence of the stars, the emphasized independence of the earth-spirit from matter, and, a typical Hermetic view, the regarding of minerals as growths. Hardly less noteworthy is this other, from a second alchemist: [153]

---

[150] *Philosophiæ ad Athenienses*, III. 3, III. 6.

[151] H. S. Redgrove, *Alchemy Ancient and Modern*, 26; M. Maier, *Scrutinium chymicum*.

[152] Basil Velentine, *The Twelve Keys*; Redgrove, *op. cit.*, 25.

[153] Benedictus Figulus, *A Golden and Blessed Casket of Nature's Marvels*, pp. 71 and 72 in A. E. Waite's English trans.

The elements and compounds, in addition to crass matter, are composed of a subtle substance, or intrinsic radical humidity, diffused through the elemental parts, simple and wholly incorruptible, long preserving the things themselves in vigor, and called the Spirit of the World.

As I have said, the correspondence between the passages quoted above and Bacon's utterances is not perfect. In those passages there is discussed a single spirit, which, furthermore, does not prey on matter but is nourished by the stars alone. The first of these discrepancies, however, is merely apparent. Alchemy was largely an application of mysticism, and the doctrine that men share a universal soul but possess individual spirits was paralleled in the case of "material growths"; that is animals, plants, and things.[154] Indeed, a chain of spiritual being was postulated, and the links were regarded as proceeding from each other. Thus a given metal differed from the rest in virtue of a specific spirit; but this was a modification or state of a common "metalline soul" which in its turn, through the principles of which it consisted, was an emanation of the "anima mundi" informing all matter; and the "anima mundi" emanated from the "spirit of the universe" and ultimately from God.[155] It would seem, then, that the theories of the alchemists rather explain than controvert Bacon's. The second discrepancy is a real one, and it may be that the influence of Heraclitus has something to do with the matter; nevertheless I think it probable that in this case also Bacon is chiefly indebted to the Hermetic philosophers, whose doctrine of transmutation includes beliefs concerning the nourishing of spirits which at once recall his. Before examining this question in detail, however, let us hear Bacon himself in the essay on Proserpine.

Bacon interprets the episode of the pomegranate seed—Proserpine's eating the seed, and her consequent detention—as follows:

Proserpine remains fixed where she is; the reason and manner whereof is accurately and admirably set forth in those two agreements between Jupiter and Ceres. For with regard to the first, most certain it is that there are two ways of confining and restraining spirit in solid and earthly

---

[154] Redgrove, 15.

[155] Redgrove, 15 and note; Janus Lacinius, *The New Pearl of Great Price*, A. E. Waite's Eng. trans. 262; Benedictus Figulus, *A Golden and Blessed Casket of Nature's Marvels*, Waite's Eng. trans., 60. French, *Distill.*, V. 107, with which compare Vincent of Beauvais, *Spec. Majus*, VIII. 60.

matter; one by constipation and obstruction, which is simple imprisonment and violence; the other by administering some suitable aliment, which is spontaneous and free. For when the imprisoned spirit begins to feed and nourish itself, it is no longer in a hurry to escape, but becomes settled as in its own land.

Despite the quaintness of his language, Bacon makes his meaning quite clear. He wishes to explain how creative energy may be understood to inform matter. Discarding physical occlusion, he postulates a closer identification analogous to the assimilation of food by the body. As we have seen, he conceives of the spirit as becoming in a sense continuous with the enclosing body through the medium of a process of absorption or transmutation. This process Bacon calls feeding; but it is worthy of note, as will presently appear, that he explains it rather as an act of procreation, by which the spirit generates more spirit from surrounding matter:[156]

... every spirit seated among the grosser parts dwells unhappily; and being in such solitude, where it finds nothing like itself, it the more strives to make and create something similar; and to increase its quantity, it works hard to multiply itself, and prey upon the volatile part of the grosser bodies.

Evidently, then, Bacon has two ideas more or less confusedly associated in his mind: that spirit feeds on matter, and that it joins with it in an act of procreation. Let us now inquire whether he can have found similar conceptions in the works of the alchemists.

The Hermetic doctrine of transmutation was founded on the belief that the "metalline soul," when not stunted in its development by somewhat indefinite "impurities," was identical with the spirit of gold; and that when released from matter and introduced in its purity into any base metal, it would draw the metalline soul there into its own state of perfection, assimilating from it what was pure and rejecting the extraneous element.[157] We have here, then, something akin to digestion, and in fact the process is very frequently called by that name.[158] Just as frequently, however, it is called generation,[159] and the transmuting agent is likened to sperm. If it is further considered that the pure metalline spirit is often

---

[156] X. 162.
[157] Bonus of Ferrara, in *The New Pearl of Great Price*, 295.
[158] *Ibid.*, 215 et seq.
[159] Michael Scott, same work, 420; Bonus of Ferrara, 283 et seq.

identified with the "anima mundi"[160] (of which, in fact, it is the metalline manifestation), it becomes apparent that the Hermetic doctrine is closely analogous to Bacon's. Equally suggestive of Bacon's theory is that upon which were founded the attempts to make the philosopher's stone. The pure metalline spirit was not conceived of as a simple principle but as a spiritual soul in a spiritual body or medium of contact with matter,[161] the one active and quick to escape, the other passive and semi-material. Furthermore, these two principles were regarded as identical with the spirits of sulphur and of mercury, the spirit of sulphur being usually identified with the active principle, though some alchemists taught the opposite. By pulverizing and distilling in a closed receptacle a mixture of sulphur and mercury, it was thought possible to extract and mingle the respective spirits. The active principle was then supposed to assimilate the other, and the result, brought to an unexplained materiality by condensation, was the famous stone. Now the union of the two spirits was technically known as "fixation": but inasmuch as it gave rise to the stone it was constantly described as a marriage;[162] and because the stone was regarded as a mineral sperm, and sperm as highly "digested" blood, it was no less frequently referred to as a digesting of the "body" by the "soul" or a nourishing of the "soul" by the "body,"

The peculiar ideas I have just described are more or less explicitly expressed in a number of Hermetic works. Bacon may have found several passages of this kind in a book entitled *Pretiosa margarita*,[163] published by the Aldine Press in 1546, which, besides the treatise from which it takes its title, contains selections from half a dozen others. Thus in the treatise:[164]

The generation of gold is of quicksilver, and its nutriment (like that of the chicken in the egg) is of the yellow substance, namely sulphur. Hence the stone is generated of the white, i. e., quicksilvers, and the nutriment of the yellow.

---

[160] Redgrove, 31.

[161] Bonus of Ferrara, 257 et seq.

[162] Redgrove, 31.

[163] This is the book translated by A. E. Waite under the title of *The New Pearl of Great Price*.

[164] *The New Pearl of Great Price*, 290.

Again, in the selection from Michael Scott:[165]

But as only that sperm which is prepared in the vital liver generates in the case of animals; so only after long and patient digestion are our mineral spirits capable of producing our Stone.

Not infrequently the gastric, sexual, and spiritual conceptions of the union became somewhat confused in the writer's mind. Thus Sir George Ripley, an English alchemist of the second half of the fifteenth century, advises us to [166]

> Put the Soule with the Body and Spirite
> Together in one that they may meete
> In his Damnes belley till he wax great,
> With giving Drinke of his owne sweate:
> For the Milke of a Cow to a Child my brother
> Is not so Sweete as the Milke of his Mother.

The process of "feeding" was applied to the completed "stone" in order to replenish or multiply it;[167] but in the case of "fixation" it was intended to furnish the active principle with a medium through which it might act on matter, and, what is especially to our purpose, to prevent it from escaping. This last fact is frequently emphasized.[168]

It is the body which retains the soul, and the soul can show its power only when it is united to the body. Therefore, when the Artist sees the white soul arise, he should join it to its body in the very same instant; for no soul can be retained without its body.

Because the "soul" might escape, the vessel in which it was liberated must be kept well shut till fixation was assured:[169]

> When your Ferments [170] to your matters be put,
> Then your Vessell close you must shut.

Let it be noted, too, that in these Hermetic prescriptions Bacon may have found a suggestion of something more specifically to his purpose than fixation in general. Says another English alchemist:[171]

---

[165] *Op. cit.*, 425.
[166] *A Short Worke* (in E. Ashmole's *Theatrum Chemicum Britannicum*).
[167] Norton's *Ordinall*, "The Eleventh Gate" (in *Theat. Chem. Brit.*)
[168] *The New Pearl of Great Price*, 256.
[169] *Theat. Chem. Brit.*, sub *Anonymi*, chap. IV.
[170] The active principle.
[171] Sir George Ripley, *The Compound of Alchymie*, "Eighth Gate" (in *Theat. Chem. Brit.*)

> But when these to sublymacyon continuall
> Be laboryd so, with hete both moyst and temporate,
> That all is whyte and purely made spirituall;
> Then Heaven upon Earth must be reiterate,
> Unto the Sowle with the Body be reincorporate:
> That Earth becom all that afore was Hevyn,
> Whych will be done in Sublymacyons sevyn.

This association of alchemistical with cosmic ideas was frequent and natural, for the alchemist imagined himself to be imitating cosmic processes. Paracelsus, for example, asserts this point of view at length, and indeed explains the earth as a fecundated egg, surrounded by its nourishing albumen the atmosphere, almost in the words of the *Pretiosa margarita*.[172]

So much for Bacon's interpretation of Proserpine's eating the pomegranate seed. Let us now turn a step backward and consider his explanation of her violent abduction. It goes as follows:[173]

> This spirit is represented as having been ravished, that is suddenly and forcibly carried off by the Earth; because there is no holding it in if it have time and leisure to escape, and the only way to confine and fix it is by a sudden pounding and breaking up; just as if you would mix air with water, you can only do it by sudden and rapid agitation: for thus it is that we see these bodies united in foam, the air being as it were ravished by the water.

Having explained to us how cosmic energy may be conceived to combine with matter, Bacon, in this passage, tells us how it may be supposed to mingle with it in such a way as to make combination possible. We are reminded of Anaxagoras and of Empedocles, and it may well be, too, that Bacon was impressed with the phenomenon of foam, which he mentions again elsewhere;[174] yet, when all is said, he is describing the making of an emulsion. He talks more like a chemist than a cosmologist, and the alchemists frequently use much the same language. Wishing to combine the "soul" of the metalline spirit with its "body," they mix sulphur and mercury together as thoroughly as possible, pounding and pulverizing the mixture. Thus Arnold de Villa Nova:[175]

---

[172] *De natura verum*, IV.
[173] XIII. 164.
[174] X. 159.
[175] *The New Pearl of Great Price*, 331. See also 412.

Our earth is not sublimed in its condition as calx, unless it be first subtly incorporated with mercury. Hence you should pound the earth, saturate it with mercury and digest them till they become one body. This must be repeated over and over again, or else the sublimation cannot take place, because the earth will not be properly incorporated with the mercury.

When sublimation occurred, the two principles, the active immeshed in the passive, as it were, and bearing it up, were supposed to rise together and combine.

Bacon tells us that for vital energy to be properly incorporated with matter it must not only be " pounded up " but also " curdled " or torpid at the time of incorporation:[176]

It is prettily added that Proserpina was carried off while in the act of gathering flowers of Narcissus in the valleys: for Narcissus takes its name from torpor or stupor; and it is only when beginning to curdle, and as it were to gather torpor, that spirit is in the best state to be caught up and carried off by earthly matter.

I will presently show that Bacon was not the first to understand Narcissus as meaning torpor and to allegorize accordingly. The point just now is his idea about creative energy. Paracelsus regarded all matter as the " coagulation " of such energy,[177] and the word is of constant occurrence among the alchemists. The Hermetic philosophers apply the term not only to the actual formation of matter but also to the union in spiritu of its principles, and not infrequently they imply their belief in a preliminary coagulation of the active principle. For example, Raymondus Lullius, describing a certain method of distillation, says:[178]

By this continual heat the body is subtilized, and the spirit condensed. The gentler the fire, and the slower the distillation, the more perfectly is the process performed.

Again, Arnold de Villa Nova tells us that:[179]

Unless the bodies become incorporeal, and the spirits corporeal, no progress will be made. The true beginning, then, of our work is the solution of our body, because bodies, when dissolved, become spiritual in their nature, and are yet at the same time more fixed than the spirit, though they are dissolved with it. For the solution of the body means the coagulation of the spirit and vice versa; each gives up something of its own nature: they meet each other half-way, and thus become one inseparable substance, like water mixed with water.

---

[176] XIII. 165.
[177] Phil. and Athen. III. 3.
[178] The New Pearl of Great Price, 356.
[179] Ibid, 316.

It should be remembered, too, that the process by which the component parts of the stone threw off their grosser selves was constantly referred to and represented as the death of the two substances.[180]

Bacon's conception of the earth-spirit as something imprisoned and ready to escape would naturally lead him to look upon the metals as more retentive of their vitality than the more porous organic bodies. This, in fact, he does:[181]

> For though the spirit which is contained in metals and minerals is prevented from getting out chiefly perhaps by the solidity of the mass, that which is contained in plants and animals dwells in a porous body, from which it could easily escape if it were not by that process of tasting reconciled to remain.

As I have said, this idea may have occurred spontaneously to Bacon; but in so far as it is concerned with metals it was already a familiar one to the alchemists, whose main reason, indeed, for pounding and calcinating the minerals they used was to set free the spirits within,[182] though as we have seen, they also had in mind the mingling of these principles. One of them, for example, declares that:[183]

> The seed of animals and vegetables is something separate, and may be cut out or otherwise separately exhibited; but metallic seed is diffused throughout the metal and contained in all its smallest parts; neither can it be discerned from its body; its extraction is therefore a task which may well tax the ingenuity of the most experienced philosopher.

The notion that the spirit of organic bodies might escape through their pores may have been suggested to Bacon by Lucretius:[184]

> No pain, however, can lightly pierce thus far nor any sharp malady make its way in, without all things being so thoroughly disordered that no room is left for life, and the parts of the soul fly abroad through all the pores of the body.

Bacon tells us that Ceres strove in vain to release her imprisoned daughter; and that two heroes, Theseus and Pirithous, descended

---

[180] Redgrove, 32; *The New Pearl of Great Price*, 38-45.
[181] XIII. 166.
[182] Redgrove, 32.
[183] Eirenheus Philalethes, *The Metamorphoses of Metals;* see Redgrove, 80.
[184] *De rer. nat.*, III. 252-255.

into Hell to rescue Proserpine, but were themselves detained there. He interprets both episodes as symbolizing the tendency of certain external agencies to cause the escape of the earth-spirit. In the case of Ceres he says as follows: [185]

The air meanwhile, and the power of the celestial region (which is represented by Ceres) strives with infinite assiduity to win forth and recover this imprisoned spirit again; and that torch which the air carries—the lighted torch in Ceres's hand—means no doubt the Sun, which does the office of a lamp all over the earth, and would do more than anything else for the recovery of Proserpina, were the thing at all possible.

Much the same view is expressed in *Historia vitæ et mortis*: [186]

With regard to the second desire, namely, that of escaping and resolving itself into air, it is certain that all thin bodies (which are always movable) move willingly to their likes when near at hand. One drop of water moves toward another, and flame to flame; but much more does this appear in the escape of the spirit into the external air, because it is not carried to a particle like itself, but to a very world of connaturals.

Once again we are reminded of Empedocles's imprisoned ether drawn back to its native sphere. We are also reminded of Lucretius, where he says: [187] "For whatever ebbs from things, is all borne always into the great sea of air." Finally, we are reminded of Paracelsus. Bacon also speaks of the influence of the sun; but this is not unnatural, for he knows that luminary as the chief source of life and of corruption.[188] As for the interpretation of Ceres's torch, Natalis Comes identifies her chariot with the sun;[189] but in any case, Bacon's interpretation of Proserpine almost involves that of Ceres.

Bacon's interpretation of the episode of Theseus and Pirithous is much more remarkable than the other: [190]

The meaning is that the subtler spirits which in many bodies descend to the earth often fail to draw out and assimilate and carry away with them the subterranean spirit, but contrariwise are themselves curdled and never reascend again, and so go to increase the number of Proserpina's people and the extent of her empire.

---

[185] XIII. 165.
[186] X. 162.
[187] *De rer. nat.*, V. 275-277.
[188] Aristotle, *De gener. et corruptione*, II. 10.
[189] *Mythologiæ*, V. 14.
[190] XIII. 166.

This would seem to mean that extra-terrestrial bodies project into the earth principles which would release the earth-spirit were it not that they themselves become earthly. Now it will be remembered that the alchemists believed the earth-spirit to be replenished by the heavenly bodies. They did not, to my knowledge, regard these bodies as tending to set the spirit free; but they professed two doctrines in connection with their art which may very well have suggested what Bacon says. One was that in the process of sublimation the active principle bore up with it the passive, but was finally held down by it when fixation occurred. The other was that a superabundance of raw material would overpower the spirits and transform them into its own nature.

It will readily be understood that the first of the doctrines explained above is analogous to that set forth by Bacon. Says Bonus of Ferrara:[191]

The force of the body should prevail over the force of the soul, and instead of the body being carried upward with the soul, the soul remains with the body, the work is crowned with success, and the spirit [192] will abide with the two in indissoluble union forever.

The process during which the "body" was supposed to be "carried upward with the soul" took place in a closed receptacle, the distilled vapors rising to the top and suggesting "heaven," as we have seen, to one author. Evaporation was followed by condensation and then repeated; so that "heaven" came to "earth" a number of times and bore up with it the earthly quintessence, till at least it was "coagulated" and "fixed." As for the second doctrine, it may very well have contributed to Bacon's idea that ethereal emnations are transmuted into more material things. Arnold de Villa Nova has this transmutation in mind when he says that "The ferment must exceed or at least equal in weight its sulphur"; and also, in regard to the proportion between crude sulphur and quintessence, that: "if there be a preponderance of the body it will quickly change the volatile sulphur into a powder of its own color."[193]

In regard to Theseus and Pirithous, Bacon tells us that only those mortals might return from Dis who first provided themselves

---

[191] *The New Pearl of Great Price*, 262.
[192] A link between "body" and "soul" sometimes postulated.
[193] *The New Pearl of Great Price*, 334.

with a certain gold branch growing like mistletoe on a tree in a deep forest; in short, the branch that Vergil has made us all familiar with. He comments as follows:[194]

As for the golden branch, it may seem difficult for me to withstand the Alchemists. if they attack me from that side; seeing they promise us by that same stone of theirs not only mountains of gold, but also the restitution of natural bodies, as it were from the gates of the Infernals. Nevertheless for Alchemy and those that are never weary of their wooing of that stone, as I am sure they have no ground in theory, I suspect that they have no very good pledge of success in practice. And therefore putting them aside, here is my opinion as to the meaning of that last part of the parable. From many figurative allusions I am satisfied that the ancients regarded the conservation, and to a certain extent the restoration, of natural bodies as a thing not desperate, but rather as abstruse and out of the way. And this is what I take them in the passage before us to mean, by placing this branch in the midst of the innumerable other branches of a vast and thick wood. They represented it as golden, because gold is the emblem of duration; and grafted, because the effect in question is to be looked for as the result of art, not of any medicine or method which is simple or natural.

In the passage quoted above, Bacon implies that the alchemists identified the golden bough with the philosopher's stone, and some of them doubtless did. A. Pernety, in his *Dictionnaire Mytho-Hermetique,* published at Paris in 1787, says as follows:

Rameau d'or . . . est le symbole de la matière des sages, suivant que l'explique d'Espagnet. Il est pris d'un arbre semblable à celui ou étoit suspendue la toison d'or. Mais la difficulté est de reconnaître cette branche et ce rameau; car les Philosophes, dit le même Auteur, se sont étudíes plus particulièrement à le cacher que toute autre chose.

I am not familiar with Pernety's authority, and have found no specific mention of the golden bough in the alchemists I have read; but I think it very probable that the symbol was traditional. Lacinius represents the metals as a grove of trees,[195] Bonus of Ferrara calls the stone "the Golden Tree,"[196] Maier describes it as a "Tree of Life" bearing rejuvenating golden apples.[197] It would be natural, too, for the alchemists to associate Vergil's golden bough

---

[194] XII. 166.
[195] *The New Pearl of Great Price,* 30-36.
[196] *Ibid,* 238.
[197] *Scrutinium chymicum,* emblem 9 and epigram 26.

with mistletoe,[198] a plant popularly believed to have the power of revealing the presence of gold.[199]

Bacon symbolizes in the Vergilian grove the difficulty of renovating natural bodies. He implies that his interpretation is original; nevertheless it was probably suggested to him by the alchemists. Says Pernety:

Ils entendent par le terme de forêt la matière terrestre dans laquelle leur vraie matière prochaine est comme confondue, et d'où il la tirent comme d'un chaos.

Bacon does not believe in the philosopher's stone. Its reproductive powers, its ability to eliminate "impurities" from natural bodies, the "impurities" themselves, indeed, and the evolution of metals which they are supposed to retard: all these he regards as dreams.[200] But when it comes to the ultimate objects which the stone is supposed to achieve, he is at one with the alchemists. He believes it possible not only to rejuvenate living beings but also to transmute metals.[201] This, it should be observed, is pretty much the position of Albertus Magnus,[202] one of the philosophers themselves. Indeed, in protesting that the performance of the miracle can be accomplished only by a profoundly scientific "art," he is in accord with many alchemists. The difference between him and them is not that he has a much maturer conception than they do of what such a scientific art should be, or that he is singular in requiring, theoretically, that it should be the result of observation and experiment; but rather that he is not sure of possessing it, whereas most of his fellows in stern criticism are.[203] It is by no means astonishing that he should adapt their symbolism to his use; he unquestionably adapts much more than that. We have seen that his conception of spirits and some of his ideas about them are paralleled in Hermetic works. In view of his somewhat disdainful

---

[198] It will be recalled that Vergil compares the bough with mistletoe, with which, indeed, he probably identified it. Cf. Æn., VI. 205 et seq.

[199] J. G. Frazer, Balder the Beautiful, II. 284, et seq.

[200] IV. 315.

[201] Ibid, 316.

[202] Cf. Thorndike, A History of Magic and Experimental Science, II. 568.

[203] See for example Paracelsus in his De alchimia. In theory he is as much an experimentalist as Bacon; but he believes himself to have made all the experiments necessary, and is dogmatical about them.

setting aside of the alchemists, it may be well to trace his indebtedness to them further.

I have said that Bacon believes in the possibility of transmuting metals. One of the passages in which he expresses this belief goes as follows: [204]

In the meantime, by occasion of handling the axioms touching maturation, we will direct a trial touching the maturing of metals and thereby turning some of them into gold: for we conceive indeed that a perfect good concoction or digestion or maturation of some metals will produce gold.

As we presently discover, Bacon means that transmutation follows when the spirit of a metal completely "digests" the substance of it, and that the process is to be regarded as a "maturation" of the metal itself. At first sight the passage seems to speak for itself. However, it is not as literally alchemistical as it appears to be, for in a measure Bacon is using the vocabulary of the alchemist in a new sense, much as he does that of the schoolman. According to the Hermetic philosophers, a metal became gold when the metalline spirit informing it was able to achieve the complete "digestion" or assimilation of its "body" by its "soul." Again, when pure metalline spirit was introduced into a base metal, it "digested" or drew into its own nature the imperfect spirit there by ejecting the "impurities" and thus making possible the complete integration of its parts. Now Bacon's spirits, closely similar to those of the alchemists though they are, do not consist of "souls" and "bodies"; and as applied to them, "digestion" means either the actual transmutation of material "humidity" into energy, or a complete inter-atomic penetration—a complete enfolding of the atoms—by the spirit. And here it becomes apparent that Bacon has borrowed much more than words. He believes that in all metals except gold this penetration is incomplete, but may be artificially completed by loosening the atomic structure of the substance and thus removing the material obstacles in the spirit's way: [205]

The second is, that the spirit of the metal be quickened, and the tangible parts opened: for without those two operations, the spirit of the metal wrought upon, will not be able to digest the parts.

Thus the unobstructed spirit of mercury, let us say, becomes the

---

[204] IV. 316.   [205] IV. 317.

spirit of gold. Who can doubt that all this is an adaptation of Hermetic doctrine?

Although the alchemists frequently veiled their meaning in mythological allegory, I have not been able to discover that any of them called the earth-spirit Proserpine, and I think it probable that Bacon took a hint from the *Mythologiæ*. Natalis Comes interprets Proserpine in the conventional way, but begins his interpretation thus:[206]

Cicero, in the second book of *De natura deorum*, writes that the vital energy of the earth was attributed to Pluto, who was called Pluto and Dis because all things arise from the earth and sink back into it.

With this compare the opening sentences in Bacon's interpretation of Proserpine:

The fable relates, as I take it, to Nature; and explains the source of that rich and fruitful supply of active power subsisting in the under world, from which all the growths of our upper world spring, and into which they again return and are resolved.

Bacon doubtless knew his Cicero as well as Comes did; but Comes introduces Pluto as an accessory detail in an essay on Proserpine, thus suggesting precisely the subordination which Bacon brings about. Furthermore, a second and more striking parallel follows. Bacon and Comes draw closely analogous conclusions from the mention of Narcissus in the myth. Says Comes:[207]

Seed, when it is filled with nourishment, will produce and gather, as it were, other seed; therefore Proserpine is said to have been carried off by Pluto as she was gathering flowers. And what flowers? The flowers of Narcissus especially, which word signifies torpor and sluggishness (torporem et segnitiem). For indeed the seed does not sprout immediately, while it is gathering nourishment, but retains this matter within it, and in a year's time gradually brings forth a shoot.

Bacon says almost exactly the same in terms of the "death" of matter in transmutation, which was followed, be it remembered, by the "nourishment of the active principle":

It is prettily added that Proserpina was carried off while in the act of gathering flowers of Narcissus in the valleys: for Narcissus takes its name from torpor or stupor; and it is only when beginning to curdle, and as it

---

[206] III. 16. 166.

[207] III. 16. Bacon does not forget Proserpine the plant-spirit. See XIII. 166.

were to gather torpor, that spirit is in the best state to be caught up and carried off by earthy matter.

If I understand the matter rightly, we have now before us the chief sources of Bacon's interpretation of Proserpine. That our author is heavily indebted to them, and not for his symbolism alone, seems to me clear. Of the philosopher, however, so curiously mediæval in much of his thinking, I will speak later. Here I should like to point out that aspect of his mind in which, perhaps, he is as much the artist as the philosopher. In this essay even more than in the others, Bacon elevates and blends his acquired conceptions into a loftier and more beautiful whole, and yet gives that whole a picturesque and striking concreteness. To the alchemist, the earth-spirit was chiefly the prolific mother of metals; Comes conceived of Proserpine as the mother of plants. Bacon units the two [208] into the majestic mother of all things on earth; and as for grimy Pluto, he relegates him to the background.

Proteus.[209]

The word *Protean* still speaks to us of the sea-god whom the wandering Ithacans held fast, unterrified by all his transformations, till the wily old fellow resumed his proper shape and used his gift of prophecy for their benefit. Bacon interprets Proteus in two ways: as the type of the scientist and as that of matter in its formity. As the following table will show, both these interpretations are in substance paralleled by Natalis Comes.

Bacon	Natalis Comes [210]
And whereas it is added in the fable that Proteus was a prophet and knew the three times; this agrees well with the nature of matter; for if a man knew the conditions, affections, and processes of matter, he would certainly comprehend the sum and general issue (for I do not say that his knowledge would extend to the parts and singularities) of all things past, present, and to come. Most excellently therefore did the ancients represent Proteus,	Others, among whom was Antigonous Carystius, handed down the opinion that Proteus was a very learned man, who wrote much on natural philosophy: on plants, minerals, the nature of wild animals, the mutual transmutation of elements, and how these are the first principles of all things that grow or are born, which, according as by their vital energies they assimilate this or that, becomes trees, or grasses, or animals. He was called

---

[208] XIII. 133.   [209] X. 416; XIII. 116.   [210] VIII. 8. 559.

him of the many shaps, to be likewise a prophet triply great; as knowing the future, the past, and the secrets of the present. For he who knows the universal passions of matter and thereby knows what is possible to be cannot help knowing likewise what has been, what is, and what will be, according to the sum of things. Therefore the best hope and security for the study of celestial bodies I place in physical reasons.	Proteus because he entered into all these things. He was also thought to be a prophet because thanks to his observation of the stars and of past events he left written predictions of many things.
The sense of this fable relates, it would seem, to the secrets of nature and the conditions of matter. For under the person of Proteus, matter—the most ancient of all things next to God—is meant to be represented.	As Proteus is almost τὸπρωτονον, that is to say first in existence, so matter, indeed, exists "in intellectu" before form and continually seeks various forms, as it is urged to by nature; for which reason Proteus is correctly said to exist in many forms.

I think it entirely probable that Bacon is chiefly indebted to Natalis Comes for the idea of embodying the scientist in the symbol of Proteus, but I am far from wishing to suggest that he owes him his conception of astronomy or of natural law. As for the first, it is doubtless the result of his own vigorous thinking;[211] as for the second, I think it reasonable to believe that, at least in the passage quoted, he has in mind Cicero, who says:[212]

Nothing occurs which was not once immanent in its causes; and in the same way, nothing will occur of which nature does not contain the causes now. It appears, then, that fate is not what it is superstitiously supposed to be, but that it is physical causation: the eternal origin of all that is, has been, or will be. It follows that one may by observation determine the causes from which things arise; and it stands to reason that from these same causes one may, though, perhaps, not always, infer future events. Since all things are caused by fate, as I have shown, therefore, if a mortal could exist who should know the linked causes of things in their entirety, nothing would be obscure to him.

It would certainly be rash to assert that the tremendous inference to be drawn from the universality and constancy of nature's laws first dawned on Bacon in the pages of *De divinatione;* I am dealing

---

[211] X. 433, 434.   [212] *De divinatione*, I, 55, 56.

here with an individual passage and with what may be chiefly verbal indebtedness. Yet who can doubt that Cicero's influence was one of the earliest and most powerful of those that contributed to the formation of Bacon's mind.

Cicero declared that if it were possible to lay bare the whole system of nature's laws, consequences of incalculable importance would follow. It is Bacon's message to humanity that the discovery on which so much depends is actually possible; and this message is picturesquely repeated in the essay on Proteus. Nature lies before us untamed, but:

> Nevertheless if any skilful servant of Nature shall bring force to bear on matter, and shall vex and drive it to extremities as if with the purpose of reducing it to nothing, then will matter (since annihilation or true destruction is not possible except by the omnipotence of God) finding itself in these straits, turn and transform itself into strange shapes, passing from one change to another till it has gone through the whole circle and finished the period; when, if the force be continued, it returns at last to itself. And this constraint and binding will be more easily and expeditiously effected, if matter be laid hold on and secured by the hands; that is, by the extremities.

The passage has a certain Aristotelian flavor; and although Bacon believes neither in Aristotle's materia prima nor in his forms, he does believe substances to pass through cycles of transmutations. He suspects that such radical changes are atomic re-arrangements, and in the investigation of them he sees the means of ascertaining the ultimate natures not only of substances but of the physical qualities which distinguish them from each other. It is by such an application of force as will reach down to the atomic root of things—to this far-removed *extremitas materiæ* which is likened to the extremities of Proteus—that Bacon hopes to bring about the transformations he wishes to study. As for the observation of unprovoked phenomena, gradual as they often are, it will not do:[213]

> For like as a man's disposition is never well known till he be crossed, nor Proteus ever changed shapes till he was straitened and held fast, so the passages and variations of nature cannot appear so fully in the liberty of nature as in the trials and vexations of art.

What Bacon expresses figuratively in the passages quoted above, he sets forth in terms of atomism elsewhere. Thus in *Cogitationes de natura rerum*:[214]

---

[213] VI. 188.   [214] X. 292.

..... the proper question is whether all bodies do not likewise pass through regular circuits and intermediate changes. For there is no doubt but that the seeds of things, though equal, as soon as they have thrown themselves into certain groups and knots, completely assume the nature of dissimilar bodies, till those groups or knots are dissolved. . . . And I know not whether this inquiry I speak of concerning the first condition of seeds or atoms be not the most useful of all; as being the supreme rule of act and power, and the true moderator of hope and works.

I need hardly say that the conditions to which Bacon refers are not merely static. In his opinion, as we have seen, Proserpine is more important than Pluto: [215]

To rest the inquiry of nature principally on the contemplation and examination of motion is the part of one who regards works. But to study or feign inactive principles of things is the part of those who would sow talk and nourish disputations. Now by inactive principles I mean those which tell us of what things are made up and consist, but not by what force or in what manner they come together. For with a view to action and the enlargement of the power or operation of man, it is not enough, nor indeed of any great use, to know of what things consist, if you know not the ways and means of their mutations and transformations.

Bacon is here emphasizing, as he frequently and significantly does, the importance of the forces determining transmutation; but for him all substances and practically all physical qualities as weight, color, hardness, elasticity, are functions of the atom or atomic group in action. To the corresponding states of atomic aggregation and activity Bacon, as is well known, gives the scholastic name of forms.

To repeat in other terms what I have said elsewhere, Bacon proposes to investigate physical phenomena in their forms or ultimate atomic causes. That these atomic conditions are what he has in mind when he talks of laying hold on Proteus by his extremities is made fairly clear by various passages. In *Cogitationes de natura rerum,* for example, he writes: [216]

Again, arguments and subtleties concerning nautral and violent motion, motion from within and motion from without, and the limits of motions, these likewise lay no hold upon the body of nature, but are rather like writings on the bark. Discarding therefore such matters, or sentencing them to be handed over to popular discourse, we should investigate those appetites and inclinations of things by which all that variety of effects and changes which we see in the works of nature and art is made up and

---

[215] X. 293.   [216] X. 295. See also VIII. 499.

brought about. And we should try to enchain Nature, like Proteus; for the right discovery and distinction of the kinds of motions are the true bonds of Proteus. For according as motions, that is, incentives and restraints, can be spurred on or tied,[217] so follows conversion and transformation of matter itself.

The means by which atomic operations are to be forced to exhibit themselves to the investigator is, specifically, the application of heat. Under ordinary circumstances, however, such application would result only in superficial changes of state, as fusion or evaporation. Matter must therefore be prevented from absorbing the infusion of energy in this way, so that finally it may be compelled to respond with atomic changes. Bacon believes that this can be accomplished by heating the substance experimented on in a closed receptacle:[218]

It is certain that of all powers in nature heat is the chief; both in the frame of nature, and in the works of art. Certain it is likewise that the effects of heat are most advanced when it worketh upon a body without loss or dissipation of the matter; for that ever betrayeth the account. And therefore it is true that the power of heat is best perceived in distillations which are performed in close vessels and receptacles. But yet there is a higher degree; for howsoever distillations do keep the body in cells and cloisters, without going abroad, yet they give space unto bodies to turn into vapour, to return into liquor. and to separate one part from another. So as nature doth expatiate, although it hath not full liberty; whereby the true and ultimate operations of heat are not attained. But if bodies may be altered by heat, and yet no such reciprocation of rarefaction and of condensation and of separation admitted, then it is like that this Proteus of matter, being held by the sleeves, will turn and change into many metamorphoses. Take therefore a square vessel of iron, in form of a cube, and let it have good thick and strong sides. Put into it a cube of wood, that may fill it as close as may be, and let it have a cover of iron, as strong (at least) as the sides; and let it be well luted, after the manner of the chemists. Then place the vessel within burning coals, kept quick kindled, for some few hours' space. Then take the vessel from the fire, and take off the cover, and see what is become of the wood. I conceive that since all inflamation and evaporation are utterly prohibited, and the body still turned upon itself, that one of these two effects will follow: either that the body of wood will be turned into a kind of "amalagma" (as the chemists call it), or that the finer part will be turned into air, and the grosser stick as it were baked and incrustate upon the sides of the vessel; being become of a denser matter than the wood itself crude.

It is sufficiently evident, I take it, that in the experiment de-

---

[217] Cf. IV. 223.   [218] IV. 221.

scribed above, Bacon is walking directly in the footsteps of the alchemists. In fact, he tells us so himself: [219]

There is nothing more certain in nature than that it is impossible for any body to be utterly annihilated; but that as it was the work of the omnipotency of God to make somewhat of nothing, so it requireth the like omnipotency to turn somewhat into nothing. And therefore it is well said by an obscure writer of the sect of chemists, that there is no such way to effect the strange transmutations of bodies, as to endeavour and urge by all means the reducing of them to nothing.

The endeavor referred to is, of course, to be made through distillation. Various passages make this quite certain. For example: [220]

... when men consider the inexorable necessity there is in the nature of matter to sustain itself, and not to turn or dissolve into nothing, they should omit no way of vexing and working it; if they would detect and bring out its ultimate operations and powers of resistance.

With this compare the following, which brings us directly back to distillation: [221]

The intention therefore of a profound and radical change of bodies is no other than this, that matter be by all proper methods vexed, and yet both these separations in the meantime prevented. For then only does matter suffer real constraint, when every way of escape is cut off.

It is quite clear, then, that the "constraint and binding" of Proteus is to be effected by alchemistical methods. Bacon does not believe in the philosopher's stone, but the Hermetic philosophers are nevertheless his teachers, and he proposes to reach the spirits of matter very much as they do.

The conclusions reached above are of some importance not only as regards the content of our essay but also from the point of view of its symbolism. As a reader of alchemistic literature, Bacon not impossibly encountered the symbol of Proteus used very much as he uses it himself. In 1629 one Grosschedel published a Hermetic treatise entitled *Proteus Mercurialis*,[222] and probably enough the same symbolism occurs in earlier books of the same kind. Furthermore, Bacon, doubtless took notice of the following passage in which Natalis Comes violently assails the Hermetic fraternity: [223]

---

[219] IV. 223.   [220] X. 299.   [221] X. 300.
[222] H. Kopp, *Die Alchemy in Alterer und Neuer Zeit*, 366-370.
[223] II. 6. 104.

Do you think to overcome Nature with fire? Fool! She, with long steps, leaves you behind, and you accomplish nothing. She deceives you with colors; she mocks you with the many forms of matter. Even thus Proteus changed himself into many shapes: now a dread serpent, now water, now fire.

Of course it is not necessary to suppose that Bacon required any suggestion at all for the detailed application of a symbol already brought to his attention in a general way as we have seen above. Yet, if he was familiar with the *Mythologiæ*, as can hardly be doubted, he probably read the passage in question; and once before he has given us an example of his adroitness in reversing the meaning of a simile.

Bacon's interpretation of Proteus, like that of Pan, curiously mingles classic and Christian sources. Thus Proteus's counting his flock of seals at noon and then lying down to sleep is explained as an allegory of the creation of plants and animals according to the Bible. All were brought forth from matter in the noonday of their maturity and, as if nature had then fallen asleep, never thereafter added to with any new species. On the other hand, Proteus's being a sea-god is reconciled with the symbolism attributed to him by the following considerations on matter:

And it may be called the servant of Neptune, inasmuch as all the operation and dispensation of matter is effected principally in liquids.

With this compare Bacon's discussion of Thales in *De principiis atque originibus*: [224]

Thales asserted Water to be the principle of things. For he saw that matter was principally dispensed in moisture, and moisture in water; and it seemed proper to make that the principle of things, in which the virtues and powers of beings, and especially the elements of their generations and restorations, were chiefly found. He saw that the breeding of animals is in moisture; that the seeds and kernels of plants (as long as they are productive and fresh), are likewise soft and tender; that metals also melt and become fluid, and are as it were concrete juices of the earth, or rather a kind of mineral waters; that the earth itself is fertilized and revived by showers or irrigation, and that earth and mud seem nothing else than the lees and sediment of water; that air most plainly is but the exhaltation and expansion of water; nay, that even fire itself cannot be lighted nor kept in and fed, except with moisture and by means of moisture.

The doctrine of Thales re-appears in many books. The following in Natalis Comes [225] is, I think, significant:

---

[224] X. 355.   [225] VIII. 1. 538.

Orpheus and all the theologians of the ancients relate that from Oceanus arose things and gods; for as Thales explains, nothing is created or decays without moisture, and all the qualities of the elements, which were called by the names of the gods, derive their being from liquids.

Deucalion,[226] Ixion,[227] and Ericthonius.[228]

We have seen that Bacon's relation to the alchemists is a peculiar one. He is undoubtedly indebted to them; yet he entirely disagrees with them on some of their most fundamental views. His interpretations of the myths of Deucalion, Ixion, and Ericthonius, are the complete expression of this disagreement.

The sub-title of the essay on Deucalion, *Renovation,* at once calls to mind that *renovatio*—that rejuvenation and renovation of men and things—which the Hermetic philosophers aimed at no less than at the transmutation of metals. The interpretation of the myth is simply a criticism of the method which most of these philosophers prescribed. Indeed, Bacon repeats here what he has said in regard to the Golden Bough, and again describes alchemistical beliefs in the language of the alchemists. The essay goes as follows:

> The poets relate that when the inhabitants of the old world were utterly extinguished by the universal deluge, and none remained except Deucalion and Pyrrha, these two being inflamed with a pious and noble desire to restore the human race, consulted the oracle and received answer to the following effect: they should have their wish if they took their mother's bones and cast them behind their backs. This struck them at first with great sorrow and despair, for the face of nature being level by the deluge, to seek for a sepulchre would be a task altogether endless. But at last they found that the stones of the earth (the earth being regarded as the mother of all things) were what the oracle meant.
>
> This fable seems to disclose a secret of nature, and to correct an error which is familiar to the human mind. For man in his ignorance concludes that the renewal and restoration of things may be effected by means of their own corruption and remains; as the Phoenix rises out of her own ashes; which is not so: for matters of this kind have already reached the end of their course, and can give no further help towards the first stages of it: so we must go back to more common principles.

Had Deucalion and Pyrrha successfully carried out what they at first conceived to be the meaning of the oracle, they would have done precisely what books on alchemy would lead us to do, if taken literally, in order to replenish the world with gold. To be exact,

---

[226] XIII. 133.   [227] VIII. 514.   [228] XIII. 132.

they would have done all there was left to do, for the maker of gold was also required to bring about the death and burial preceding exhumation. The precepts I refer to are represented pictorially in *The New Pearl of Great Price*.[229] We see the slaying of a king, his burial, the removal of his bones from his tomb, their miraculous rising in resurrection. Finally we see the royal personage, his might increased a thousand fold, crowning his sons with golden crowns. The king represents the crude materials of the philosopher's stone; his death and the putrefaction of his body, the pounding, calcinating, etc., whereby the spiritual elements of the stone (represented by the bones) are freed from matter; his resurrection, the union of the elements in the stone; the crowning of his sons, the creation of gold by the transmutation of base metals. The analogy between myth and allegory could not be more complete; for let us remember that the King's bones could not only perfect lead into gold but dead bodies into living beings. Indeed, such renovation was deemed possible even without the philosopher's stone. The clogged spirit, it was thought, might be set free and allowed to regain its full powers; the decayed substance might be reduced to primal matter. Then the two might be brought together again.[230] The preliminary process of dissolution was technically known as "putrefaction," and the doctrine of renovation originated to some extent in the belief that life sprang from death, as Pythagorism and the Church taught and as inaccurate observation seemed to prove. The art of renewing and re-creating organic bodies was professed by most of the alchemists. Paracelsus tells us how to turn old wood to new,[232] and assures us that a dead snake, subjected by him to putrefaction under proper conditions, arose from its remains in a multitude of little snakes.[233] Indeed, so familiar to alchemy was the idea of resurrection that several of the philosophers symbolized their art in the Phoenix, and the Apothecaries' Company adopted that fabulous bird as a crest.[234]

Bacon believes no more in "putrefaction" than he does in the philosopher's stone:

matters of this kind have already reached the end of their course, and can

---

[229] 38-47.
[230] Paracelsus, *De natura rerum*, I.   [231] Redgrove, 32.
[232] Paracelsus, *op. cit.*, VI.   [233] *Ibid.*
[234] Hulme, *Natural History Lore and Legend*, 177.

give no further help towards the first stages of it: so we must go back to more common principles.

According to Bacon's theory of spirits, a body in the condition contemplated by the alchemists has lost its moisture and its spirit and has furthermore suffered at least molecular distintegration;[235] according to his atomic theory, it has, presumably, undergone atomic change. It seems clear that sometimes, at least, Bacon regards his two theories as consistent;[236] we may therefore venture the hypothesis that in the present passage he conceives of a decayed body as having lost energy, matter, and, to some extent at least, the ultimate structure of its substance. If such is his view, he is of course right in saying that a decayed body no longer contains the elements of its renovation. The alchemists, however, speak rather of substances than of bodies. Now a decayed substance still consists of atoms, and it must be supposed to contain some energy, for it has physical qualities which according to Bacon's own views are functions of the atom in action. That Bacon discounts this residual energy as not constituting an individual "spirit" does not seem possible, for he tells us to seek "more common principles." I take the whole passage to mean that a decayed substance is no longer in a condition to react to a comprehensive process of renovation, and that we must superinduce in it the form, or atomic equivalent, of each of its original physical qualities separately.

The importance which Bacon attaches to a knowledge of the forms of qualities as essential to the understanding and to the making of substances is well known. Doubtless, his theory of forms is partly of Aristotelian origin; but it should not be forgotten that the idea of creating substances by joining their characteristic qualities to matter was fundamental in alchemy. It should be remembered, too, that certain substances were supposed to be the material embodiments of these qualities, which thus came to be regarded, at least in a measure, as states of matter,—a view more in keeping with Bacon's than the Aristotelian view. Thus sulphur was supposed to embody the principles of color, hardness, and combustibility; and mercury those of fusibility, malleability, and lustre.[237] Considered from this point of view, the one was the saturated receptacle of the yellowness and hardness of gold; the

---

[235] X. 157, 158.   [236] IV. 219 et seq.   [237] Redgrove, 18-21.

other, the basic substance of metals, or something so closely approaching to it as to make extraction readily practicable. The stone, considered in this manner, was regarded as a quintessence of gold so charged with its characteristic qualities as to impart them to other metals. Allusions to these beliefs are of continual occurrence in Hermetic works. Thus Bonus of Ferrara: [238]

For this reason the tincture is said to be derived rather from the quality and form, or sulphur, than from the quantity, or quicksilver.

And again, in regard to sulphur: [239]

Hence, on account of its redness, its operation can be extended to a great quantity of any kind of metal, so as to tinge and perfect it into gold.

And elsewhere: [240]

In the same way fixed sulphur is said to be the cause of the hardness of metals, as we see in iron and brass. But quicksilver, whether fixed or not, is the cause of metallic fusion.

As for the basic nature of mercury, at least when duly refined, Arnold de Villa Nova tells us that: [241]

Quicksilver is the matter and element of all metals alike; all of them when melted are converted thereto, and it also combines with them.

In other words, the alchemists mingled and confused with their doctrine of spirits theories of a purely physical nature. Now this is precisely what Bacon does.

So much for Bacon's interpretation of the myth of Deucalion. Bacon is unquestionably a pupil of the alchemists; but he is a critical pupil, an insurgent. In his interpretation of the myth of Ixion he returns to the charge:

For as for that natural magic which flutters about so many books, embracing certain credulous and superstitious traditions and observations concerning sympathies and antipathies, and hidden and specific properties, with experiments for the most part frivolous, and wonderful rather for the skill with which the thing is concealed and masked than for the thing itself; it will not be wrong to say that it is as far differing in truth of nature from such a knowledge as we require, as the story of King Arthur of Britain, or Hugh of Bordeaux, and such like imaginary heroes, differs from Cæsar's commentaries in truth of story. For it is manifest that Cæsar did greater things than those imaginary heroes were feigned to do,

---

[238] *The New Pearl of Great Price*, 237.
[239] *Ibid*.
[240] *Ibid*, 227.
[241] *Ibid*, 308.

but he did them not in the fabulous manner. Of this kind of learning the fable of Ixion was a figure; who designing to embrace Juno, the Goddess of Power, had intercourse with a fleeting cloud, out of which he begot Centaurs and Chimæras.[242]

The idea of symbolizing false learning in the myth of Ixion may have been suggested to Bacon by the following in *Mythologiæ*: [243]

And indeed, those who pursue glory rather than virtue, or who embrace false learning instead of real, necessarily commit themselves to the unseemly consequences: monstrous Centaurs are brought forth by the cloud.

The alchemists themselves, however, speak of the results of wrong methods in similar terms, as indeed is natural in view of the fact that the creation of the stone is so often conceived of as a birth. Thus Michael Scott [244] declares that: "Those who wish to bring forth the child before the proper period produce an abortion"; and John Dastin warns us against attempting to compound the stone of unfit materials: [245]

> For where is made unkindly geniture,
> What followeth but things abominable,
> Which is to say Monstrum in Nature?

Bacon again thunders against alchemy in his interpretation of the myth of Ericthonius. Indeed, just as Ixion stands for the beclouded alchemist, so Ericthonius represents the monstrous "birth." The essay goes as follows:

The poets tell us that Vulcan wooed Minerva, and in the heat of desire attempted to force her; that in the struggle which followed his seed was scattered on the ground; from which was born Ericthonius, a man well made and handsome in the upper parts of the body, but with thighs and legs like an eel, thin and deformed: and that he, from consciousness of this deformity, first invented chariots, whereby he might show off the fine part of his body and hide the mean.

This strange and prodigious story seems to bear this meaning: that Art (which is represented under the person of Vulcan, because it makes so much use of fire) when it endeavours by much vexing of bodies to force Nature to its will and conquer and subdue her (for Nature is described under the person of Minerva, on account of the wisdom of her works) rarely attains the particular end it aims at; and yet in the course of

---

[242] It will be recalled that too-enterprising Ixion was mocked by Jupiter with a cloud in the image of his wife.
[243] VI. 16. 412.
[244] *The New Pearl of Great Price*, 426.
[245] *Theatrum chemicum Britannicum*.

contriving and endeavouring, as in a struggle, there fall out by by the way certain imperfect births and lame works, specious to look at but weak and halting in use: yet impostors parade them to the world with a great deal of false shew in setting forth, and carry them about as in triumph. Such things may often be observed among chemical productions, and among mechanical subtleties and novelties; the rather because men being too intent upon their end to recover themselves from the errors of their way rather struggle with Nature than woo her embraces with due observance and attention.

The essay on Ericthonius reads peculiarly in the light of that on Proteus. Bacon doubtless refers to an uncritical " vexing " of matter; but in any case he does not always think so ill of alchemistic methods as he seems to here. Indeed, it is reasonable to believe that he was fully cognisant of the genuine discoveries made through their agency. In the *Advancement of Learning,* for instance, he says: [246]

And yet surely to Alchemy this right is due, that it may be compared to the husbandman whereof Æsop makes the fable, that when he died told his sons that he had left unto them gold buried under ground in his vineyard; and they digged over all the ground, and gold they found none, but by reason of their stirring and digging the mould about the roots of their vines, they had a great vintage the year following: so assuredly the search and stir to make gold hath brought to light a great number of good and fruitful inventions and experiments, as well for the disclosing of nature as for the use of man's life.

This judgment does not, of course, invalidate the others; imposture and self-delusion were rife among the alchemists,[247] and both resulted in the parading of things " specious to look at." It does, however, restrict it within proper limits. Bacon does not reject that method of " vexing " matter for which he has acknowledged his indebtedness elsewhere, and to the fruitfulness of which he bears witness in the passage just quoted; he rejects one particular application of it, and denounces as merely specious the results to which this application leads.[248]

Bacon's associating the myth of Ericthonius with alchemy may, I think, be traced to the alchemists themselves; and also to Natalis

---

[246] VI. 127.

[247] See H. C. Bolton, *The Follies of Science at The Court of Rudolph II.*

[248] I do not mean to ignore the fact that in this and the preceding interpretation Bacon is not talking exclusively of alchemy. His language shows, however, that he is thinking chiefly of that art.

Comes, who links the two in remarks no more favorable to the Hermetic brotherhood, or their "sympathies" and "antipathies" of matter, than Bacon's are: [249]

> They say that Vulcan, cast out of heaven because of his deformity, was nothing but either sulphur or mercury, because neither will combine with anything that is not of its own nature, and is thus separated from everything else. In the same way they explain Minerva's having been loved by Vulcan as symbolizing what they believe to be the sympathy of sulphur and iron for mercurial water, which they call Minerva. As these are separated from each other in the process of putrefaction (because they are of different natures) they say that Minerva fled from Vulcan. But let us pursue their nonsense no further.

It is in this part of his work that Comes inveighs against the perverse folly of the alchemists who think to overcome nature with fire and are mocked by her Protean elusiveness. Not impossibly the specious "births" were partly suggested to Bacon by that passage. Ericthonius himself, however, is indirectly associated with applied physical science in the *Mythologiæ:* [250]

> From Vulcan's seed, which was scattered on the ground, was born a monster. What does this mean, good heaven? What was this horrid monster? The nature of upper ether does not descend pure to earth; that heat which is so important in generation is impure and mingled with gross matter. Therefore it is said that the seed of Vulcan, falling on the ground, gave rise to the animal world, whose varieties are expressed by the form of Ericthonius. Vulcan is always to be understood as turbulent and gross fire helpful in generation. He it was who made Pandora, the gift of all the gods. In fact, he has a part in the inventions of Ceres, Bacchus, Pallas, and all the other gods; he instructed her in all the arts.

Atalanta.[251]

The myth of Atalanta may be called Bacon's favorite, for he alludes to it no less than nine times in his works.[252] His interpretation of it is always the same; therefore what he says about it in *De sapientia veterum* is typical. The essay goes as follows:

> Atalanta, who was remarkable for swiftness, was matched to run a race with Hippomenes. The conditions were that if Hippomenes won he was to marry Atalanta, if he lost he was to be put to death; and there seemed to be no doubt about the issue, since the matchless excellence of Atalanta in running had been signalised by the death of many competitors. Hippo-

---

[249] II. 6. 104. [250] II. 6. 103. [251] XIII. 142.
[252] I. 275, 323; VI. 34, 35, 69, 419; VIII. 101, 149; XIII. 142.

menes therefore resorted to an artifice. He provided himself with three golden apples and carried them with him. The race began. Atalanta ran ahead. He seeing himself left behind bethought him of his stratagem, and rolled forward one of the golden apples, so that she might see it,—not straight forwards, but a little on one side, that it might not only delay her but also draw her out of the course. She, with a woman's eagerness, attracted by the beauty of the apple, left the course, ran after it, and stooped to take it up. Hippomenes in the meantime made good way along the course and got before her. She however by force of her natural swiftness made good the loss of time and was again foremost; when Hippomenes a second and a third time interrupted her in the same way, and so at last by craft not speed won the race.

The story carries in it an excellent allegory, relating to the contest of Art with Nature. For Art, which is meant by Atalanta, is in itself, if nothing stand in the way, far swifter than Nature and, as one may say, the better runner, and comes sooner to the goal. For this may be seen in almost everything; you see that fruit grows slowly from the kernel, swiftly from the graft; you see clay harden slowly into stones, fast into baked bricks: so also in morals, oblivion and comfort of grief comes by nature in length of time; but philosophy (which may be regarded as the art of living) does it without waiting so long, but forestalls and anticipates the day. But then this prerogative and vigour of art is retarded, to the infinite loss of mankind, by those golden apples. For there is not one of the sciences or arts which follows the true and legitimate course constantly forth till it reach its end; but it perpetually happens that arts stop in their undertakings half way, and forsake the course, and turn aside like Atalanta after profit and commodity,—

Leaving the course the rolling gold to seize.

And therefore it is no wonder if Art cannot outstrip Nature, and according to the agreement and condition of the contest put her to death or destroy her; but on the contrary Art remains subject to Nature, as the wife is subject to the husband.

That, having conceived of such an interpretation as the above, Bacon should recur to it often, is natural: his dominant conviction as a scientific reformer is precisely that if on the one hand untested speculation must be avoided, on the other a narrow interest in limited practical application must also be regarded as injurious to true scientific progress. The point at present, however, is how he came to interpret the myth in this particular way. Boccaccio, characteristically enough, sees in the myth an allegory of the venality of women; Comes, of the corrupting power of gold in general. Both of these obvious explanations may have influenced Bacon to some extent, but neither coincides with his. The sub-title of the essay, *Profit,* shows clearly enough that he has the mercenary investigator in mind. Such a person, however, impresses him as childish rather than corrupt. " For I do not run off like a child after golden apples," he says in one place,[253] " but stake all on the victory of Art over Nature in the race." The notion of regarding mythical golden apples as symbols of the showy trifles that immature people snatch at, occurred to him as early as 1604. The Commons were assured of obtaining from the King the substance of their demands, but with customary seditiousness began to haggle over the letter of the law. Then Bacon raised his voice in warning:[254] " That we be not in Tantalus' case: Spectat aquas in aquis et poma fugacia captat." As a symbol of greed, the myth of Tantalus was conventional;[255] Bacon skillfully applied it to express at once a stupid unconsciousness of possessing essentials and a crude eagerness in grasping at trifles.

It is possible that the myth of Tantalus contributed something to Bacon's interpretation of that of Atalanta; but that something does not account for what chiefly distinguishes his explanation from those, for example, of Boccaccio and Comes. Bacon applies his allegory to scientific investigation. In doing so, he makes three noteworthy statements: that art is by rights more expeditious than nature; that it is frustrated by the greed and incompetence of its practitioners; that its purpose is to overtake nature and " put her to death or destroy her." The last of these assertions is certainly very peculiar, even allowing for figurative speech. To what may we attribute it, and the others also? I believe we shall be placing ourselves on the right track if we compare the passage in question with the following, which occurs in *De augmentis scientiarum:*[256]

It was not ill said by the alchemists, " That Vulcan is a second nature, and imitates that dexterously and compendiously which nature works circuitously and in length of time."

The alchemists once again appear upon the scene, and with one of the corner-stones of their theoretic edifice. Furthermore, who, if not the alchemists, attributed failure in their art to lack of disinterested fervor and patient assiduity. Who represented the " kill-

---

[253] VIII. 149.
[254] Spedding, *Francis Bacon and His Times*, I. 455.
[255] Wilson, *The Arte of Retorique*, Clar. Press Ed., 196.
[256] VIII. 480.

ing" and "destroying" of matter in gruesome emblems? But this is not all; as I shall presently show, one alchemist used precisely the myth of Atalanta as a symbol of his pursuit.

It was one of the chief contentions of the alchemists that they did not falsify or violate nature, but rather that, by hastening the natural evolution of metals towards gold, they outdistanced it. "For," says Ianus Lacinius,[257] "Nature has left only a comparatively small thing for him to do,—the completion of that which she has already begun." And again:[258]

For all common metals there is a transient and a perfect state of inward completeness, and this perfect state they attain either through the slow operation of Nature, or through the sudden transformatory power of our Stone.

And once more:[259]

Nature requires so many years for that purpose, they do not see how our elixir can bring about the change in a moment of time. We answer that the digestion of gold and of our elixir are alone complete; but whereas gold is a compound, and is only sufficiently digested for its own purposes, the elixir is the form of gold, and its digestion suffices not only for itself, but is so exuberant, and capable of such indefinite multiplication, as to make up in a brief space of time what is wanting in the common metals.

The Hermetic philosopher regarded himself almost as a high priest; the secrets of his art were sacred mysteries which God imparted only to the pure in heart. Thus in Norton's *Ordinall* we see the neophyte receiving the holy book on his knees,[260] while the sage who delivers it to him bids him "receive the gift of God under the sacred seal," and angels hovering above proclaim that because the aspirant has withheld his hands from injustice and has turned away from iniquity, therefore God has anointed him. In the text are many warnings against entering upon the solemn vocation with any but the purest motives:

> Who lucre coveteth this Science shall not finde,
> But he that loveth Science for her owne kinde,
> He may purchase both for his blessed minde.

Unseemly haste must also be avoided, for it leads to failure:

> All Auctors writing of this Arte
> Saye haste is of the Devils parte:

---

[257] *The New Pearl of Great Price*, 153.   [258] *Ibid.*, 176.
[259] *Ibid.*, 215.
[260] See *Theatrum chemicum Britannicum*.

> The little Boke writ of the Philosophers feast
> Saith, omnis festinatio ex partis diaboli est.

And again

> No man sooner faileth in heate and colde
> Then doth the Master which is hasty and boulde:
> For no man sooner maie our Worke spill
> Then he that is presuminge his purpose to fulfill.

I do not mean to imply that Bacon borrowed his lofty sense of the high seriousness of science, but assuredly the alchemists taught him nothing contrary to it; his own words to the King are proof of it:[261]

> Your majesty standeth invested of that triplicity which in great veneration was ascribed to the ancient Hermes; the power and fortune of a King, the knowledge and illumination of a Priest, and the learning and universality of a Philosopher.

By killing and destroying nature Bacon doubtless meant doing away with its mystery, piercing the husk in order to sieze the kernel of principles, of "forms" within; nevertheless, as we have seen, his language is that of the alchemist. The conception of investigation as a chase or pursuit is distinctly alchemistic too. Lacinius, discussing the "form" of gold, says as follows:[262]

> It is also the fugitive slave, and blessed is he who can overtake him, for his nature adapts itself to all things.

It was probably this idea which led Michael Maier to entitle his alchemistic emblem-book *Atalanta fugiens*. I have not been able to discover any edition of this work earlier than that of 1617, but it is entirely possible that other books of the sort bore the same title. Throughout the seventeenth century a deluge of alchemistic treatises appeared, especially in Germany, under mythological captions,[263] as for example a *Balneum Dianæ*, a *Proteus Mercurialis*, an *Ædypus chymicus*. It was Bacon's practice rather to elaborate than to create; otherwise one might accept his use of the myth as original and as signifying nothing more than compliance with the tendency of the age. As the matter stands, it is not unreasonable to surmise that among the impressions which led to his choice was that produced on him by some work on alchemy. Indeed, I think

---

[261] VI. 90.
[262] *The New Pearl of Great Price*, 202.
[263] H. Kopp, *op. et loc. cit.*

it far from unlikely that the essay is chiefly directed against alchemy itself; for, with the possible exception of the astrologers, the Hermetic philosophers were the typical scientists of the time, and in theory and practice exhibited in a striking manner precisely the faults with which Bacon reproached the whole class.

Dædalus and Icarus.[264]

"Through the clouds of fable which gathered round his life and adventures," says Sir James Frazer commenting on Apollodorus's account of Dædalus, "we may dimly discern the figure of a vagabond artist as versatile as Leonardo da Vinci and as unscrupulous as Benvenuto Cellini."[265] In fact, this mechanical genius has an unsavory reputation in the classics. When he designed the famous laberynthine prison for King Minos of Crete, "he had fled from Athens," says Apollodorus, "because he had thrown down from the acropolis Talos, the son of his sister Perdix; for Talos was his pupil, and Dædalus feared that with his talents he might surpass himself." He had also prostituted his ingeniousness to the guilty passion of Minos's wife; and he again betrayed his employer by contriving the escape of Theseus. Imprisoned himself together with his son Icarus, he invented and made wings for both; or as Servius explains the matter,[266] he invented and made sails for both their boats. Sought relentlessly by the King, and about to be surrendered by his host Cocalus, he contrived a boiling-hot showerbath which despatched Minos at once.

Dædalus's dark career was of course familiar to all in Bacon's England; his fame as the great inventor of antiquity had given rise to the adjective *Dedalean,* explained by Blount as follows:[267]

Dedalean: intricate or perplexed, also expert or cunning. A derivative from Dædalus, an expert Artificer, who first invented the Saw, Ax, Sail and Sail-yards for a ship, which gave occasion for the Fable of Dædalus his wings, etc.

As for Icarus, his name, even more than now, was a byword for rash aspiration.[268] Indeed, given the strongly ethical tendencies

---

[264] XIII. 129, 157.
[265] Apollodorus, *Library,* trans. by Sir J. G. Frazier, II, 120.
[266] *Com. in Virg. Aen.,* VI. 19.
[267] Thomas Blount, *Glossographia.*   [268] Cf. *Oxford Dictionary.*

of the English, Dædalus's fate also—that of a fugitive despite his wicked brilliancy—probably suggested a moral lesson to many. Bacon, therefore, who emphasizes the moral aspect of both cases, is following the trend of the times. He is also following the example of Natalis Comes, who parallels him rather closely. He is not merely accepting the opinions of others, however; and while his unfavorable comments on inventors seem paradoxical, coming from him, they are really in keeping with his general principles and are largely justified by the circumstances.

Bacon's interpretation of the myth, in so far as it concerns Dædalus himself, goes as follows:

The parable may be interpreted thus. In the entrance is noted that envy which is strongly predominant in great artists and never lets them rest; for there is no class of men more troubled with envy, and that of the bitterest and most implacable character.

Then is touched the impolitic and improvident nature of the punishment inflicted; namely banishment. For it is the prerogative of famous workmen to be acceptable all over the world, insomuch that to an excellent artisan exile is scarcely any punishment at all. For whereas other modes and conditions of life cannot easily flourish out of their own country, the admiration of an artisan spreads wider and grows greater among strangers and foreigners; it being the nature of men to hold their own countrymen, in respect of mechanical arts, in less estimation.

The passages which follow concerning the use of mechanical arts are plain enough. Certainly human life is much indebted to them, for very many things which concern both the furniture of religion and the ornament of state and the culture of life in general, are drawn from their store. And yet out of the same fountain come instruments of lust, and also instruments of death. For (not to speak of the arts of procurers) the most exquisite poisons, also guns, and such like engines of destruction, are the fruits of mechanical invention; and well we know how far in cruelty and destructiveness they exceed the Minotaurus himself.

Very beautiful again is that allegory of the labyrinth; under which the general nature of mechanics is represented. For all the more ingenious and exact mechanical inventions may, for their subtlety, their intricate variety, and the apparent likeness of one part to another, which scarcely any judgment can order and discriminate, but only the clue of experiment, be compared to a labyrinth. Nor is the next point less to the purpose; viz. that the same man who devised the mazes of the labyrinth disclosed likewise the use of the clue. For the mechanical arts may be turned either way, and serve as well for the cure as for the hurt and have power for the most part to dissolve their own spell.

Moreover, the unlawful contrivances of art, and indeed the arts themselves, are often persecuted by Minos; that is by the laws: which condemn them and forbid people to use them. Nevertheless they are secretly preserved, and find everywhere both hiding-places and entertainment; as was well observed by Tacitus in his times, in a case not much unlike; where speaking of the mathematicians and fortune-tellers, he calls them " a class of men who in our state will always be retained and always prohibited." And yet these unlawful and curious arts do in tract of time, since for the most part they fail to perform their promises, fall out of estimation, as Icarus from the sky, and come into contempt, and through the very excess of ostentation perish. And certainly if the truth must be told, they are not so easily bridled by law as convicted by their proper vanity.

Whatever Bacon's attitude to the myth itself, he is here criticizing the applied science of his time, which he finds largely fraudulent and otherwise more harmful than beneficial. This judgment is in a measure biased. Bacon was still mediæval in being almost exclusively a theorist. The elaborate system of classification which occupies so important a place in his works, and which doubtless deceived him as to the extent of his accomplishment, betrays the mind of the schoolman. His ignorance as to actual achievement in the field of applied science has been commented on.[269] Yet the fact remains that the applications of science most in evidence in his day were such as to justify his unfavorable impression. The manufacture of arms, the preparation (hardly less talked about) of mysterious and deadly poisons, alchemy, astrology, a barbarous and dangerous art of medicine, the ingenious contrivances of rogues: these, judging by the evidence at our disposal, were the arts most discussed.

Fire-arms as such were no novelty in Bacon's times; yet their reputation for murderous efficiency in war dated from 1525, and since then a succession of improvements in their construction had made them more and more formidable. At the spectacular battle of Pavia, the arquebuse had swept away the pike and become the infantry weapon of all Europe; the far deadlier Spanish musket had supplanted the arquebuse, and improved by Gustavus Adolphus had given terrible proof of its powers. Once a portable cannon, to be held with one hand and touched off with the other, the musket had been transformed by the invention of the lock; and cavalry pistol-fire had swept away the lance. Then rifling had been discovered. Meanwhile the Germans were using breech-loading field-pieces; and they and the Dutch, explosive shells. Nor was this all. The new and manageable weapons were coming into general use, with the

---

[269] VI. 436 et seq.

added danger to civil life that a pistol could be readily concealed about the person. As early as 1550 it was declared that even peasants and shepherds used fire-arms in Germany. And in a measure England saw all this from afar, as a portent; for bows had not been entirely discarded in the army as late as 1627.

Bacon may well have had his misgivings as he noted the mechanical ingenuity of the different types of lock; the perverse versatility that produced dagger-pistols, buckler-pistols, whip-pistols; the exquisite carving and engraving lavished upon these weapons.[270] It is true that he did not hesitate to advocate war, and as a political expedient; but even had he known Sir John Napier as the inventor of logarithms, he would not improbably have shaken his head at the fervor of the following, in Sir John's hand, dated June 2, 1596:[271]

A Burning Mirror for burning ships by the sun's beams. A piece of Artillery contrived so as to send forth its shot not in a single straight line but in all directions, in such a manner as to destroy everything in the neighborhood. A round Chariot of Metal constructed so as both to secure the complete safety of those within it, and moving about in all directions to break the enemy's array by continual charges of shot of the arquebuse through small holes. These inventions, beside devices of sailing under water and divers other devices and stratagems for harassing the enemies, by the grace of God and the work of expert craftsmen I hope to perform.

How different from Bacon's notes! And interest in the devastating piece of artillery was so great that Napier was asked to reveal the secret of the weapon on his death-bed.

Poison has long been pre-eminent as a safe means of removing obstacles, and Bacon doubtless read startling pages on its use in Tacitus;[272] but Nero's Locusta was a bungler compared with the Borgias, and the Borgias were far from being the last to make Europe whisper with raised eye-brows. Spectacular murders followed each other; poisons that worked gradually and left no trace were much heard about;[273] and not alone on the Continent.[274] Nor was it only the skilled assassin who made poison a name of

---

[270] For beautiful illustrations of these weapons, and for much in the preceding paragraph, see W. W. Greener, *The Gun and Its Development*.

[271] J. Timbs, *Stories of Inventors and Discoverers*, 88.

[272] *Annales*, XIII. 15, 16.

[273] J. Beckmann, *A History of Inventions, Discoveries, and Origins*, I. 47-63.

[274] Bacon's part in the famous Somerset case will be remembered.

terror in Bacon's day; the unskilled physician slew many more than he did. In his *Historial Expostulation against The Beastlye Abusers bothe of Chyrurgerie and Physyke*,[275] Dr. John Halle gives a hair-raising account of the epidemic of murderous quackery which afflicted England. The following case is one of many:

> One Robert Nicols, a false deceiver, and moste ignoraunte beaste, and of the profession of vagaboundes (as were his former felowes) hath in tymes passed boasted him selfe to have been the servant of Maister Vicary, late sargeant chyrurgien to the queenes highness. But now the matter being put in triall, he sayeth he was apprentice with a priest, among whose wicked and prodigious doynges, which are infinite, one very notable chaunced in the yere of our Lorde 1564, the 26 of September. He poured in a purgation to an honest woman of good fame, one Riches, wydowe, of Linton (a paryshe of three myles distant from Maydestone), whiche within three or foure houres at the moste, purged the lyfe out of hir body, so violent was this mortal potion.

As might be expected, such practitioners as the "ignoraunte beaste" named above found it expedient to keep moving, and Bacon may well have been reminded of Dædalus by their roving lives. Says Dr. Halle:

> It cannot be without suspicion, therefore, either of the lacke of cunnyng, or of a deceivable false conscience, that a chirurgien or phisitien shall refuse to fixe himselfe constantly in some dwellyng place and to become a wanderynge fugitive, as these were and are, of whom I have wrytten.

Another of their practices may have recalled the famous clue. Halle complains that these men are often sorcerers,

> so that it seemeth to be a common composition among them, the one to tormente the bodies of both man and beastes that another may be sought unto to remedy the same.

He protests that such remedies are forbidden by the Christian faith, and adds:

> Farthermore, if none such (as God in his holy lawe hath commanded) were suffred to lyve, there could no such inconvenience chaunce, whereby any man should have neede to seke to them for helpe seynge that there is never any neede of their ayde but where the effect is firste caused, through the wycked workyng of those damnable artes.

Here the good doctor exposes others beside the quacks; and when he informs us with indignation that such persons profess to be guided

---

[275] Percy Society, vol. 11.

by astrology, he reflects on no less a man than Paracelsus. Small wonder that Bacon thinks ill of the profession.[276]

At once an art of healing and of enrichment, alchemy stood prominent among the applied sciences, as innumerable books on the subject prove. It also counted its conscious quacks by the thousands, and Chaucer was by no means the last to hold them up to scorn. The bitterest in their derision are the genuinely anointed. Queen Elizabeth took no chances. Cornelius de Launoy, having promised to produce gold and diamonds for Her Majesty, was given a fair chance to make good, after which he went to the Tower; four years later, in 1570, John Bulkely, Oxford student, and William Bedo, stationer, "who proposed to cast a figure for the recovery of lost money, and professed to have many alchemical secrets for diminishing and lessening the coin of the realm," went to the Tower too.[277] A less mysterious alchemy turned unprofitable things into seeming wine. Robert Greene is loud in his complaints. Nor was chemistry the only hand-maid of the rogue. Greene describes the horse-thief trudging along.[278]

having a long staffe on his necke, and a blacke buckram bag at his backe, like some poore Client that had some writing in it, and there he hath his saddle, bridle and spurs, stirhops and stirhop leathers so quaintly and artificially made that it may bee put in the slop of a mans hose.

I refrain from discussing "the arts of procurers," but in any case I have said enough, I think, to explain Bacon's attitude. Dr. Halle's book, which is almost sufficient in itself to accomplish this purpose, certainly does so in the matter of that mutual acrimony which Bacon ascribes to "artists." In a poem addressed to his colleagues, the doctor begs that there shall be no quarrelling in the sick-room, and adds:

> And when alone with your foreman,
> One of you is presente,
> Defame nor dispraise in no wise
> The same that is absente.
> For noughte can more discomforte him,

---

[276] VI. 416. The work in question is the *Filum labyrinthi*. It may be of interest to add that there is a *Filum Ariadnæ* among the alchemistical books mentioned by Kopp, and that one of Maier's books is entitled *Viatorum . . . vel Ariadneo filo in Labyrintho*.

[277] M. W. Durrant in *Archæologia*, vol. 37.

[278] The Second Part of *Conny-Catching*.

Symbols of Scientific Speculation 115

> That lies in griefe and peyne,
> Then heare that one of you doth beare
> To other such disdeine.

Incidentally, the *Historiall Expostulation* reminds us that Bacon had frequent occasions to observe the "impolitic and improvident nature" of banishment. The worst that ever seemed to happen to any of the murderous quacks was to be "banisht the towne." As for the fact that the skilled artisan prospers in exile, Bacon had an illustration of it before his eyes in the case of the Flemish silk-weavers who found refuge in England in 1585 and established the industry there.

Bacon's interpretation of the flight of Icarus, with which he couples one of the myth of Scylla and Charybdis, is largely a discussion of excess and defect according to Aristotle; but the *Ethics* is not his only source, and his interpretation is scientific as well as ethical. On Icarus he comments as follows:

> It is an easy and familiar fable. The path of virtue goes directly midway between excess on the one hand and defect on the other. Icarus, being in the pride of youthful alacrity, naturally fell a victim of excess. For it is on the side of excess that the young commonly sin, as the old on the side of defect. And yet if he was to perish one way, it must be admitted that of two paths, both bad and mischievous, he chose the better. For sins of defect are justly accounted worse than sins of excess; because in excess there is something of magnanimity,—something, like the flight of a bird, that holds kindred with heaven; whereas defect creeps on the ground like a reptile. Excellently was it said by Heraclitus, "Dry light is the best soul." For when the moisture and humours of earth get into the soul, it becomes altogether low and degenerate. And yet here too a measure must be kept: the dryness, so justly praised, must be such as to make the light more subtle, but not such as to make it catch fire. But this is what everybody knows.

In a general sense, Bacon's interpretation is conventional; in a more special one, it is paralleled by Diodorus, and, as I shall presently show, by Lucian and Natalis Comes. What is said, however, about the desirableness of a moderate dryness of soul [279] reminds one of the alchemists. Thus Bonus of Ferrara, explaining the preparation of the Stone: [280]

---

[279] The idea that a "wet soul" is earthly may have been suggested by Heraclitus who says: "Where the earth is dry, the soul is wisest and best."

[280] *The Pearl of Great Price*, 246.

When the humid and the dry, and the hot and the cold, are so evenly balanced that there is an equilibrium of the elements, they are perfectly united, and the compound is indestructible.

And a few pages further on: [281]

Then if all elements are evenly combined without being touched by hand, the artist is a rich man . . . The right moment must be seized here, as in all other things. When you are baking bread or sweetmeats, or any other solid substance, the moment will arrive when they are perfectly done; and if after that moment you leave them in the oven ever so short a time, they will be marred, burnt, and destroyed. Haly compares the preparation of our Stone to that of soap, which is spoiled if boiled beyond a certain point. Hence the artist must be extremely watchful, and as soon as the substance has reached its most subtle stage, he must put an end to the digestive process; if he pushes it any further, the combined forces of the fire and the volatile part of the substance overcome its fixed part, and the whole evaporates.

As I have shown, Bacon might have been led to interpret the myth of Dædalus and Icarus as he does by the conventions and circumstances of his time, with no other literary sources than Aristotle and perhaps alchemistical literature; yet, as will now appear, Natalis Comes parallels him fairly closely, and what has been set forth in the preceding pages makes it appear practically certain, it seems to me, that Bacon used the *Mythologiæ*. I think it probable, therefore, that this book had at least a contributive influence in the present case. It might be expected to have shared such influence with many others; but as far as I know, it did not. For example, Servius, Diodorus Siculus,[282] and Pausanias,[283] rationalize Dædalus's adventures, but not ethically, nor do they comment on his enviousness; and while Diodorus explains Icarus's rashness with a passing " quæ iuvenum levitas est," he does not dwell on it at length. The *Mythologiæ* interprets as follows: [284]

Without doubt, injustice is the source of all ills and all calamities; and Dædalus, because through envy he cast Calus (*sic.*) from a tower, himself incurred many misfortunes, and learned that not even the friendship of kings insures impunity to the wicked. Indeed what gifts of mind but will lead to wretchedness if coupled with iniquity? Dædalus was ambitious and therefore sought the friendship of the great; but he well knew, and tried to convince his son of it, that it is safer to choose a middle course. For great success is wont to be accompanied by great wickedness

---

[281] *Ibid.*, 264, 265.
[282] *Bibliotheca*, IV. 77.
[283] *Descr. of Greece*, IX. 11.
[284] VII. 16. 528.

and great calamities. It was for this reason that he admonished Icarus, when they were about to take their flight for Sicily, that the middle course is the best . . . Nor did the poets preserve the memory of these things for any other reason but that of showing us that there is no safety in excess, whether of wealth or of anything else; and that he is wisest who practices moderation and neither looks down upon the humble nor incurs the envy of the multitude. Lucian, in his *Astrology*, illustrates by this fable the rashness and giddiness of youth, which does not pursue what is profitable, but wandering in the clouds and impatient of method and sober judgment, suddenly, plunges into the sea.

Truly, to compare this homily with the enlightened sagacity of our essays is to be convinced that England was blessed in her freedom from Rome, and that Bacon, despite much in his thinking that was still mediæval, profited nobly by that blessing.

Comes's reference to Lucian is misleading, for that writer does not employ the myth to illustrate the foolishness of youth but to emphasize his denunciation of the folly of astrology. He says as follows: [285]

The story of Dædalus also is a rare and wonderful tale; but I suspect that he was no scorner of astrology. Rather, obsessed with it himself, he taught his son these beliefs. Icarus, assured by his youthful temerity, and seeking the impossible with his head in the clouds, turned aside from truth and wandered from reason; wherefore he plunged into that ocean whose waters are mere fancies and groundless opinions.

As may be seen, Lucian's interpretation is even more to Bacon's purpose than Comes's, and it is quite possible that Bacon read it. If he did, he may in his own mind have anticipated that passage in the *Filum Labyrinthi* [286] where he says:

He thought also, that knowledge is uttered to men in a form as if everything were furnished; for it is reduced into arts and methods, which in their divisions do seem to include all that may be. And how weakly soever the parts are filled, yet they carry the shew and reason of a total; and thereby the writings of some received authors go for the very art; whereas antiquity used to deliver the knowledge which the mind of man had gathered, in observations, aphorisms, or short and dispersed sentences, or small tractates of some parts that they had diligently meditated and laboured; which did invite men, both to ponder that which was invented, and to add and supply further.

It is in favor of a pithy concreteness that he interprets the myth of Scylla and Charybdis, thus incidentally relived of its hackneyed moral symbolism: [287]

---

[285] *Of Astrology*, IX. 11.   [286] VI. 418.   [287] XIII. 158.

We are meant to understand that in every knowledge and science, and in the rules and axioms appertaining to them, a mean must be kept between too many distinctions and too much generality,—between the rocks of the one and the whirlpools of the other. For these two are notorious for the shipwreck of wits and arts.

When it comes to practice, however, Bacon is not always proof against the mediæval elaborateness he reprehends.

Æsculapius.[288]

In his reflections on Æsculapius, Bacon gives us a beautiful example of his skill in that kind of figurative speech discussed in this paper. In his hands the mythical founder of medicine becomes an original symbol of the unhappy state of that science in the seventeenth century; then, gracefully and naturally associated with a more august figure, an eloquent illustration of what Bacon felt the destinies of medicine to be. The literary sources are few and simple; the interpretation is chiefly based on what the writer saw about him and on what he felt in his heart. Indeed these pages contain a pathetic and almost fugitive personal allusion which gives them an added subtle meaning. Bacon fleetingly associates the statesman with the doctor in the hard lot which opinionated ignorance imposes on both; and truly, was he not the anxious physician of a state ill with headstrong crudeness and fast approaching a crisis?

The reflections I have alluded to above are as follows:

This variable composition of man's body hath made it an instrument easy to distemper; and therefore the poets did well to conjoin Music and Medidcine in Apollo; because the office of meddicine is but to tune this curious harp of Man's body and to reduce it to harmony. So then the subject being so variable hath made the art by consequent more conjectural; and the art being conjectural hath made so much the more place to be left for imposture. For almost all other arts and sciences are judged by acts or masterpieces, as I may term them, and not by the successes and events. The lawyer is judged by the virtue of his pleading, and not by the issue of the cause. The master in the ship is judged by the directing his course aright, and not by the fortune of the voyage. But the physician and perhaps the politique, hath no particular acts demonstrative of his ability, but is judged most by the event; which is ever but as it is taken; for who can tell, if a patient die or recover, or if a state be preserved or ruined, whether it be art or accident? And

---

[288] VI. 242. et seq. See also IX. 23, 26.

therefore many times the impostor is prized, and the man of virtue taxed. Nay, we see the weakness and credulity of men is such, as they will often prefer a montabank or witch before a learned physician. And therefore the poets were clear-sighted in discerning this extreme folly, when they made Æsculapius and Circe brother and sister, both children of the sun, as in the verses,

> Apollo's son from whom that art did grow
> Jove struck with thunder to the shades below.[289]

And again,

> Now by the shelves of Circe's coast they run
> Circe the rich, the daughter of the sun.[290]

For in all times, in the opinion of the multitude, witches and old women and imposters have had a competition with physicians.

At this point let us interrupt an already long quotation and consider the sources involved. The lines from Vergil are more a suggestion than a model; yet I have discovered nothing to make me think that Bacon had a more immediate source. They are chosen felicitously enough; for the injustice of Æsculapius's fate is apparent, and Circe, the mixer of drugs, was also the typical sorceress —the Acrasia, the Armida—of the Renaissance. The conceit that Apollo's lyre is his attribute as the god of medicine occurs in Boccaccio: [291]

According to Theodontius, he was the first to discover the virtue of herbs and to apply them to the needs of man. Therefore he was called not only the inventor but the god of medicine, since many who are sick recover health through his remedies. And because he discovered the right rhythm of the pulse, it is said that Mercury, prince of numbers, granted him the lyre; by which was meant that even as the strings of the lyre may be skillfully touched to produce a melody, so the various beating of the pulse may, by a good physician, be so ordered as to produce health in the harmony of a well regulated body.

Boccaccio implies that he has a source, but I have not been able to find it; and on the other hand the *Genealogiis deorum* was widely known in England and parallels Bacon closely elsewhere.

Bacon's assertion that the multitude regarded "witches and old women" as worthy of competing with physicians is amply supported by Dr. Halle. In an address to the "Company and Brotherhood of Chirurgiens of London," [292] he complains that the profes-

---

[289] *Aen.* VII. 772. [290] *Ibid.*, 11. [291] *Geneal. deor.*, V. sub. *Apollo*.
[292] *Percy Society Publications*, intro. to Dr. Halle's book.

sion is disgraced by "smythes, cutlers, carters, coblars, coopers, coriars of leather, carpenters, and a great rable of women;" and the first "beastlie deceaver" pilloried in the *Hystoriall Expostulation* is a woman. That the people were largely responsible appears from the following racy passage in the account of a male charlatan:

> Well, for jesting a lyttel agaynste the madnes of thys deceaver, I hadde a dagger drawne at me not longe after. The wordes that I spake were to his hostes, when I sawe him goe by, in thys wise. Is this (quod I) the cunnyng sothsayer, that is sayde to lye at your house? Sothsayer, quod shee; I knowe no suche thynge by him, therefore ye are to blame so to name him. Why, quod I, suche men and suche enformed me that he can tell of thynges loste, and helpe children and cattell bewitched and forspoken, and can tell by lokyng in ones face, what markes he hathe on his bodie, and where, and tell them what they have done, and their fortune to come. Yea, and all this in deed he can doe, quod she. Why, then, he is a sothesayer and a sorcerer, quod I. Well, quod she, yf he have so muche cunnynge in his bellye, he is the happyer, and it is the more joye of him. Nay, quod I, it were mere folyshnes for him to carye his cunnyng in his bellye. And why? quod she. Why, quod I, thynke you that men of lernyng and knowledge cary their cunnynge in their bellies? Wher else, quod she, and why not? Mary, quod I, yf he should beare his cunnyng there, he should alwayes waste it when he wente to the privye, and so in time he should lose all his cunnyng. This beyng merylye spoken, turned me afterwards not to a little displeasure, even at their handes, where I had deserved and loked for friendship as of dutie; but I must cease to marveyle any longer at this, when almoste everie suche abhominable vylaine is defended, upholden, and mayntayned, by suche as of righte, and according to the holesome lawes of this realme, should punish them for these their abusions. Yet surelie the grieffe were the lesse, yf onely the blynde, and supersticious antiquitie had a regarde and love to suche deceavers. But nowe a great number that have borne an outwarde shewe of great holynes, and love to Gods holie worde; we see them seke daylie to such divelishe wyches and sorcerers, if their fynger doe but ake, as though they were Goddes, and could presentlie helpe them with wordes, although they knowe that God in his Israell, hath called them an abhominacion, and hath farther commaunded that none suche should be suffred among them to lyve.

It was not only the multitude that believed in Circe. "Dr. Dee,"[293] who if neither an old woman nor a witch was a learned counterpart of both, determined for Leicester the auspicious day on which to crown Elizabeth, was called to Court to interpret the omen of a comet and to counteract a sorcerous attempt upon his

---

[293] For an amusing account of this man's experience in England and Germany, see H. C. Bolton, *op. cit.*, first five chapters.

royal mistress, and by her was made Chancellor of St. Paul's Cathedral and Warden of Manchester College. It constitutes a curious side-light on the times that the rabble gutted this man's house and destroyed his books and instruments, declaring him to be a sorcerer. It regarded as deep learning what mystified it,—but not too much; and the upper classes were in precisely the same position. The Court knew that when the Doctor gazed muttering upon his "shewstone" he was not summoning the Devil but invoking angels, who in fact came, and communed with him in the disordered language of his subconsciousness. All high science ended in God, as Bacon himself tells us, and was mystically one in all its branches. Good Dr. Hall is scandalized that the quacks should profess to cure by astrology; but it may be doubted whether ignorance of that science is not their chief offence in his eyes, for he admonishes the medical neophyte that:

> Not onlye in chirurgery,
> Thou oughtest to be experte;
> But also in astronomye,
> Bothe prevye and aperte.

Bacon attributes to discouragement [294] the physician's proficiency in all learning save his own,[295] but this is only part of the truth. The physician was a sage. Bacon himself was a sage, who claimed all knowledge as his province. He knew that such knowledge was a thing to fill more than Vincent de Beauvais' *Speculum naturale;* he felt that omniscience was an ocean extending far beyond the Columns of Hercules, and that the ships to explore it were many experiments. Yet he felt no misgivings; for beside the Renaissance man's boundless confidence in the powers of the human mind, based on divine antiquity, he had not a little of his belief in the miraculous. He was of two minds as to whether the classic myths did not afford a short-cut to knowledge; and it is not without significance that, having set forth what physicians may hope to accomplish, he continues: [296]

---

[294] VI. 244.

[295] Cf. Petrarch, *Rer. sen.*, V. 4: "I have known and been most friendly with many doctors who were eloquent, cultured, learned in many sciences, but only of no account as doctors." The parallel may, of course, be fortuitous and as for Bacon's "Parables, which are a divine poesy," in VIII. 409, it is the expression of a widely known doctrine; yet see III. 320.

[296] VI. 245.

What that they should do, the nobleness of their art doth deserve; well shadowed by the poets, in that they made Æsculapius to be the son of the Sun, the one being the fountain of life, the other as the second stream; but infinitely more honoured by the example of our Saviour, who made the body of man the object of his miracles, as the soul was the object of his doctrine.

Atlas [297] and Scylla.[298]

Bacon's criticism of the scientific thought of his times finds peculiarly sweeping and sharp expression in two of his interpretations: that of Atlas and that of Scylla. In the first, he stings with his mockery the intellectual cowardice of clinging blindly to authority; in the second, he vigorously lashes the triviality of observation and experiment intended rather to intrench accepted doctrine than to subject it to inquisition. In both, his applications of myths are largely original, yet recognizably suggested, I believe by earlier applications.

In regard to Atlas, forever burdened with a sky which, it was thought, would fall if not supported, Bacon says as follows:

> For the mind of man is strangely eager to be relieved from suspense, and to have something fixed and immovable, upon which in its wanderings and disquisitions it may securely rest. And assuredly Aristotle endeavors to prove [299] that in all motion there is some point quiescent; and as he very elegantly interprets the ancient fable of Atlas, who stood fixed and supported the heaven on his shoulders, to be meant of the poles or axletree of heaven, whereupon the conversion is accomplished; so do men earnestly desire to have within them an Atlas or axletree of the thoughts, by which the fluctuations and dizziness of the understanding may be to some extent controlled; fearing belike that their heaven should fall.

It will be noticed that Bacon's idea is not really analogous to Aristotle's; for it deals with a desire, whereas the other is concerned with what is conceived to be a physical fact. The analogy is a strained one, and we are justified in suspecting that the association of ideas is due to an external cause. In fact, Natalis Comes furnishes us with a plausible one when, having interpreted Atlas as a hard-beset statesman and Hercules as a sagacious friend who assisted him in his perplexity,[300] he closes with the following original epistle to some retiring acquaintance, informing us that this

---

[297] IX. 94.   [298] VI. 549; VIII. 26.   [299] *De motu anim.*, 3.

[300] It will be recalled that Hercules, according to Apollodorus and others, held up the sky while Atlas went to fetch the golden apples which the hero was in quest of.

composition " is by no means irrelevant to a proper understanding of the fable: " [301]

I rejoice that you are returning to the Muses relieved of the great burden of public tasks which your country placed upon you; for unremitting toil, so it is said, will at last tame even lions. It is for this reason that Mother Nature requires night to follow day; for this reason are we taught that wise Hercules gave welcome respite to the shoulders of Atlas . . . Believe me, he is happiest who spends his days far from the madding crowd, in rustic peacefulness, watching the stream flow by. For happiness is denied to man except in quiet . . . What makes us serene and cheerful is above all a quiet mind.

Retiring to the country and leaving all perplexities to Hercules is not the panacea that Comes proclaims it to be. It involves the explaining away of persistent facts; and as where there is no certainty there can be no agreement, it also involves endless inconclusive controversy. This it did throughout the Middle Ages and was still doing in the seventeenth century; and Bacon vigorously protests against the triviality and folly of the whole proceeding. In the transcript of *Valerius Terminus*,[302] a passage in reprehension of inconclusive and self-deceiving investigators ends as follows:

which is the reason why the learning that now is hath the curse of barrenness, and is courtesan-like, for pleasure, and not for fruit.

The passage is annotated in Bacon's own hand:

Nay to compare it rightly, the strange fiction of the poets of the transformation of Scylla,[303] seemeth to be a lively emblem of this philosophy and knowledge; a fair woman upwards in the parts of show, but when you come to the parts of use and generation, barking monsters; for no better are the endless distorted questions which ever have been, and of necessity must be, the end and womb of such knowledge.

Even more than by the general vigor of expression to be noted in these utterances, one is impressed by what at first sight appears to be the prodigious nimbleness of imagination displayed. The unproductiveness of science is compared with barrenness in women;

---

[301] VII. 1. 466.

[302] VI. 49.

[303] The nymph Scylla, it will be remembered, having provoked the jealousy of Circe, was so transformed that the heads of dogs grew from the lower part of her body; whereupon she threw herself into the sea, and endowed with immortality by her lover Glaucus, became a standing menace to passing ships.

and specifically with deliberate barrenness in courtesans; and immediately afterwards, with the deformed barrenness of Scylla. The whole thing is highly effective, rapidly adding to the general idea of sterility those of willfulness, triviality, unnaturalness, clamorousness; nevertheless the imaginative aspect of it still impresses one, the passage per saltum from courtesans to Scylla seeming almost fantastic. As a matter of fact, the ideas involved are quite naturally connected, as will appear if we consider their sources.

We have seen that Boccaccio identifies the unproductiveness, in a sense, of pure speculation with what he calls the barrenness of Minerva; and although Bacon parallels him in a passage of much later date than the first of those quoted, it is probable that he was already acquainted with *De genealogiis deorum* when he wrote *Valerius Terminus*. The supposition is not, however, imperative in the present case. In Bacon's times, the word *barren* was much more generally used in the senses of sterile, fruitless, and unproductive, than it is now; and on the other hand it was much more likely to recall its literal meaning in the Bible, where it very frequently occurs. Bacon, then, would naturally use the word, and by it would not improbably be put in mind of some such comparison as he makes. Barrenness as a misfortune or curse is typically biblical, and we may feel pretty sure, I think, that Bacon's expression was suggested to him by the Scriptures. But the barrenness of which Bacon treats is willfully iniflcted upon learning by those who prostitute science to mere dilettantism or to the trivial appeasing of their minds; and the writer aptly compares it to the state of those unfortunates who, in an age by no means familiar with birth-control, were singular in their enforced adoption of the practice. With courtesans in his thoughts, it was not fantastic, but on the contrary quite natural, for Bacon to think of Scylla. Fulgentius,[304] followed by Boccaccio,[305] interprets Scylla as the type of the traffic-infesting courtesan, going into gross but striking details that recall mad Lear's tirade against woman.

Eolus[306] and Hylas.[307]

Partly, perhaps, from a sense of artistic fitness, Bacon, in most of his interpretations, concerns himself with large and philosophic

---

[304] *Mythologicon*, II. 12.
[305] X, sub *Scylla*.
[306] IX. 410.
[307] IV. 249.

subjects; but in those of the myths of Eolus and Hylas he comes to gripes with individual facts, and thus puts himself to the test by which he has found his contemporaries wanting. The facts in question are the nature of the wind and the attenuation of sound by water. The first of his interpretations is conventional, though with a significant difference; the second, as far as I can discover, is original.

In regard to Eolus, Bacon says as follows:

> The poets have feigned that the kingdom of Eolus was situated in subterranean dens and caverns, where the winds were imprisoned, and whence they were occasionally let loose . . . There is doubtless a large quantity of air contained in the earth, which probably exhales by degrees, and must certainly from particular causes some times rush out in a body.

Various authors with whom Bacon was probably familiar explain the myth much as he does. Servius remarks [308] that: "Indeed it is natural for hollow places to be full of wind." Boccaccio goes into considerable detail: [309]

> It was feigned that the winds were raised by Juno against Jove because they are believed to come out of the earth, which is represented by Juno, and to be sent forth as by a breathing of the earth itself . . . It was also said that they were imprisoned in caverns under the guardianship of Eolus because the Eolides (the islands over which Eolus ruled and which are named after him) are full of caverns, and these are full of air and water, the stirring of which, producing heat, gives rise to evaporation; and the vapors which result, not having room in a restricted space, come forth, and if the opening is a small one, they come forth impetuously, and with a prolonged, sonorous sound.

Boccaccio's words betray his source. Aristotle tells us that: [310] "After a rainfall, the earth, evaporating by reason of the sunshine and of internal heat, gives out a breathing which is the substance of the wind"; and classifying the various winds, he says: [311]

> The Anaphysma, which means almost a breathing, is a wind that whirls upward from the earth and is emitted by some cavern or fissure.

It will be noticed that Bacon is more reserved in his expression than either of his predecessors. In fact, he regards exhalation from caves as but one of many causes, chief of which the action of the sun in expanding the air and producing vapor.[312] Even so, he does not

---

[308] *Com. in Virg. Aen.*, I. 52.
[309] IV, sub *De ventis*.
[310] *Meteorologicorum*, II. 4.
[311] *De mundo*, IV.
[312] IX. 421, 422.

ground his acceptance of the explanation on tradition only, but also on recently reported evidence.[313] He probably expresses his true position in regard to the whole matter when he says: [314]

> The nature of the winds is generally ranked among the things mysterious and concealed; and no wonder, when the power and nature of the air, which the winds attend and serve (as represented by the poets in the relation of Æolus to Juno)[315] is entirely unknown.

Curiously enough, he accepts unreservedly the current belief that pent-up winds are the cause of earthquakes: [316]

> It requires a great force of subterraneous air to shake or cleave the earth, but a less to raise the water. Hence it is that earthquakes are uncommon, but swellings and risings of the waters are more frequent.

It is, then, to pent-up air that he attributes the swelling of the earth when he says: [317]

> But in earthquakes the earth swells suddenly and manifestly; and oftentimes there burst forth springs of water, wreaths and balls of flame, and strong and strange winds; and stones and ashes are hurled up into the air.

But in this passage he is adducing proofs of the expansive force of the spirits informing all matter, and is therefore thinking of the air in terms of a more universal agency. It is probably with this idea in mind that he gives the following interpretation, which I believe to be individual, of a myth of Pan and Typhon: [318]

> The same thing [319] is alluded to in that other circumstance of the catching of Typhon in a net: because however it be that vast and strange swellings (for that is the meaning of Typhon) take place occasionally in nature,— whether of the sea, or the clouds, or the earth, or any other body— nevertheless, all such exuberancies and irregularities are by the nature of things caught and confined in an inextricable net, and bound down as with a chain of adamant.

In Servius,[320] Boccaccio,[321] and Natalis Comes,[322] Typhon represents pent-up and inflamed air which causes earthquakes and vol-

---

[313] *Ibid.*, 412.   [314] *Ibid.*, 381
[315] Bacon disagrees with Boccaccio in his interpretation of Juno. He is, however, in agreement with Natalis Comes.
[316] IX. 411.   [317] X. 208.   [318] XIII. 99.
[319] The self-preserving powers of nature.
[320] *Com. in Virg. Aen.*, III. 578.
[321] IV. sub *De Typhoeo*.   [322] VI. 22.

canic eruptions. As for the restraint imposed by nature upon her own destructive forces, it is asserted by Comes [323] in his interpretation of the myth of Pan and Cupid, and it is suggested, though unintentionally, by Lucretius.[324] Furthermore, Bacon himself suggests a net when, in regard to the creative expansiveness of the informing spirits, he says: [325]

> Generation or vivification is likewise the combined work of the spirit and the grosser parts, but in a very different manner. For the spirit is entirely detained, but swells and moves locally . . . Vivification therefore always takes place in a matter tenacious and viscous, but at the same time soft and yielding . . . And this appears in the matter of all things . . . for there is manifest in them all a matter hard to break through, but easy to yield.

Bacon mentions Hylas in connection with an experiment in acoustics which he proposes. Let a man duck down under water, pulling an inverted tub over his head; let him then speak, and in the "sharp and exile" tones which will be heard above the surface, those in observation there will have proof that sound is diminished in volume and intensity when it passes from water to the air. In support of this assertion Bacon adds:

> A man would think that the Sicilian poet [326] had knowledge of this experiment; for he saith that Hercules' page, Hylas, went with a water pot to fill it at a pleasant fountain that was near the shore, and that the nymphs of the fountain fell in love with the boy, and pulled him under the water, keeping him alive; and that Hercules missing his page, called him by his name aloud, that all the shore rang of it; and that Hylas from within the water answered his master, but (that which is to the present purpose) with so small and exile a voice, as Hercules thought he had been three miles off, when the fountain indeed was fast by.

Aristotle would seem to have observed the fact thus charmingly illustrated, for he says [327] that sound " is heard in air and in water, but less in the latter." I think it probable, however, that Bacon's interpretation (if such it can properly be called) originated in his experiment and in the myth itself. Theocritus says that "a thin voice came from the water," and one disposed to read between the lines and accustomed to Hermetic accounts of experiments might very well indulge at least a passing surmise. Bacon does not ex-

---

[323] Vide ante sub *Pan.*
[324] *De rer. nat.*, V. 363-404. See also Ovid, *Metam*, I. 57-60.
[325] X. 158.   [326] Theocritus, in Idyl XIII.   [327] *De Anima*, II. 8.

plicitly adduce the myth as evidence, but it may be suspected that if he had found encouragement in Servius or Comes he would have cited it in *Sylva sylvarum* just as he does that of Eolus in *Historia ventorum*.

Prometheus.[328]

Of the many legends which from remote antiquity gathered around the name of Prometheus, Bacon relates the following. Prometheus, having created men out of animal scraps and clay, stole fire from heaven for their benefit. They, however, denounced him for the theft to Jupiter, who in reward not only sanctioned their use of fire, but conferred perpetual youth on them. This they at once lost, for the ass on whose back they placed it exchanged it for a drink of water with the serpent guarding a certain pool. Prometheus forgave mankind but not Jupiter, whom he presently mocked as follows. Having slaughtered two bulls, he stuffed the hide of one with the flesh of both, the other with the bones, and offered Jove his choice for a sacrifice. To punish him in his pride as the creator of men, Jove sent to these a vase of plagues by the hands of the bewitching maid Pandora, manufactured at his behest by Vulcan. Pandora failed to make wise Prometheus open her deadly vase; but she persuaded his brother Epimetheus, who repenting too late, was in time to shut in only the one blessing sent with so many curses: the faculty of hope. Prometheus, seized, at length, by Jupiter, and accused of theft, impiety, and the attempted ravishment of Minerva, was chained to a peak in the Caucasus mountains. There, by the famous eagle, he was subjected to a torment which might have proved eternal, for his torn liver grew and healed again each night However, he was finally set free by Hercules who, it is said, crossed the sea between them in a cup given to him by Apollo.

Fulgentius interprets Prometheus as the providence of God which, having created man's body, breathed into it the heavenly spark of the soul.[329] Servius, instead,[330] and Augustine,[331] regard Prometheus as an enlightened leader and reformer who, so to speak, invented civilization. Boccaccio[332] combines both views, attributing to Prometheus a two-fold symbolism. Natalis Comes, as we

[328] XIII. 144.
[329] *Mythologicon*, II. 9.
[330] *Com. in Virg. bucol.*, VI. 42.
[331] *De civ. Dei*, XVIII. 8.
[332] IV, sub *De Prometheo*.

shall presently see, agrees rather with Servius than with Fulgentius, but explains Prometheus and Epimetheus as human forethought and thoughtlessness more than as individuals. Bacon is indebted both to Comes and to Boccaccio, and interprets the whole myth as a history of mankind which, having described the creation of the first human beings, traces the progress of civilization in a course marked by forethought and intelligence, and yet by thoughtlessness and rashness also.

Bacon begins his interpretation of the myth with an explanation of Prometheus for the two-fold nature of which he is probably indebted to Boccaccio:

Prometheus clearly and expressly signifies Providence; and the one thing singled out by the ancients as the special and peculiar work of Providence was the creation and constitution of Man. For this one reason no doubt was, that the nature of man includes mind and intellect, which is the seat of Providence; [333] and since to derive mind and reason from principles brutal and irrational would be harsh and incredible, it follows almost necessarily that the human spirit was endued with providence not without the precedent and intention and warrant of the greater providence.[334]

With this compare the beginning of Boccaccio's interpretation: [335]

I think it well to inquire how we are to understand this Prometheus. He must be understood to have a two-fold nature, even as created man has First, then, he is the true and omnipotent God, who made man out of clay . . . Secondly, he is the man Prometheus, of whom Theodontius says that he inherited kingly power from his father Japhet, but being young and in love with learning abdidcated in favor of his brother Epimetheus and betook himself to Assyria where he consorted with the most famous Chaldeans of the day. Thence he retired to the top of Mount Caucasus and there studied the course of the stars and many other things. Descending from the mountain, he began teaching astrology and the ways of civilized life to his fellow men, who were entirely barbarous; and so successfully did he labor that he left them in a state of civilization.

The rest of Boccaccio's interpretation, and indeed of his narrative, is scanty as compared with Bacon's, no mention being made, for example, of Jupiter's gift of immortality nor of Prometheus's mocking sacrifice; and it differs from Bacon's in the explanation of Pandora's vase and of Prometheus's torment.

Natalis Comes gives all the episodes to be found in Bacon, and,

---

[333] That is, of forethought or prudence.
[334] Cf. Thom. Aquin., *Sum. Theol.*, I. 119; and for that matter, *Gen.* II. 7.
[335] IV, sub *De Prometheo*.

what is perhaps significant, practically no others. That Bacon is considerably indebted to him appears, I think, from the following table.

Bacon	Natalis Comes [337]
The nature of man includes mind and intellect, which is the seat of providence. The followers of Epimetheus are the improvident . . . and on this account it is true that they suffer many distresses.	Prometheus, as Zezes correctly interprets, is mind, which foresees things long before they happen. Epimetheus is the knowledge we acquire after the fact, and his daughter is repentance.
Nevertheless we see that man in the first state of his existence is a naked and defenseless thing, slow to help himself, and full of wants. Therefore Prometheus applied himself with all haste to the invention of fire;[336] which in all human necessities and business is the great minister of relief and help . . . For through it most operations are effected, through it the arts mechanical and the sciences themselves are furthered.	In truth men were at first primitive; they knew nothing of ploughing nor of any art—But gradually experience and necessity taught them to do better—In truth daily discomfort made them prudent—Hence it is said that Prometheus or prudence discovered fire; and by means of this, later, all the arts. For indeed there is no art which does not depend on fire.[338]
Pandora has been generally and rightly understood to mean pleasure and sensual appetite, which after the introduction of civil arts and culture and luxury is kindled up as it were by the gift of fire . . . And from her have flowed forth infinite mischief upon the minds and bodies and fortunes of men . . . For from this same fountain have sprung wars, and civil disturbances and tyrannies.	The ancients tell us that Jove, enraged at the invention of Fire, sent all sorts of evil to men; for there is no calamity that does not arise from voluptuousness, which is served by many arts. Indeed, together with the arts there arose kings, and war and robbery, and anxiety and all the distresses of life.
Having described the state of man in respect of arts and matters intellectual, the parable passes to	It is said that Prometheus offered to God flesh in one oxhide, bones in another; for with the coming of

---

[336] This passage decidedly recalls Plato's words in the *Protagoras*, and that work doubtless contributed to Bacon's interpretation, though it could not have been his only source.

[337] IV. 6. 211.

[338] Comes presumably paraphrases Fulgentius (or Boccaccio, who quotes him) in his remarks about the importance of fire to industry; but these writers say what they do in connection with Vulcan.

Religion; for with the cultivation of the arts came likewise the worship of things divine; and this was immediately seized on and polluted by hypocrisy. Therefore, under the figure of that double sacrifice is elegantly represented the person of the truly religious man and the hypocrite.[339]

The school of Prometheus on the other hand, that is the wise and forethoughtful class of men, do indeed by their caution decline and remove out of their way many evils and misfortunes; but with that good there is this evil joined that they stint themselves of many pleasures and of the various agreeableness of life, and cross their genius, and (which is far worse) torment and wear themselves away with cares and solicitude and inward fears. For being bound to the column of necessity, they are troubled with innumerable thoughts (which because of their flightyness are represented by the eagle), thoughts which prick and gnaw and voluptuousness and luxuries, not only are right and law sacrificed to convenience, but even the gods come to be held in contempt. Few indeed are those who care more for the worship of God than for fat profits.

It is said that the eagle of Jove incessantly tears Prometheus's liver, because the minds of prudent men are always distracted with various cogitations . . . Prometheus's liver is said to have grown at night in proportion as it was devoured by day because nature determines alternate times of quiet and of anxiety and cogitation.

---

[339] Cf. VIII. 487, where Bacon gives a different interpretation of the sacrifice:

Certainly astronomy offers to the human intellect a victim like that which Prometheus offered in deceipt of Jupiter. Prometheus, in the place of a real ox, brought to the altar the hide of an ox of great size and beauty, stuffed with straw and leaves, and twigs. In like manner astronomy presents only the exterior of the heavenly bodies (I mean the number of the stars, their positions, motions, and periods), as it were the hide of the heavens; beautiful indeed and skillfully arranged into systems; but the interior (namely the physical reasons) is wanting, out of which (with the help of astronomical hypotheses) a theory might be devised which would not merely satisfy the phenomena (of which kind many might with a little ingenuity be contrived), but which would set forth the substance, motion, and influence of the heavenly bodies as they really are.

With this compare Boccaccio, I, sub *De Paue*:

As for his being covered with a spotted leopard skin, it was said of him to suggest the beauty of the eighth sphere, painted with the splendor of the stars, by which the things of nature are covered and hidden even as a man is covered by a garment.

corrode the liver; and if at intervals, as in the night, they obtain some little relaxation and quiet of mind, yet new fears and anxieties return presently with the morning.

But I must now return to a part which, that I might not interrupt the connection of what precedes, I have purposely passed by. I mean that last crime of Prometheus, the attempt upon the chastity of Minerva. For it was even for this offence—certainly a very great and grave one—that he underwent that punishment of the tearing of his entrails. The crime alluded to appears to be no other than that into which men not infrequently fall when puffed up with arts and much knowledge,—of trying to bring the divine wisdom itself under the dominion of sense and reason: from which attempt inevitably follows laceration of the mind and vexation without end or rest.[340]

Theophrastus, in certain commentaries, left it written that Prometheus was said to have brought fire from heaven to men because he was the first to instruct mortals in divine matters and in philosophy, and the first to direct their gaze in speculation towards those heavenly and eternal bodies; which opinion is confirmed by what Æschylus wrote. Duris the Samian also wrote that Prometheus was tortured because he loved Pallas.[341]

Natalis Comes dwells at length on Prometheus's mixing animal particles with his clay, a legend alluded to, as he points out, by various classical writers. As for the interpretation of the episode, he says as follows:

For it is said that Prometheus, when he made man, mixed the indidvidual elements in his work, and that because of the proportions of these elements he was able not only to unite the energies of individual bodies but to give to those the impulse and habits of friends.[342] Such as have attempted a more fanciful explanation say that Prometheus united in men the timidity of the hare, the craftiness of the fox, the vanity of the peacock, the ferocity of the tiger, and the irascibility and great-heartedness of the lion.

---

[340] It will be noticed that Bacon elaborates on Comes, giving us what is in a measure a new interpretation of Prometheus's torments.

[341] Comes, it will be observed, cites Theophrastus, Pherecydes, Zezes, etc.; but my examination of such fragments of these authors as we possess does not lead me to believe that Bacon is directly indebted to them.

[342] Nam fama est Prometheum cum hominem fingeret portiones captas e singulis elementis suo operi admiscuisse: atque pro ipsorum elementorum temperamentis non solum vires singulis corporibus addidisse, sed etiam motus amicorum et mores.

The second of these interpretations occurs in Horace [343] and elsewhere,[344] but the first I have found only in Comes. Its peculiar language probably betrays its source, for in the *Timaeus* Plato says: [345]

And for these reasons, and out of such elements which are in number four, the body of the world was created, and it was harmonized by proportion, and therefore has the spirit of friendship; and having been reconciled to itself, it was indissoluble by the hand of any other than the framer.

Let us now hear Bacon, who says as follows:

Nor is it without meaning added that in the mass and composition of which man was made, particles taken from the different animals were infused and mixed up with the clay; for it is most true that of all things in the universe man is the most composite, so that he was not without reason called by the ancients the little world. For though the Alchemists, when they maintain that there is to be found in man every mineral, every vegetable, etc., or something corresponding to them, take the word *microcosm* in a sense too gross and literal, and have so spoiled the elegance and distorted the meaning of it, yet, that the body of man is of all existing things both the most mixed and the most organic, remains not the less a sober and solid truth. And this is indeed the reason it is capable of such wonderful powers and faculties; for the powers of simple bodies, though they be certain and rapid, yet being less refracted, broken up, and counteracted by mixture, they are few; but abundance and excellence of power resides in mixture and composition.

A comparison of Bacon's interpretation with Comes's makes it seem probable that the *Mythologiæ* suggested the association of Prometheus with the general conception of the complex composition of man's body and the many powers resulting; but for the origins of the ideas included in that conception we must evidently look elsewhere.

Bacon himself refers to the Greeks as originating the idea that man is a miniature universe, and to the alchemists as driving that idea to literal exaggeration. Of the former, Empedocles clearly implies, at least, not only that man's body is the richest in admixture but also that it owes to this fact its functional superiority over all other bodies, organic or otherwise.[346] Bacon recalls Anaxagoras,

---

[343] *Carm.*, I. 16. 13.
[344] *Scriptores rerum mythicarum latini*, II. 63.
[345] Jowett's Plato, III. 451.
[346] Gomperz, *Greek Thinkers*, I. 247.

though by contraries, when in the *Advancement of Learning* he says that: [347]

of all substances which nature hath produced, man's body is the most extremely compounded. For we see herbs and plants are nourished by earth and water; beasts for the most part by herbs and fruits; man by the flesh of beasts, birds, fishes, herbs, grains, fruits, water, and the manifold alterations dressings, and preparations of these several bodies, before they come to be his food and aliment.

Plato comes to mind in connection with Bacon's implied assertion that God moulded man's body of many elements with a view to its perfection; for in the *Timaeus*, which, as we have seen, was probably Come's source, he tells us that: [348]

... the creator compounded the world out of all the fire and all the water and all the air and all the earth.... His intention was, in the first place, that the animal should be as far as possible a perfect whole and of perfect parts.

And again, in the same work: [349]

For the Deity, intending to make this world like the fairest and most perfect of intelligible beings, framed one visible animal comprehending within itself all other animals of a kindred nature.

As for Bacon's relating the powers of man's body to its being " the most organic," Aristotle taught him no less.

We now come to ideas which, as far as I know, have not been associated with Prometheus by any of Bacon's predecessors. They are to the effect that man's denouncing Prometheus to Jupiter symbolizes scientific enlightenment, and his losing Jove's gift, the opposite; that the torch-race in the Promethean Games represents the advance of science through cooperation; that Hercules's crossing the sea in a goblet is an allegory of the Incarnation, or of fortitude triumphing over bodily frailty; and finally that the whole myth of Prometheus teaches the lesson that the world was created for man's use. The last two ideas are not of a scientific nature, but I include them in this part of my inquiry as illustrating Bacon's constant tendency to associate his scientific with his religious thinking.

The first of the interpretations enumerated above goes as follows:

---

[347] VI. 241. [348] Jowett, III. 452 [349] *Ibid.* 450.

There follows a remarkable part of the parable. Men, we are told, instead of gratulation and thanksgiving fell to remonstrance and indignation, and brought an accusation before Jupiter both against Prometheus and against Fire; and this act was moreover by him so well liked, that in consideration of it he accumulated fresh benefits upon mankind. For how should the crime of ingratitude towards their maker, a vice which includes in itself almost all others, deserve approbation and reward? and what could be the drift of such a fiction? But this is not what is meant. The meaning of the allegory is, that the accusation and arraignment by men both of their own nature and of art, proceeds from an excellent condition of mind and issues in good; whereas the contrary is hated by the gods, and unlucky. For they who extravagantly extol human nature as it is and the arts as received; who spend themselves in admiration of what they already possess, and hold up as perfect the sciences which are professed and cultivated; are wanting, first, in reverence to the divine nature, with the perfection of which they almost presume to compare, and next in usefulness towards man; as thinking that they have already reached the summit of things and finished their work, and therefore need seek no further. They on the other hand who arraign and accuse nature and the arts, and abound with complainings, are not only more modest (if it be truly considered) in their sentiment, but are also stimulated perpetually to fresh industry and new discoveries. And this makes me marvel all the more at the ignorance and evil genius of mankind, who being overcrowed by the arrogance of a few persons, hold in such honor that philosophy of the Peripatetics, which was but a portion, and no large portion either, of the Greek philosophy, that every attempt to find fault with it has come to be not only useless but also suspected and almost dangerous.

The lines quoted above express the very pitch of Bacon's teaching, and it is not unreasonable to regard them as originating in his general understanding of the myth; yet they recall passages with which he was doubtless familiar. Take for example, the following in Lucretius: [350]

To say again that for the sake of men they have willed to set in order the glorious nature of the world and therefore it is meet to praise the work of the gods calling as it does for all praise, and to believe that it will be eternal and immortal, and that it is an unholy thing ever to shake by any force from its fixed seats that which by the forethought of the gods in ancient days has been established on everlasting foundations for mankind, or to assail it by speech and utterly overturn it from top to bottom; and to invent and add other figments of the kind, Memmius, is all sheer folly.

Bacon is not sufficiently a child of the Renaissance to endorse Lucretius unconditionally. He precisely believes that God willed

---

[350] *De rer. nat.*, V.

to set in order the glorious nature of the world for the sake of men. But in so far as Lucretius attacks reverence for human authority, Bacon is at one with him, and not impossibly follows in his footsteps. Again, take this in Cicero:[351]

> The arguments of Chrysippus appeared to you of great weight; a man undobutedly of great quickness and subtlety (I call those quick, who have a sprightly turn of thought, and those subtle, whose minds are seasoned by use as their hands are by labor). "If," says he, "there is anything which is beyond the power of man to produce, the being who produces it is better than man. Man is unable to make what is in the world; the being, therefore, that could do it is superior to man. What being is there but a god superior to man? Therefore there is a God."—Chrysippus adds: "If there are no gods, there is nothing better than man; but we cannot, without the highest arrogance, have this idea of ourselves."

Now Bacon's assertion that it is arrogance to believe man's works as perfect as God's is not identical with those quoted above, but it might readily be suggested by them,[352] though of course the "vanitas vanitatum" of the schoolmen implies a comparison with heavenly perfection.

Bacon's interpretation of the fable that man entrusted his newly acquired immortality to an ass and thus lost it goes as follows:

> Now for the gift which men are said to have received as the reward of their accusation, namely the unfading flower of youth; it seems to show that methods and medicines for the retardation of age and the prolongation of life were by the ancients not despaired of, but reckoned rather among those things which men once had and by sloth and negligence let slip, than among those which were wholly denied or never offered. For they seem to say that by the true use of fire, and by the just and vigorous accusation and conviction of the errors of art, such gifts might have been compassed; and that it was not the divine goodness that was wanting to them therein, but they that were wanting to themselves; in that having received this gift of the gods, they committed the carriage of it to a lazy and slow-paced ass. By this seems to be meant experience; a thing stupid and full of delay, whose slow and tortoise-like pace gave birth to that ancient complaint that life is short and art is long. And for my own part I certainly think that those two faculties—the Dogmatical and the Empirical—have not yet been well united and coupled; but that the bringing down of new gifts from the gods has ever been left either to the abstract philosophies, as to a light bird; or to sluggish and tardy expe-

---

[351] *De nat. deor.*, III. 10.

[352] I think it probable that Bacon's allusion to Chrysippus in XIII. 76 is nothing more than an echo of *De nat. deor.*, I. 15: "Et haec quidem in primo libro de natura deorum," etc.

rience, as to an ass. And yet it must be said in behalf of the ass, that he might perhaps do well enough, but for that ancident of the thirst by the way. For if a man would put himself fairly under the command of experience, and proceed steadily onward by a certain law and method, and not let any thirst for experiments either of profit or ostentation seize him by the way and make him lay down and unsettle his burthen in order that he may taste them,—such a man I do think would prove a carrier to whom new and augmented measures of divine bounty might be well enough entrusted.

I need hardly point out that the passage given above contains hardly less matter fundamental to Bacon's views than the other. Here he expresses again what he has said in regard to Pan's finding Ceres and to Atalanta's losing the race to Hippomenes, and here he adds the necessary complement to what he sets forth there. Doubtless, the ideas which he symbolizes were urgently present to his mind when he wrote the essay, and, as in the case of man's apparent ingratitude to Prometheus, their embodiment was probably suggested to him by the meaning which he attached to the myth in general. It is perhaps worth noticing that in Comes's rendering of the myth (or rather, in his translation of Nicander's) mankind is said to have forfeited immortality " nam tardi dorso imposuerunt pondus aselli ": the slow-paced ass again. Bacon's readiness to believe in the possibility of retarding old age " by the true use of fire " points once more to the influence of the alchemists. How near he is to giving credence to their " elixir," despite his protestations, may be seen in the *Historia densi et rari,* where he says: [353]

Take thought about finding the menstruums of special substances. For it seems possible that there are liquids and pulps which have such sympathy with certain bodies, that on their application they will readily open their parts and gladly take them in; at the same time intenerating and renewing themselves in their juices. For this bears upon one of the magnalia naturæ; namely, the possibility of refreshing and nourishing from without the most radical humours of things, as in flesh, bones, membranes, woods, and the like. There is likewise, even in those things which operate by separation and penetration, a certain sympathy and conformity; as aqua-fortis does not dissolve gold, nor common nitro-muriatic acid silver.

It should not be forgotten, however, that Bacon's deep faith in the possibilities of science speaks in all his words. What else

---

[353] X. 232.

inspired him to that noble vision of the torch-bearers, passing the light on and on, if they will but unite their efforts, in ever-growing splendor?

In regard to the two non-scientific interpretations, the last appears natural enough if we remember that for Bacon Prometheus represents Providence as well as forethought. The idea itself comforted the ancients, as Tully shows us, and was a commonplace in Christian writers.[354] The first interpretation is much more striking. It is set forth as follows:

> Very few therefore are they to whom the benefit of both portions falls,— to retain the advantages of providence and yet free themselves from the evils of solicitude and perturbation. Neither is it possible for any one to attain this double blessing, except by the help of Hercules; that is, fortitude and constancy of mind, which being prepared for all events and equal to any fortune, foresees without fear, enjoys without fastidiousness, and bears without impatience. It is worth noting too that this virtue was not natural to Prometheus, but adventitious, and came by help from without; for it is not a thing which any inborn and natural fortitude can attain to; it comes from beyond the ocean, it is received and brought to us by the Sun; for it comes of Wisdom, which is the Sun, and of meditation upon the inconstancy and fluctuations of human life, which is the navigation of the ocean: two things which Virgil has well coupled together in those lines:—
>
> > Ah, happy, could we but the causes know
> > Of all that is! Then should we know no fears:
> > Then should the inexorable Fate no power
> > Possess to shake us, nor the jaws of death.
>
> Most elegantly also is it added for the consolation and encouragement of men's minds, that that mighty hero sailed in a cup or pitcher; lest they should too much mistrust the narrowness and frailty of their own nature, or plead it in their own excuse as though it were altogether incapable of this kind of fortitude and constancy: the true nature of which was well divined by Seneca when he said:[355] "It is true greatness to have in one the frailty of man and the security of God."

The symbolism of the passage I have just quoted was probably familiar to Bacon's times in several sources. The Greek hero is already a symbol of fortitude in Prodicus's famous apologue of the choice of Hercules, and continues to be so in the middle ages[356] and the Renaissance.[357] His is the philosophical courage of stoic

---

[354] See for example Lactantius, *Div. inst.*, II. 11.
[355] *Epist.* 53.
[356] *De gen. deor.*, XIII, sub *De Hercule*.
[357] *Mythologiae*, VII. 1.

wisdom; and wisdom—no one who has read Plato's *Republic* will ever forget it—is as the sun, and shines on us from heaven. The Neo-Platonists lost themselves in the contemplation of that light, and Plotinus implies that symbolism specifically of Hercules.[358] The sea, which the hero crosses, is interpreted as the troubled sea of life, as it commonly is in the case of Ulysses,[359] who, as reason and fortitude, seeks to guide the lower faculties, his crew, journeying with him in their common body, the ship. Much the same symbolism, I need hardly add, has been employed by countless poets. But the myth speaks of a vessel, and Bacon doubtless remembered passages in which man and his body appear under this figment. The righteous man is not as a weaker vessel; he knows how to possess his vessel in sanctification; he is indeed a chosen vessel. Or, to descend to less august examples, he is an earthen pot floating down the stream of life and unafraid despite the iron pots around him. Last but by no means least, let us remember Plato and that pleasant passage in the *Gorgias* where Socrates says: [360]

Well, well, as you say, life is strange. For I tell you I should not wonder if Euripedes' words were true, when he says:

Who knoweth if to live is to be dead,
And to be dead, to live.

and we really, it may be, are dead; in fact I once heard one of our sages say that we are now dead, and the body is our tomb, and the part of the soul in which we have desires is liable to be over-persuaded and to vacillate to and fro, and so some smart fellow, a Sicilian, I daresay, or Italian, made a fable in which—by a play of words—he named this part, as being so impressionable and persuadable, a jar, and the thoughtless he called uninitiate: in these uninitiate that part of the soul where the desires are, the licentious and fissured part, he named a leaky jar in his allegory, because it is so insatiate.

Bacon is evidently impressed with the aptness and beauty of the

---

[358] *Ennead* IV. 3. 31, with which compare V. 5. 6-9. Bacon nowhere mentions the early Neo-Platonists; but it would be strange if he were ignorant of them, and he recalls them more than once. Compare his remarks on wisdom in IX. 262 with *Ennead* I. 2. 6. For that matter, the enlightened discontent which he advocates in our essay is preached by Plotinus in I. 2. 7. Others beside myself have suspected that he may owe something to the Neo-Platonists. See J. A. Stewart, The *Myths of Plato*, 242, note 1.

[359] *De geneal. deor.*, XI, sub *De Ulixe*; *Mythologiae*, IX. 1; Porphyry, *On The Cave of The Nymphs*, 16, 17.

[360] Lamb's Plato, 415.

symbol we have been discussing. He returns to it in his essay *Of Adversity,* and in our own essay makes a second application of it. In both cases he impresses upon it a Christian connotation. The first of these interpretations is as follows:

> ... Hercules, when he went to unbind Prometheus (by whom human nature is represented), sailed the length of the great ocean in an earthen pot or pitcher; lively describing Christian resolution, that saileth in the frail bark of the flesh thorough the waves of the world.

Bacon does not mention the sun, this time, but he may well have thought of *Mal.* IV. 2 and other biblical passages.[361] The second interpretation goes thus:

> Such are the views which I conceive to be shadowed out in this so common and hacknied fable. It is true that there are not a few things beneath which have a wonderful correspondency with the mysteries of the Christian faith. The voyage of Hercules especially, sailing in a pitcher to set Prometheus free, seems to present an image of God the Word hastening in the frail vessel of the flesh to redeem the human race. But I purposely refrain myself from all licence of speculation in this kind, lest peradventure I bring strange fire to the altar of the Lord.

Bacon's words incline me to believe that he was familiar with certain incidents in the myth of Prometheus which indeed are strikingly suggestive of the Atonement. Hercules binds himself vicariously, with a crown of olive, for Prometheus,[362] and finds in Chiron a substitute who shall die in his place.[363] Prometheus, on his part, is nailed to Mount Caucasus,[364] offers to live immortal that the wounded Chiron may die,[365] and is venerated by the ancients as their great martyred benefactor.[366] I suspect that some Alexandrine exegesist did in fact explain the voyage of Hercules as an allegory of the Advent, for Julian makes a mocking reference to the hero's having walked across the sea;[367] but under the circumstances Bacon hardly needed to be shown the way.

---

[361] *Rev.*, I. 16; *Psa.*, 19. 4, 84. 11.
[362] Apollodorus, *Library*, II. 5. 11.
[363] Ibid., 5. 4.
[364] *Op. cit.*, I. 7. 1.
[365] II. 5. 4.
[366] Hyginus, *Astronom.*, II. 15; Servius, *Ecl.* VI. 42; Pliny, *Nat. Hist.*, XXXVII. 2.
[367] *Orations*, VII.

Sphinx.[368]

In a general sense, the symbolism of the Sphinx has long been conventional. Whatever is enigmatic and disquieting has at one time or another, we may feel sure of it, been compared with the famous woman-headed monster who waylaid travelers near the gates of Thebes and tore them to pieces with her lion's claws when they failed to solve her riddle. Spenser embodied the Inquisition in the monster; Alciati, the nature of ignorance; Comes, the claws and the winged flightiness of fortune, the human reasonableness and the leonine strength with which they must be born. Bacon chose this embodiment for his conception of "science," by which, let us remember, he meant knowledge in general; for says Blount in his *Glossographia:*

Science: cunning, skill, learning, knowledge. The seven Liberal Sciences are these: Grammar, Logick, Rhetorick, Astronomy, Geometry, Arithmetick, and Musick.

And Bacon fully supports this definition:

Now of the Sphinx's riddles there are in all two kinds: one concerning the nature of things, another concerning the nature of man; and in like manner there are two kinds of kingdom offered as the reward of solving them: one over nature and the other over man. For the command over things natural—over bodies, medicines, mechanical powers, and infinite other of the kind—is the one proper and ultimate end of true natural philosophy; however, the philosophy of the School, content with what it finds, and swelling with talk, may neglect or spurn the search after realities and works. But the riddle proposed to Œdipus, by the solution of which he became King of Thebes, related to the nature of man; for whoever has a thorough insight into the nature of man may shape his fortune almost as he will, and is born for empire; as was well declared concerning the arts of the Romans,—

> Be thine the art,
> O Rome, with government to rule the nations,
> And to know whom to spare and whom to abate,
> And settle the condition of the world.

In the light of this passage, the essays composing *De sapientia veterum* acquire, perhaps, an added interest; for, evidently they fall under the two heads laid down here.

It is characteristic of Bacon, and indeed fundamental to his teaching, that he regards knowledge as a kingdom yet unconquered,

---

[368] XIII. 159.

as a riddle to be solved. Not unnaturally it presents itself to his mind as something that may become tormenting and cruel; all the more so as in its aspect of statesmanship he knows it but too well to be a Sphinx. As in the discourse on Æsculapius, we seem to hear a personal sharpness of tone when he says:

Again Sphinx proposes to men a variety of hard questions and riddles which she received from the Muses. In these, while they remain with the Muses, there is probably no cruelty; for so long as the object of meditation and inquiry is merely to know, the understanding is not oppressed or straitened by it, but is free to wander and expatiate, and finds in the very uncertainty of conclusion and variety of choice a certain pleasure and delight; but when they pass from the Muses to Sphinx, that is from contemplation to practice, whereby there is necessity for present action, choice and decision, then they begin to be painful and cruel; and unless they be solved and disposed of they strangely torment and worry the mind, pulling it first this way and then that, and fairly tearing it to pieces. Moreover the riddles of the Sphinx have always a twofold condition attached to them; distraction and laceration of mind, if you fail to solve them; if you succeed, a kingdom. For he who understands his subject is master of his end; and every workman is king over his work.

Who can doubt that the symbol came spontaneously to Bacon's mind? And it came to his mind as a statesman. Indeed, it seems to me that he has said few things more self-revealing than these. Compared, let us say, with a Huxley, he surely regards pure science like a Lord-Chancellor taking his pleasure; but—and this Gilbert failed to appreciate—he regards knowledge like a Lord-Chancellor anxiously considering the welfare of the state. Or let us say that he regards it like a Prometheus, "troubled with innumerable thoughts (which because of their flightiness are represented by the eagle), thoughts which prick and gnaw and corrode the liver." By doing so we may discern a contributive influence which perhaps led Bacon to think of the Sphinx, and incidentally, we may find in the interpretation of the eagle's wings an added reason for believing him indebted to Comes.

In an entirely secondary way, Comes's interpretation of the Sphinx itself may have something to do with Bacon's: Comes symbolizes the lacerating anxieties which beset men; the life-and-death importance of facing them with a clear mind. Alciati also may have exerted some little influence. Bacon deals rather with the discomfort of ignorance than with the conscious power of knowledge, and not improbably he was acquainted with the *Emblematum flumen*. If so, he may have remembered how the multiform Sphinx is declared to symbolize different kinds of ignorance, its conundrum different types of men (nam vir ipse, bipesque, tripesque, et quadrupes idem est), and Œdipus, in contrast with the ignorant and hasty, who are devoured, the prudent judge of human nature, concerning whom Alciati closes with a

> Primaque prudentis laurea, nosse virum.

In some small measure, such a recollection may have contributed towards his writing:

> Nor is that other point to be passed over, that the Sphinx was subdued by a lame man with club feet; for men generally proceed too fast and in too great a hurry to the solution of the Sphinx's riddles; whence it follows that the Sphinx has the better of them, and instead of obtaining the sovereignty by works and effects, they only distract and worry their minds with disputations.

All this is at least possible; but these ideas are fundamental with Bacon (here, in a new embodiment, we have the barking dogs of Scylla) and, once again, the symbol was a commonplace. Not impossibly it was more or less a commonplace as a representation of philosophy. In John Healey's *Young Man's Call* there occurs the following:

> It is the philosopher's Sphinx, which however it may seem to propound toyes, yet devoureth all (as that did) who fall unwisely into its embraces.

The *Young Man's Call* was published in 1678, and Healey may have been indebted to Bacon as Sandys surely was; but it is also possible that he was using an expression which had occurred to many.

How multiform and widespread the symbolism of the Sphinx was in Bacon's times may be further seen in a book already mentioned in this paper; I mean Michael Maier's alchemistic emblem-book entitled *Atalanta fugiens* and later *Scrutinium chymicum*. In this little work there appears a picture of Œdipus and the Sphinx which is explained in part as follows:

> Know, oh investigators, what the Philosophers declared long since: not without the making of many errors is the truth to be discovered; and nothing rends the heart with such pain as falling into error in this art. For indeed, he who thinks he has the whole world in his grasp finds that

he has nothing. It is this that the ancient Philosophers wished to stamp on our minds when they told us of the Sphinx: a symbol of the difficulty and vexatiousness of the art. Not only to the Thebans, and to the Egyptians before them, but to all aspirants to the art did the Sphinx propound her enigmas; and even as she stood on guard at the gates of Thebes, so, even today, she stands at the entrance to the works of the philosophers. He who passes by and goes his way receives no hurt from the monster; but he who, trusting in his boldness and his intelligence, attempts to solve the enigma,—he, I say, if he fails, prepares his own destruction: that is, the laceration of his heart and the loss of his substance. . . . The Philosophical Sphinx knew and spoke the human language (or perhaps I should say the Greek tongue); aye, and propounded subtle and enigmatic questions, rich in learning and piercing keen, which the run of men did not find it easy to answer, nor brutish men even to apprehend. Such are the doctrines of Philosophy, as he who is versed in them can readily understand.

I need hardly say that if Bacon read the eloquent outburst quoted above he was interested and impressed, though he may have disagreed with Count Maier in his conception of an investigator. One might even be tempted to postulate indebtedness; for Maier,[369] already prominent as a physician and noted for his active part in the Rosicrucian controversy, greatly added to his reputation by the numerous Hermetic works which he published up to his death in 1622, and furthermore visited England. As far as I can discover, however, *Atalanta fugiens* first appeared in 1617. On the other hand, the passage sounds too spontaneous to be itself an imitation; and the safest inference to be drawn from its resemblance to Bacon's essay is that Count Maier, like Bacon though in a different field, had already discovered to his cost that the ways of knowledge are alluring but dark and full of pitfalls. In short, when in its general meaning a symbol becomes a matter of every-day speech, it is perhaps idle to seek further for the cause of its particular adaptations.

Bacon disposes as follows of certain minor points in his interpretation:

Science, being the wonder of the ignorant and unskilful, may be not absurdly called a monster. In figure and aspect it is represented as many-shaped, in allusion to the immense variety of matter with which it deals. It is said to have the face and voice of a woman, in respect of its beauty and facility of utterance. Wings are added because the sciences and the

---

[369] See Redgrove and Bolton.

discoveries of science spread and fly abroad in an instant; the communication of knowledge being like that of one candle with another, which lights up at once. Claws, sharp and hooked, are ascribed to it with great elegance, because the axioms and arguments of science penetrate and hold fast the mind, so that it has no means of evasion or escape; a point which the sacred philosopher also noted: " The words of the wise are as goads, and as nails, driven deep in." Again, all knowledge may be regarded as having its situation on the heights of mountains; for it is deservedly esteemed a thing sublime and lofty, which looks down upon ignorance as from an eminence, and has moreover a spacious prospect on every side, such as we find on hill-tops. It is described as infesting the roads, because at every turn in the journey or pilgrimage of human life, matter and occasion for study assails and encounters us.

The symbolical portrait of knowledge which Bacon gives us above has a certain felicitous and evident congruity with our conception of the Sphinx,—chiefly, I suspect, because the elements of it, which collectively represent the monster to us, are already associated in our minds with wisdom, the conveyance of information, etc. Philosophy has been a fair woman since Boethius and earlier. That the words of the wise are as nails we all learned long age;[370] also that there is no evasion or escape from the horns of a dilemma. The mountains are consecrated to wisdom by Moses and Christ alike, though Bacon may also have had in mind the lofty seat of Ovid's Fame, with its vast prospect before it. And the wings of Fame, in Ovid or Virgil, may have been present to him also, perhaps giving added point to the expression that much, good and bad, spreads on the wings of rumor. That knowledge is Protean is something that all men think whether they have said it before or not; that it is a monster to the ignorant was a fact as familiar to Bacon's contemporaries as the gaping of the vulgar, for the word *monster* was current in the now obsolete meaning of a marvel or prodigy. That all our paths are infested with knotty problems is a truism which we are never allowed to forget.

With the essay on the Sphinx the first part of this investigation may fitly come to a close. In so far as regards the scientific symbolism concerned, it has, I trust, justified my assertion that Bacon's figurative use of classical mythology is not original. Indeed, I believe it to have shown in a fairly convincing way that most of the mythological interpretations of a scientific nature which delight us

---

[370] It is perhaps superfluous, therefore, for me to recall that the expression occurs in *Eccl.* 12. 11.

in Bacon's works may be traced to the chief contemporary authority on such matters, Natalis Comes. The parallels which link the two authors are strikingly numerous, and some are so close in peculiar detail as to be unmistakably significant. Again, the *Mythologiæ* does not merely parallel turns of expression; it frequently furnishes the key to perplexing twists of thought. Extraordinary as the thing may seem, I believe there is no question but that Bacon took over the bulk of his semi-Empedoclean cosmology from Natalis Comes. His universe in the essay on Cœlum is precisely the universe evolved by Comes from a blending of Empedoclism and Christian doctrine. His assertions in the essay on Cupid about the formlessness of Chaos are incomprehensible without the elucidation afforded by the corresponding statesments in the *Mythologiæ*.

The last point touched upon above is of some importance, for Bacon's peculiar utterances in regard to the formlessness of Chaos have been identified with those of the schoolmen to the effect that immediately after the creation of heaven and earth the latter [371] "was unadorned and in disorder." Bacon's assertions are not identical with those of the schoolmen. His conception of the first act of creation is notably different from theirs: [372]

> ... the confused mass and matter of heaven and earth was made in a moment, and the order and disposition of that chaos or mass was the work of six days.

Bacon is not talking of a distinct heaven and a distinct earth but of a preliminary chaos. Describing [373] "the state of things as it was before the work of the six days," he tells us that matter existed in intrinsic reality but not in distinct aggregations. We have here, then, something analogous to Empedocles's primordial mass, with which Bacon in fact identifies it through Comes and the symbol of Cupid. I do not doubt that the schoolmen and their exegetical problem were present to his mind, or that he owes them his quibbling conception of formlessness; but to all intents and purposes they are talking of one thing, he of another. I believe that Bacon adopts Comes's Empedoclism because it is Christian Empedoclism, just as he favors Democritus because Democritus [374] "came some-

---

[371] V. 276.
[372] VI. 136. See also X. 386.
[373] X. 353.
[374] XIII. 114. See also X. 386.

what nearer to the truth as declared in the divine narrative." In matters involving faith, Bacon is as mediæval as Aquinas.

The fact that Bacon is heavily indebted to Natalis Comes does not diminish the importance of his indebtedness to the alchemists. The sustained Hermetic symbolism of the interpretations of Proteus, Proserpine, Deucalion, Ixion, Ericthonius, and Atalanta, bears witness in a remarkable manner to Bacon's familiarity with alchemistic thought and literature; and the content of those essays and of Bacon's other writings on physical science justifies the drawing of important conclusions from this evidence. It can hardly be doubted that Bacon's theory of spirits and his method of distillation were both suggested to him by the Hermetic philosophers. Indeed, I think it probable that his doctrine of forms is largely derived from the same source. It is true that he urges the importance of this last belief with a personal earnestness. The following, for example, impresses one: [375]

For it seems to me that there can hardly be discovered any radical or fundamental alterations and innovations of nature, either by accidents or essays of experiments, or from the light and direction of physical causes; but only by the discovery of forms.

With this passage, however, compare the following in Bonus of Ferrara: [376]

Know, then, that a knowledge of the essence and nature of a thing is obtained from a knowledge of its first principles, or proximate causes. We cannot understand the changes of bodies, or even of quicksilver itself, if we have no radical knowledge of its essential properties.

That Bacon regarded his forms more or less in an alchemistic light may be inferred from various passages in his works. These passages have a two-fold interest, for they also make it clear that Bacon had alchemistic views as to the states of matter most receptive of forms. In *De augmentis,* for example, he says as follows: [377]

But I must here stipulate that magic, which has long been used in a bad sense, be again restored to its ancient and honorable meaning. For among the Persians magic was taken for a sublime wisdom, and the knowledge of the universal consents of things; and so the three kings who came from the east to worship Christ were called by the name of Magi. I however

---

[375] VIII. 513.

[376] *The New Pearl of Great Price,* 244.

[377] VIII. 513.

understand it as the science which applies the knowledge of hidden forms to the production of wonderful operations; and by uniting (as they say) actives with passives, displays the wonderful works of nature.

"They," of course, are the alchemists, and the "actives" and "passives" are the alchemists' terms for the forms and the ultimate matter of things. Bonus of Ferrara, for one, can tell us as much: [378]

It should be observed that, as everything is composed of matter and form, and is what it is by virtue of its form, a thing has the more being the more it possesses of the form. Quantity does not enter into the definition of form, since quantity and passivity belong to matter.

The terms *active* and *passive* were usually applied to the elements of the philosopher's stone, of which the mercury, or the essence derived from it, was, of course, the passive ingredient. Many alchemists, however, extended the idea if not the term to the metal to be transmuted, and required that it should be brought to a receptive passiveness by a process of refinement [379] or even by reduction to fundamental matter. Thus Sir George Ripley: [380]

> As the Philosopher in the boke of *Meteors* [381] doth wryte,
> That the lykenesse of bodys Metalline be not transmutable,
> But after he added theis words of more delyte,
> Without they be reduced to theyr beginning materiable.
> Wherefore such bodies which in nature be liquable,
> Minerall and mettaline may be Mercurizate.

Considered from the mystic point of view, the active ingredient of the stone becomes the "sperm" and the passive the "menstrum" from which the stone is generated: [382]

When it is thus purified it unites with purified sulphur to produce the glorius Elixir, and the complete perfection of gold and silver, just as the female menstrual blood combines with the male sperm to make a man.

Here again the idea of generation is extended to the transmuting of base metals, which became in fact if not in name the "menstruums" of gold; or at least contain in their common metalline substratum this "menstruum" or "seed" of gold: [383]

---

[378] *The New Pearl of Great Price*, 236.
[379] *The New Pearl of Great Price*, 347 seq.
[380] *Compound of Alchymie* (*in Theatr. chem. Brit.*).
[381] Cf. *Meteorologicorum*, I. 3.
[382] *The New Pearl of Great Price*, 395.
[383] *Ibid.* 182.

In order to effect this ultimate change, there is no need to reduce the common metals to their first matter, for they already contain that proximate first matter, which may, by comparison, be called the seed of gold.

In view of such passages as the above, the following in Bacon becomes significant: [384]

The conversion of silver, quicksilver, or any other metal into gold, is a thing difficult to believe; yet it is far more probable that a man who knows clearly the natures of weight, of the colour of yellow, of malleability and extension, of volatility and fixedness, and who has also made diligent search into the first seeds and menstruums[385] of minerals, may at last by much and sagacious endeavour produce gold than that a few grains of an elixir should in a few moments of time be able to turn other metals into gold.

It will be noticed that in this passage Bacon conceives of gold as the union of forms and a specific materia prima and that he calls that fundamental substance by its technical alchemical names. Elsewhere he shows us that he believes this substance to grow naturally into gold: [386]

The second kind of axiom, which is concerned with the discovery of the latent process, proceeds not by simple natures, but by compound bodies, as they are found in nature in its ordinary course. As, for instance, when inquiry is made from what beginnnigs, and by what method and by what process, gold or any other metal or stone is generated, from its first menstrua and rudiments up to the perfect mineral.

Presumably the inquiry is to lead to a hastening of nature in typical Hermetic fashion.

The middle ages were perhaps nearer to Bacon's England than to Galileo's Italy, and Bacon was by no means entirely divorced from his times. His profession of universality smacks of the mediæval thesaurus, his mind is mediævally asimilative rather than modernly constructive, he has the schoolman's love of classification and his preoccupation with religious issues, he has the mediæval thinker's tendency to slip into metaphysics. In his vigorous but more or less unreasoning hostility to the mystic aspects of astrology and alchemy and to the almost mystic deference paid to Aristotle, he

---

[384] VIII. 515.

[385] Cf. I. 531 and note in which Bacon's use of the word is, mistakenly, I believe, referred to Aristotle.

[386] VIII. 172. This belief was probably general, however. See Redgrove, 25.

can better be compared to Petrarch than to Galileo. One is constantly impressed with the fact that the materials of Bacon's conceptions come to him from the world around him and frequently overpower his reason. He knows that he is in a wilderness because he discerns clearings, not because he can lift himself bodily above it. His intuitions are the more remarkable. He denounces astrology and, far more constructively than Petrarch, proposes, at least in general conception, the proper substitute; saturated though he is with alchemistical notions, he has the mental vigor to throw off much that is superstitious and yet to grasp firmly and retain what he feels to be the rudiments of experimental science; living in the shadow of Aristotle he can yet, with the help of the alchemists, progress from metaphysical forms to such as lead him to the discovery of the nature of heat. His is not a supreme genius that towers above its age, but rather a robust and sagacious common sense that pushes its way through contemporary thinking and with rare good judgment seizes upon the best.

PART II

SYMBOLS OF WORLDLY WISDOM

In the interpretations heretofore discussed, Bacon appears to us as the scientist; in those now to be considered he stands forth as the statesman and the man of the world. Now briefly, now at length, he gives utterance to his views on kings, courtiers, favorites, and councilors; on policies and expedients; on insurrections, wars, and treaties; on life, human nature, youth and age. These aphorisms, it seems to me, should be of special interest. The scientific thinking of any man is bound to be more or less impersonal, more or less the expression of his reasoning powers alone; but in his thoughts on men and life we may hope to see reflected his entire nature and character. And few are the historical figures about whom we are more curious, in this respect, than we are about Francis Bacon. We have only to read Strachey's brilliant book *Elizabeth and Essex* to understand that even to the keenest minds Bacon is ultimately an impenetrable mystery. For obviously he was not the great serpent, the political Mephistopheles so picturesquely portrayed there. He did not play diabolically with the world; the world played with him, and presently tossed him aside. The thing is astonishing, for he was notably endowed with some of the gifts that make for permanent worldly success. He had an observing eye, a persuasive tongue, a vigorous mind, an unusual power of industry. Why did his life end in such ignominious failure? If he had been overthrown as Napoleon was, we should understand the matter; but apparently he was pushed over by a few rapscallions whom a man in his position should have been able to suppress, in one way or another, with the greatest ease. I say apparently; for though I have no pretentions to omniscience it seems to me obvious that it was Bacon's own limitations that wrought his undoing, and that they had long been undermining his career when he tripped on a clod, as it were, and crashed down. Some of these limitations may be discernible between the lines in the following paragraphs. Let us see.

Orpheus.[387]

Famous and beautiful is the myth of Orpheus, the supreme musician, who by his art all but rescued his wife Eurydice from Hades; and later, playing in the wilderness, drew to him the wild things of nature and held them entranced, assembled in gentle understanding, till the fierce Bacchæ broke the spell and tore to pieces the beneficent magician. It is as a benefactor, a civilizer of man, that Orpheus is understood by Plato;[388] and Horace,[389] Lactantius,[390] Servius,[391] Boccaccio,[392] and Natalis Comes[393] interpret the myth in this sense, explaining the trees, rocks, and wild animals as primitive men, and the music of Orpheus as the persuasive eloquence of an enlightened leader. It is Orpheus who, dissuading his fellows from the wandering life of beasts, induces them to dwell together in a law-abiding way. It is he, indeed, who introduces law among them, and the institution of marriage, and the conception of the sacredness of human life. He differs from Prometheus, then, in advancing the moral rather than the material welfare of mankind. Truly impressive is Bacon's interpretation. He regards Orpheus not as a man but as the symbol of philosophy or human enlightenment, and the myth as an allegory at once of the excursions of intelligent curiosity into the dark depths of physical science and of the more successful efforts of reason in the field of social organization,—which last, however, subject as it is to outbursts of primitive violence, periodically rends, as it were, its own informing principles and relapses into brutish anarchy.

In the opening paragraph of his essay on Orpheus, Bacon, I believe, points clearly to one source, at least, of his interpretation. The paragraph in question goes as follows:

> The story of Orpheus, which though so well known has not yet been in all points perfectly well interpreted, seems meant for a representation of universal Philosophy. For Orpheus himself,—a man admirable and truly divine who being master of all harmony subdued and drew all things after him by sweet and gentile measures,—may pass by an easy metaphor for philosophy personified. For as the works of wisdom surpass in dignity

---

[387] XIII. 110.
[388] *Laws*, III.
[389] *Epistola ad Pisones*, 391 seq.
[390] *Div. instit.*, I. 5.
[391] *Georg.* IV. 520.
[392] *De gen. deor.*
[393] VII. 14.

and power the works of strength, so the labours of Orpheus surpass the labours of Hercules.

The closing sentence in the paragraph quoted above at once recalls the following passage in *De rerum natura:* [394]

For if we must speak as the acknowledged grandeur of the thing itself demands, a god he was, a god, most noble Memmius, who first found out that plan of life which is now termed wisdom, and who by trained skill rescued life from such great billows and such thick darkness and moored it in so perfect a calm and in so brilliant a light. Compare the godlike discoveries of others in old times: Ceres is famed to have pointed out to mortals corn, and Liber the vine-born juice of the grape; though life might well have subsisted without these things, as we are told some nations even now live without them. But a happy life was not possible without a clean breast; wherefore with more reason this man is deemed by us a god, from whom come those sweet solaces of existence which even now are distributed over great nations and gently soothe men's minds. Then if you shall suppose that the deeds of Hercules surpass his you will be carried still farther away from true reason.

The actual parallelism of the two passages quoted in the preceding paragraph is limited to the sentences with which they close; and though both writers are talking about bringers of enlightenment, Lucretius has reference to Epicurus, not to Orpheus. Nevertheless, the sentences in question make it appear probable, it seems to me, that Bacon had Lucretius in mind; and what the latter says immediately afterwards adds, I think, to this probability, for he proceeds as follows:

For what would yon great gaping maw of Nemean lion now harm us and the bristled Arcadian boar? Aye, or what could the bull of Crete do and the hydra plague of Lerna, fenced round with its envenomed snakes? Or how could the triple-breasted might of threefold Geryon, how could the birds with brazen arrowy feathers that dwelt in the Stymphalian swamps do us such mighty injury, and the horses of Thracian Diomede breathing fire from their nostrils along the Bistonian borders and Ismara?—But unless the breast is cleared, what battles and dangers must then find their way into us in our own despite! What poignant cares inspired by lust then rend the distressful man, and then also what mighty fears! And pride, filthy lust, and wantonness! What disaster they occasion! And luxury and all sorts of sloth? He therefore who shall have subdued all these and banished them from the mind by words, not arms, shall he not

---

[394] V.

have a just title to be ranked among the gods? And all the more so that he was wont to deliver many precepts in beautiful and godlike phrase about the immortal gods themselves and to open up by his teachings all the nature of things.

Lucretius does not assert that the eloquence of his philosopher subdued wild beasts and monsters, but he says something so closely similar as to put us in mind of the myth of Orpheus; and not only in its literal but also in its allegorical sense. Those " precepts in beautiful and godlike phrase about the immortal gods," too, recall Horace's " interpresque Deorum . . . Orpheus." It would not be at all surprising, then, if Lucretius had suggested to Bacon the transition from Orpheus the enlightened leader to Orpheus the philosopher. The Roman poet was not necessarily alone in doing so, however. The cultured Elizabethan surely knew the dying words of Socrates, and therefore remembered that " Philosophy . . . is the noblest and best of music." [395] He knew his Seneca also,—that letter,[396] for example, in which the writer holds with Posidonius that in the Golden Age " government was under the jurisdiction of the wise." For that matter, he probably knew his Posidonius, and Macaulay [397] long ago pointed out the resemblances between Bacon's ideas and the Stoic's. As for the final transition from the philosopher to philosophy, it has already occurred in the author just mentioned, as appears in a passage quoted and discussed at length by Seneca, who says:

Up to this point I agree with Posidonius; but that philosophy discovered the arts of which life makes use in its daily round I refuse to admit, nor will I ascribe to it an artisan's glory. Posidonius says: " When men were scattered over the earth, protected by caves or by the dugout shelter of a cliff or by the trunk of a hollow tree, it was philosophy that taught them to build houses."

Bacon's views on the practical aspects of philosophy coincide with the Greek's and may in some measure have been influenced by them; but the Renaissance in general had revolted against the purely contemplative and was not indifferent to the betterment of life. In any case, his attitude accounts for the fact that the essays on Orpheus and Prometheus to some extent overlap. The musician also sought to capture for humanity the spark of a useful scientific curiosity:

---

[395] *Phædo.*   [396] *XC.*   [397] Essay on Bacon.

The meaning of the fable appears to be this. The singing of Orpheus is of two kinds: one to propitiate the infernal powers, the other to draw the wild beasts and the woods. The former may be best understood as referring to natural philosophy; the latter to philosophy moral and civil. For natural philosophy proposes to itself, as its noblest work of all, noth-thing less than the restitution and renovation of things corruptible, and (what is indeed the same thing in a lower degree) the conservation of bodies in the state in which they are, and the retardation of dissolution and putrefaction. Now certainly if this can be effected at all, it cannot be otherwise than by due and exquisite attempering and adjustment of parts in nature, as by the harmony and perfect modulation of a lyre. And yet being a thing of all others the most difficult, it commonly fails of effect; and fails (it may be) from no cause more than from curious and premature meddling and impatience.

Here we recognize once more the alchemistic bent of Bacon's thinking and are led to recall his interpretation of Apollo's lyre. As for the general symbolism of Orpheus's descent to Hades, it may well have been suggested by Fulgentius,[398] who interprets the descent of Æneas in a closely similar way. Fulgentius regards the sixth book of the *Æneid* as an allegorical treatise on the arcana of philosophy, explains the golden bough as intellectual preparation or instruction, and ushers Æneas into the depths with a: "He, then, as we have said, having possessed himself of the golden bough—that is, of instruction—proceeds into the infernals and studies the secrets of knowledge."[399]

With truly philosophical spaciousness the essay on Orpheus contemplates the status of enlightenment in human society. It is far from repeating the *omnia vanitas* of the age of fear and darkness; indeed it makes a stoic application of the mediæval *memento mori* which is as characteristic of the Renaissance as it would have been shocking to the piety of earlier days. Accounting for the fact that Orpheus subdues the wild creatures after his unsuccessful attempt to rescue Eurydice from Hades, Bacon says:

And this application of Philosophy to civil affairs is properly represented, and according to the true order of things, as subsequent to the diligent trial and final frustration of the experiment of restoring the dead body to life. For true it is that the clearer recognition of the inevitable necessity of death sets men upon seeking immortality by merit and renown.

---

[398] *Expositio Verg. contin.*

[399] Tum ille, ergo, ut antea diximus, ramum aureum, id est doctrinam adeptus, inferos ingreditur et secreta scientiæ scrutatur.

There is no lack here of the hopefulness of the times. Yet Bacon had not read his Plato [400] in vain nor considered unthoughtfully the vicissitudes recorded by history. The essay closes with a passage that anticipates Vico but displays none of the Italian's mystic optimism:

> But howsoever the works of wisdom are among human things the most excellent, yet they too have their periods and closes. For so it is that after kingdoms and commonwealths have flourished for a time, there arise perturbations and seditions and wars; amid the uproars of which, first the laws are put to silence, and then men return to the depraved conditions of their nature, and desolation is seen in the fields and cities. And if such troubles last, it is not long before letters also and philosophy are so torn in pieces that no traces of them can be found but a few fragments, scattered here and there like planks from a shipwreck; and then a season of barbarism sets in, the waters of Helicon being sunk under the ground, until, according to the appointed vicissitude of things, they break out and issue forth again, perhaps among other nations, and not in the places where they were before.

Perseus,[401] *Achelous,*[402] *Diomedes,*[403] *and Typhon.*[404]

In the four essays on Perseus, Achelous, Diomedes, and Typhon, Bacon discusses war: offensive, defensive, religious, and revolutionary. His views on the subject are, I believe, largely derived from Machiavelli's, though on the other hand, these may be traced in the military writings of the time. He believes that a state of preparedness for war, and even war itself are beneficial to the state; he advocates the conquest of remote colonies; he recommends that absolute authority be given to commanding generals, and dwells upon the prudence, astuteness, resoluteness, with which these should be gifted. Civil war he brands as a pestilent evil, and—here expressing his personal opinion, I think—judges no less severely of religious war. His symbolism, and in a measure some of his ideas, are chiefly derived from Fulgentius, Boccaccio, and Natalis Comes.

In the essay on Perseus—or rather, in the essays, for Bacon returns to the subject in his *De augmentis*— [405] it is first related

---

[400] *Republic*, VIII, for example.
[401] XIII. 102.
[402] XIII. 136.
[403] XIII. 126.
[404] XIII. 84.
[405] VIII. 457.

Symbols of Worldly Wisdom

how Perseus, having been commanded by Pallas to slay Medusa, received a shield and a mirror from the goddess, a helmet from Pluto, and winged sandals from Mercury. Equipped with these, the account continues, and with the eye and tooth lent him by the aged Græææ, Perseus flew swiftly against the monster. Although he surprised her asleep with her sisters, and though in any case his helmet made him invisible, he still faced great danger, for the mere sight of her was deadly; but the mirror now stood him in good stead and directed his arm. As the monster's head fell, presently to be fastened to the victor's shield, the winged horse Pegasus leaped from her spouting blood. Such, as Bacon relates it, is the myth. The interpretation follows. Perseus, the wise general, is guided by Pallas or wisdom in undertaking a war which is just, for Medusa symbolizes the tyrant; possible of achievement, for she alone of the Gorgons is vulnerable; and advantageous, for such the wise Romans judged wars waged far from home to be. To his wisdom the good general further owes his watchfulness and his prudence: a mirror to the plans of the enemy, a shield to the forces he commands himself. And he has other qualities besides. In striking, and even more in pursuing his advantage, he is as swift as winged feet. Sole commander,[406] in this ideal war, he masks his purposes as with a magic visor. Indeed, sinister things of darkness do his bidding: the peering eye of the traitor and the sharp tooth of the maker of dissension work for him in secret. Relentless as fate, he conquers; and the winged horse of fame spreads his renown, and the terror of his reputation, like Medusa's head on a shield, turns men to stone at his approach. The whole thing is decidedly vivid, and the Renaissance *condottiero* emerges from it in all his disquieting complexity. Curiously enough the sketch for this portrait was done long before the Renaissance.

If we turn to the chapter on Perseus in Fulgentius's *Mythologicon*,[407] we shall find that King Phorcus left his realm to his three daughters, of whom the eldest, being as wise as the serpent, assumed the direction of affairs and was said, figuratively, to have the head of a snake. Despite her sagacity, however, Prince Perseus sailed to the conquest of her Kingdom in his winged ships and robbed her of both crown and life. Enriched with her wealth,

---

[406] VIII. 461. [407] I. 26.

which he bore off as he might a foeman's head, Perseus now invaded the kingdom of Atlas who, unable to cope with an enemy of such resources, retreated into the mountains, and was therefore said to have been turned into stone. " But," continues Fulgentius, "let me also expound a more subtle meaning which the Greeks attached to the story of Medusa." He then proceeds to explain the Gorgons as three aspects of fear, and Perseus as the warrior endowed at once with valour and with wisdom. Perseus advances upon the Gorgons with averted face, for the brave soldier disdains to notice fear; he bears a mirror, for even the brave are sensible of the terrors of battle, which may, indeed, be reflected in their faces. The brave conquer the terror they feel. Then winged fame spreads their renown. Obviously, we have here something similar to Bacon's interpretation. We shall find a closer approach to it, however, in Boccaccio.

Boccaccio's version of the myth of Perseus differs from Fulgentius's in representing Pegasus as preexistent to Medusa's death and indeed instrumental in bringing it about. According to this account of the combat, Perseus, though shod with the winged buskins, is mounted on Pegasus's back when he slays the monster. Boccaccio's interpretation is clearly based on his predecessor's, but elaborates on it considerably. It goes in part as follows:[408]

> Perseus mounted on the horse Pegasus symbolizes the man led by desire of fame. . . . The shield of Pallas is to be understood, I think, as prudence, by means of which we make ourselves acquainted with the plans of the enemy and defend our own forces against ambush and attack. The buskins of Mercury signify, in my opinion, quickness and alertness in carrying things out.

In the chapter on Medusa, Perseus is touched upon again:[409]

> . . . Thus the prudent general shrewdly anticipates what the enemy may attempt and so takes measures to defend himself, thus making fruitless all his antagonist's plans. From the union of prudence and courage in the general springs Pegasus,—that is fame.

Obviously, here and in Fulgentius we have the nucleus of Bacon's interpretation.

---

[408] *De gen. deor.*, XII.   [409] *Op. cit.*, X.

If Boccaccio elaborates on Fulgentius, Bacon does so, and much more considerably, on both. Around the suggestion furnished by them he builds up a fairly extensive theory of offensive war. Most of the ideas expressed by him were current in his times; but it is sufficient to read such a book as Ayala's *De iure et officiis bellicis* to appreciate how much contemporary theory was indebted to Machiavelli, and the *Essays* make it appear highly probable that Bacon was directly influenced by that author. To him [410] may probably be traced the opinion (concerning which, however, Bacon was not always of one mind) [411] that it is advantageous to wage wars of conquest far from home; to him [412] the precepts that in war rapidity of execution is the best warrant of secrecy, vigor of action ineffectual unless sustained, leadership weak if entrusted to many, treachery a justifiable weapon in a good cause, luck the last thing in which a good general should place his faith; it is Machiavelli's leader who must be cool not only when planning but also when swords clash and a sudden manoevre, an artful shout of victory, a misunderstood command, may change the fortunes of the day. Of course, Machiavelli was not the last reader of Livy nor the only one to observe the vicissitudes of recent history; and some of Bacon's rules of war are as old as war itself. That soldiers fight most willingly in a righteous cause is laid down by Onosander; [413] and that it is desirable to catch the enemy napping, even as Perseus did, is surely a matter of immemorial common sense. Less obvious is Bacon's reason for interpreting the Grææ as he does; yet Natalis Comes [414] explains them as prudence and subtleness, and their eye as the peering curiosity of the busy-body.

So much for Perseus and offensive war. We now turn to defensive warfare and the myth of Achelous. That river-god, it will be remembered, contending with Hercules for the hand of Deianeira, turned into a bull; but the hero overthrew him and broke off one of his horns, in exchange for which he received the cornucopia or horn of plenty. It will be noticed that Hercules appeared upon the scene as an outsider and as it were an invader; for the King-

---

[410] *Discorsi sopra la prima deca di Tito Livio*, II, 4.
[411] XII. 237.
[412] *Op. cit.*, III. 3; III. 32; III. 12; III. 36; II. 1; III. 11.
[413] *The General*, IV.
[414] VII. 12. 495.

dom of Æneus, Deianeira's father, was hard by the Achelous. In any case, Bacon regards him in that light, his interpretation of the myth being as follows:

> The fable alludes to military expeditions. The preparation for war on the part defensive (which is represented by Achelous) is various and multiform. For the form assumed by the invader is one and simple, consisting of an army only, or perhaps a fleet. Whereas a country preparing to receive an enemy on its own ground sets to work in an infinity of ways; fortifies one town, dismantles another, gathers the people from the fields and villages into cities and fortified places; builds a bridge here, breaks down a bridge there; raises, and distributes forces and provisions; is busy about rivers, harbours, gorges of hills, woods, and numberless other matters; so that it may be said to try a new shape and put on a new aspect every day; and when at last it is fully fortified and prepared, it represents to the life the form and threatening aspect of a fighting bull. The invader meanwhile is anxious for a battle, and aims chiefly at that; fearing to be left without supplies in an enemy's country; and if he win the battle, and so break as it were the enemy's horn, then he brings it to this: that the enmy, losing heart and reputation, must, in order to recover himself and repair his forces, fall back into his more fortified positions, leaving his cities and lands to the conqueror to be laid waste and pillaged; which is indeed like giving him Amalthea's horn.

The question whether or not it is better to await an invader within one's own frontiers was a frequent source of dispute among the leaders of antiquity; and judging by Ayala's book, which may be taken to express the views of Philip II's generals, it was still a moot question in Bacon's times. Machiavelli [415] lays down the doctrine that a rich country not thoroughly organized for war should not wait to be invaded. Now Bacon's England found itself in the position contemplated by this precept, and as a maritime power, also, would naturally favor meeting an enemy beyond its borders. It seems to me probable, therefore, that Bacon, in his essay, sees the matter from the English point of view. As for his symbolism, it is not at first sight evident why the struggle between Hercules and the river-god should have suggested an invasion. It is true that Cæsar and other Roman writers frequently call the wings of an army cornua; it is also true that Plutarch [416] interprets the fight between Theseus and the Minotaur as a naval engagement in which the hero, invading Crete, routs Taurus, the Cretan admiral. These, however, would seem to be but faint suggestions of Bacon's allegory.

---

[415] *Discorsi*, II. 12.   [416] Life of Theseus.

The real source is probably to be found in Strabo, who discussing the alluvial land formed around its islands by the Achelous, says as follows:[417]

This accumulation of soil anciently formed the tract Paracheloitis, which the river overflows, a subject of contention, as it was continually confounding boundaries which had been determined by the Acarnanians and the Ætolians. For want of arbitrators, they decided their dispute by arms. The most powerful gained the victory. This gave occasion to a fable, how Hercules overcame Achelous in fight, and received in marriage, as the prize of his victory, Deianeira, daughter of Æneus. ... Some writers add that this was the horn of Amalthea, which Hercules broke off from the Achelous and presented to Æneus as a bridal gift.

I am the more inclined to believe that this passage is Bacon's chief source because it is unmistakably George Sandys's in his translation of the *Metamorphoses,* where, explaining the myth of Achelous, he says:

Now the strife between the Ætolians and Acarnanians (whose Countryes are watred by that River) concerning their bounders (arbitrated, for want of umpires, by the sword, wherein the stronger prevailed) was the ground of this fiction of Hercules his subduing of Achelous. Deianira, the daughter of Æneus (for it should seeme that the Ætolians had the better) the reward of his victory.

Having become acquainted with Bacon's views on war in general, we now pass to his opinion of religious wars, or indeed of all violent religious coercion. He states his position in the essay on Diomedes. Diomedes did not fear to wound Venus in battle, but his impiety led to his death; for his host, King Danaus, fearing that certain calamities which had befallen the people might be due to his presence, had him murdered. Even his comrades suffered by his sacrilegious act; for when they bewailed his death they were turned into swans.

Bacon sees in the myth of Diomedes an allegory of the man "who makes it his declared object to persecute and overthrow by violence and the sword some religious worship or sect, though a vain and light one." We know from the *Essays* that Bacon recommended leaving that sort of thing to the extreme Puritans,[418] a circumstance which throws light on his ambiguous comment that religious persecutors are doubtless moved by their superior intelli-

---

[417] *Geography,* X. 2. 19.   [418] XI. 91.

gence (as Diomedes was by Pallas) and by their "hatred of evil and honest zeal." He goes on to say that while such reformers may have their hour of triumph, they usually find it a short hour and (violence provoking violence and outraged piety sanctioning hate) are persecuted as savagely as were their victims:

And where it is said that the very grief and lamentations of his comrades were not tolerated, but visited with punishment, the meaning is that whereas almost every crime is open to pity, insomuch that they who hate the offense may yet in humanity commiserate the person and the calamity of the offender,—and it is the extremity of evil to have the offices of compassion interdicted,—yet where religion and piety are in question, the very expressions of pity are noted and disliked.

It may be doubted whether Bacon's denunciation of religious war was intended to be as unqualified in the case of a war against a non-Christian people; and indeed it has been pointed out [419] that the author of the *Advertisement Touching a Holy War* was probably not unfavorable to something approaching a crusade, though in all likelihood he would, had he finished his dialogue, "have limited his approval to a war against the Turks; and that not simply as Infidels, but as dangerous neighbors to all Christendom." I am inclined to believe that the note of downright protest in his essay is sounded chiefly against more unnatural animosities, and that the passage I have quoted, and indeed the whole interpretation, was suggested by Natalis Comes, who, with an unctuousness taught him by the Inquisition,[420] declares the fate of Diomedes to symbolize the just punishment of all impiety, and adds about his comrades that:[421]

They were turned into swans while uttering cries of sorrow because it is not safe, or wise, or pious to grieve over the misfortunes of wretches whose sufferings are decreed by Divine Providence because they have offended against God.

We now come to the last of Bacon's allegories of war: his interpretation of the myth of Typhon. The gigantic monster Typhon,

---

[419] XIII. 179.

[420] Comes frequently cringes, but it should be added in justice to him that Dante is even sterner than he in reprehending the commiseration of sinners, and that in our own days life would be safer if our juries had some of Torquemada's iron in their blood.

[421] VII. 5. 477.

who breathed fire and was belted with serpents, rebelled against Jupiter, and having captured the king of the gods, cut out his sinews. These, however, Mercury stole from him and returned to Jove who, having recovered from his injuries, finally slew the rebel. Bacon, commenting on this fable, describes the growth of disaffection to an absolute king: the soliciting of nobles for aid and leadership, the increasing turbulence of the people; finally open rebellion:

which because of the infinite calamities it inflicts both on kings and peoples is represented under the dreadful image of Typhon, with a hundred heads, denoting divided powers; flaming mouths, for devastations by fire; belts of snakes, for the pestilences which prevail, especially in sieges; iron hands, for slaughters; eagle's talons, for rapine; feathery body, for perpetual rumours, reports, trepidations and the like. And sometimes these rebellions grow so mightily that the King is forced, as if carried off on the shoulders of the rebels, to abandon the seat and principal cities of his Kingdom, and to contract his forces, and betake himself to some remote and obscure province; his sinews both of money and majesty being cut off. And yet if he bears his fortunes wisely, he presently by the skill and industry of Mercury recovers those sinews again; that is to say, by affability and wise edicts and gracious speeches he reconciles the minds of his subjects, and awakens in them an alacrity to grant him supplies, and so recovers the vigour of his authority. Nevertheless, having learned prudence and caution, he is commonly unwilling to set all upon the toss of fortune and therefore avoids a pitched battle, but tries first by some memorable exploit to destroy the reputation of the rebels: in which if he succeed, the rebels, feeling themselves shaken and losing their confidence, resort first to broken and empty threats, like serpent hisses, and then finding their case desperate take to flight. And then is the time, when they are beginning to fall to pieces, for the king with the entire forces and mass of his kingdom, as with the mountain Ætna, to pursue and overwhelm them.

That civil strife is the ruin of a state was already a dictum in classical times, and the policy which Bacon recommends to a king is as old as monarchy and older. Nevertheless I think it possible that for the formulation, at least, of his doctrines Bacon is to some extent indebted to Machiavelli. The dependence of the multitude on the nobility, the importance to a ruler of standing firm during the first moment of crisis, the power of fair words, the tendency of undisciplined forces to lose heart and disband: all this recalls memorable passages in the *Discorsi*.[422] Had Bacon listened even

---

[422] I. 43; I. 56; III. 8; etc.

more attentively to the wise Florentine it might have been the better for the Stuarts and for his own fortunes. Here and elsewhere he betrays a contempt for the plain people which smacks less of Machiavelli than of Guicciardini and, probably, of his own bias. There is in his words a scorn which was to be shared and dearly rued by Charles I when he says: [423]

> Or who can hear that in that memorable expedition of the gods against the giants the braying of Silenus's ass had a principal stroke in putting the giants to flight, and not be sure that the incident was invented in allusion to the vast attempts of rebels, dissipated as they commonly are by empty rumours and vain terrors?

The revolt of the giants is regarded as the type of rebellion by Servius, Fulgentius, Boccaccio, and many others. Nevertheless, it is safe to assert that the chief source of Bacon's symbolism in the essay on Typhon is the *Mythologiæ*, which interprets the monster as follows: [424]

> Some are of the opinion that Typhon was a fierce and active man, who, having collected a band of turbulent men and exiles, tried to drive Jupiter from his kingdom. Because of his power he was described as having a vast body; because he inflamed others against Jove, it was said that he breathed fire and cut out Jove's sinews. These, we are told, were stolen from him by Mercury and returned to Jupiter, because the latter's eloquence presently reconciled those who had rebelled.

Probably, as was his custom, Bacon enriched and amplified his recollection of this passage, not impossibly attributing to Typhon the hundred heads of Hydra, the iron hands of the Gorgons, and the feathers of Virgil's Fame, which last, as we shall see, he adopted as a symbol of seditious murmurings. His mention of pestilence, instead, is paralleled by Comes, who in a second interpretation of Typhon explains the monster as the burning and unhealthy air of summer.

Metis,[425] *The Cyclops,*[426] *Pan's Crook,*[427] *and Pandora's Box.*[428]

In the essays on Metis and the Cyclops, and in certain passages on Pan's crook and Pandora's box, Bacon sets forth a number of

---

[423] XIII. 77. I believe this interpretation to be original with Bacon.
[424] VI. 22. 435.
[425] XIII. 134.
[426] XIII. 87.
[427] XIII. 97.
[428] XII. 129.

his views on government. His opinions are very much those of his times, as formulated, especially, by Machiavelli and Guicciardini. This does not, and indeed should not seem to mean, that Bacon advocates oppression. He stands for strictly and even unscrupulously paternalistic government; but his own record, from the early days when he incurred the displeasure of Elizabeth to those long after when he aroused the resentment of James, proves him to have been rather liberal than otherwise in his leanings. He unquestionably disliked the common people, and indeed his writings hardly glow with love for his fellow man; yet he was rather the weak victim of his own servants than the oppressor of his sovereign's people. I suspect that Bacon hated no man, but loved nobody as he did his own thoughts.

The whole mechanism of kingly government in the seventeenth century (or perhaps I should say of princely government in the sixteenth) emerges from Bacon's essay on Metis, about whom we are told that she was married, and when pregnant swallowed, by Jupiter, who presently brought forth their child Minerva from his head. Bacon interprets the myth as follows:

This monstrous and at first sight very foolish fable, contains, as I interpret it, a secret of government. It describes the art whereby kings so deal with the councils of state as not only to keep their authority and majesty untouched, but also to increase and exalt it in the eyes of their people. For kings by a wise and sound arrangement tie themselves to their councils with a bond like that of wedlock, and deliberate with them concerning all their greatest matters, rightly judging that this is no diminution to their majesty. But when the question grows ripe for a decision (which is the bringing forth) they do not allow the councils to deal any further in it, lest their acts should seem to be dependent upon the council's will; but at that point (unless the matter be of such a nature that they wish to put away the envy of it) they take into their own hands whatever has been by the council elaborated and as it were shaped in the womb; so that the decision and execution (which, because it comes forth with power and carries necessity, is elegantly represented under the figure of Pallas armed) may seem to emanate from themselves.

The passage quoted above might be traced to Cornutus, but Comes also interprets the myth of Metis approximately as Bacon does:[429]

Jupiter took to wife Μῆτιν, that is to say, counsel; for prudence is

---

[429] II. 1. 74.

necessary to the proper conduct of domestic affairs. She is said to have become pregnant because such measures as one takes should be the fruit of counsel. Jupiter swallowed his wife and brought forth from his head because the head is the principal seat of reason. From reason arises Pallas armed . . . by all of which is meant that wise counsel should be taken into the mind and thought upon, that from it may arise those wise actions which are the safest defense of all things.

It will be noticed that Comes's interpretation is not specifically a political one; also that it lacks what one might be deceived into calling Bacon's cynical tone. Bacon may conceivably have supplied these elements himself; but I think it probable that for the first at least he was partly indebted to Machiavelli, who in the *Prince* [430] says as follows:

However, a wise prince must follow a third course,[431] appointing in his state sagacious men; and to those only must he give leave to tell him the truth, and only as to those things he questions them about. But he must question them about everything, and listen to their opinions; then decide in his own way.

It is not impossible that James I, when he read Bacon's essay, smiled a wry smile, and not only at the author's estimate of kingly wisdom, but also at his bland ignoring of parliaments. Likewise, it is not impossible that Machiavelli, had he perused *De sapientia veterum,* would have grinned a shrewd grin at Bacon's belief in the gullibility of the public. Machiavelli says himself (and Bacon may have been influenced by it) that a prince should wear a mask of virtue, and seem to do of his own initiative what perhaps he is forced to do; but he is too keen a judge of men not to know that an underlying scepticism is as characteristic of crude human nature as a passing tendency to gape, especially where the superior attainments of others are concerned. He makes no bones about saying that the plain people are cynical as to the accomplishments of their rulers, and Bacon's parliamentary experiences might very well have led him to the same conclusion. The Florentine's reason for advising a prince to make his final decisions himself is far less complimentary to princely advisers. He shrewdly remarks that should a stupid potentate place himself in the hands of his whole council he would be pushed and pulled a dozen ways; and did he make him-

---

[430] Chap. 23.

[431] The other two being to listen to all indiscriminately or to none.

self the mouthpiece of one councillor he would presently become his subject also. "We may safely believe," he concludes, "that it is prudent rulers that produce wise councillors; not wise councillors that produce shrewd rulers." Is it fanciful to see in Bacon's attitude the unworldly complacency of the man of learning?

If Bacon pays royalty few compliments in the essay on Metis, he gratifies it with even fewer in that on the Cyclops. He is here dealing with those darker ministers of kings who are not advisers but ruthless instruments, and he does not mince his words. Indeed he is so outspoken that he must have been confident of being understood to refer to conditions abroad. Certain it is that the essay at once recalls what is perhaps the most dramatic chapter in the *Prince*.

Having told how the Cyclops murdered Æsculapius at Jupiter's behest, and were then done away with by Apollo, Bacon interprets the myth in the following words:

This fable seems to relate to the doings of kings; by whom cruel, and bloody, and exacting ministers are in the first instance punished and put out of office. But afterwards by counsel of the Earth, that is by ignoble and dishonourable counsel, they take them into service again, when they have need either of severity of executions or harshness in exactions. They on their part, being by nature cruel and by their former fortune exasperated, and knowing well enough what they are wanted for, apply themselves to this kind of work with wonderful diligence; till for want of caution and from overeagerness to ingratiate themselves, they at one time or another (taking a nod or an ambiguous word of the prince for a warrant) perpetrate some execution that is odius and unpopular. Upon which the prince, not willing to take the envy of it upon himself, and well knowing that he can always have plenty of such instruments, throws them overboard, and leaves them to the course of law and the vengeance of the friends and relatives of their victims, and to popular hatred; and so amid much applause of the people and great acclamations and blessings on the king, they meet at last, though late, the fate they deserve.

Bacon's interpretation of Earth is not improbably his own; "it is right earth," he says elsewhere [432] of the self-seeking. But the rest at once recalls Machiavelli: [433]

Therefore he placed over that province Master Ramiro d'Orco, a cruel and expeditious man, to whom he gave full powers. He in a short time reduced the people to obedience and unity, with much credit to himself. Later the Duke judged that so much severity was unadvisable, for he thought it

---

[432] XII. 158.   [433] *The Prince*, chap. 7.

might become hateful. Therefore he sent a civil court to sit in the province, under a good chief justice, and accessible to the lawyers of all. And because he knew that the measures taken in the past had aroused hatred; therefore, in order to clear the air, he determined to show that for whatever cruelties had been committed not he was to blame but the harsh nature of his minister. And choosing his opportunity, he had him thrown on the public square in two pieces, with a stick and bloody knife by his side.

Such things as this were not rare, in those days; yet Bacon can hardly have forgotten this passage.

Machiavelli says nothing about the Cyclops, though it may not be entirely fanciful to note that Orco means ogre; but Natalis Comes discusses these monsters at length,[434] and more than once recalls passages in Bacon. He interprets them as a tribe of fierce robbers, "blasphemers of God and inclined to ferocity, the worst being their prince, Polyphemus. But," he adds, "since God invariably punishes all temerity, all cruelty, all wickedness, they received condign punishment at last." As for Polyphemus, he is not only cast down by the gods but falls into the hands of his former human victims: [435]

He was deprived of his eye by a mere man, Ulysses; for those who rise up in arrogance above their station shall be overwhelmed not only by the anger of the gods but by the strength of their fellow men.

Polyphemus, Comes adds, was conquered by wine even before Ulysses overcame him, "for no man may be wicked and also prudent." This last reminds one of a passage in the *Essays*[436] wherein Bacon remarks that the desperate men sometimes employed by princes are necessarily imprudent. Bacon's meaning is not that wickedness is in itself imprudent, but that the blind ambition of such men makes them reckless; and in general, I do not mean to imply that Machiavelli and Comes are his only sources, to the exclusion of contemporary reality. The fact remains, however, that he frequently reflects the influence of their two chief works, and that in these are contained a striking illustration of the practice he is discussing and the classical instance of an assassin's being employed by the king of the gods.

It would appear from what has gone before that Bacon was

---

[434] IX. 8; X, sub *De Cyclopibus*. [436] XII. 207.
[435] IX. 8. 647.

strongly averse to oppressing the people but not to fooling them. This was the general attitude of contemporary statesmanship, and Bacon repeatedly implies his belief that the commonalty, for their own good, should be regarded as children. Thus in the essay on Pan:[437]

Also the sheep-hook is a noble metaphor, alluding to the mixture of straight and crooked in the ways of nature. But the staff is curved chiefly towards the top; because all the works of Divine Providence in the world are wrought by winding and roundabout ways—where one thing seems to be doing, and another is doing really—as in the selling of Joseph into Egypt, and the like. So also in all the wiser kinds of human government, they who sit at the helm can introduce and insinuate what they desire for the good of the people more successfully by pretexts and indirect ways than directly, so that every rod or staff of empire is truly crooked at the top.

The justification of the ways of the anointed contained in this passage has from time immemorial constituted the church the right hand of monarchy; and that the people should be misled for their own good is a doctrine not merely general in Bacon's times but clearly implied in Plato's *Laws* and *Statesman*. Bacon's ideas, then, are venerably conventional. As for his symbolism, it was perhaps suggested by that of the pastoral staff, or crosier, which is an emblem not only of the bishop's paternal authority but also of the duty enjoined on him to jab and punish the obdurate, to support the wavering, and to catch and as it were hook the souls of men and draw them to salvation: "Curva trahit quos recta regit, pars ultima pungit." Or as Durandus [438] puts it:

It resembles and is called a crook in allusion to that used by shepherds to draw back and recall the sheep of their flock which have gone astray.

In the 1612 edition of the *Essays*,[439] Bacon gives us a concrete application of his theory. Discussing the remedies for popular discontents, he says:

Also the part of Epimetheus may become Prometheus in this case. Hee when greifes and evills flewe abroade yet kept hope in the bottome of the vessell. The politike and artificiall nourishing of some degree of hopes, is one of the best antidotes against the poyson of discontents; and it is a

---

[437] XIII. 97.

[438] *Rationali Divin. Off.*, III. 15. See also A. W. Pugin, *Glossary of Ecclesiastical Ornament*, 212 seq.

[439] XII. 381.

certaine signe of a wise governement if it can hold by hope where it cannot by satisfaction.

In the 1625 edition he commits himself even more uncompromisingly to the same views, which are not merely repeated but considerably emphasized: [440]

> The case of Epimetheus mought well become Prometheus, in the case of discontentments; for there is not a better provision against them. Epimetheus, when griefs and evils flew abroad, at last shut the lid, and kept hope in the bottom of the vessel. Certainly, the politic and artificial nourishing and entertaining of hopes, and carrying men from hopes to hopes, is one of the best antidotes against the poison of discontentments. And it is a certain sign of a wise government and proceeding, when it can hold men's hearts by hopes, when it cannot by satisfaction; and when it can handle things in such manner, as no evil shall appear so peremptory but that it hath some outlet of hope: which is the less hard to do, because both particular persons and factions are apt enough to flatter themselves, or at least to brave that they believe not.

If I rightly understand the essay from which the passages above are quoted, Bacon symbolizes in the myth of Pandora's box not the preventing of discontent but the staving off of revolution. He has in mind, at this point, a moment of acute crisis. Such an interpretation is justified, I think, by the context; but in any case, how believe anything else? In 1625 Bacon had behind him a career which, it seems to me, makes any other supposition untenable. Even considered as an expedient, however, his remedy is a dangerous one, and it is strange that he should not say so. Machiavelli recommends similar measures in time of war,[441] but chiefly in the sense of minimising partly fancied terrors on the eve of battle. As for the nourishing of prolonged hopes, he knows full well that the people "are apt enough to flatter themselves," but he is eloquent on the possible consequences.[442] The truth of the matter, one is tempted to conclude, is that on the one hand Bacon had seen little worse than parliamentary crises, and that on the other he failed to grasp what these foreshadowed. Continental statesmanship ruled with a paternal hand of iron. Machiavelli had already made a clear distinction: either you have a truly representative government, in which case you deceive the people at your peril; or

---

[440] XII. 129.
[441] *Discorsi*, III. 29.
[442] Op. cit., I. 52.

you have an absolute prince whose failures to keep his word you leave to be explained by Polyphemus.

Even as in the field of science Bacon lacked the cool concreteness of a Galileo, so in that of politics he could not bring himself to the hard, clear ruthlessness of a Machiavelli. His conscience as a man is frequently at war with his theories as a statesman, and the result is a curious casuistry. The matter of promises furnishes a case in point. Discussing self-advancement, he says: [443]

> As for evil arts, if a man would set down for himself that principle of Machiavel "that a man seek not to attain virtue itself, but the appearance only thereof; because the credit of virtue is a help, but the use of it is cumber," ... or that other principle of Lysander, "that children are to be deceived with comfits and men with oaths," and the like evil and corrupt positions, whereof, as in all things, there are more in number than of the good; certainly with these dispensations from the laws of charity and integrity, the pressing of a man's fortunes may be more hasty and compendious. But it is in life as it is in ways, the shortest way as commonly the foulest, and surely the fairer way is not much about.

It has been suggested that Lysander's precept, which Bacon found quoted in Montaigne,[444] suggested the interpretation of Pandora's box. It may have influenced him to some extent; but in any case Bacon is here in contradiction with that interpretation. It might be objected that his words add one more hypocrite to the self-appointed judges of Machiavelli; but I do not think that anybody really familiar with him would second the objection. Here we have the man in contradiction with the statesman; if, indeed, we do not have the statesman in contradiction with himself.

It is not merely on the ground of morals that Bacon is in disagreement with himself in the matter of Pandora's box; when it comes to individual conduct, he flatly reverses his interpretation on the ground of expediency: [445]

> But in hope there seems to be no use. ... For matter of hope cannot always be forthcoming; and if it fail, though but for a moment, the whole strength and support of the mind goes with it. Moreover the mind suffers in dignity, when we endure evil only by self-deception and looking another way, and not by fortitude and judgment. And therefore it was an idle fiction of the poets to make hope the antidote of human diseases, be-

---
[443] IX. 293.
[444] *Essais*, XI. 18. He is quite as likely to have found them in Plutarch.
[445] XIV. 87.

cause it mitigates the pain of them; whereas it is in fact an inflammation and exasperation of them rather, multiplying and making them break out afresh.

The *Meditationes sacræ* were doubtless approached in a fitting mood; but the point is that the judgment delivered here is a sound one politically as well as otherwise, and that the passage is introduced by considerations on the ingratitude of inflamed hopes that recall the *Prince*.[446] It is hard to understand how the same man could pen the interpretation in the *Essays*. The fickleness of Elizabeth might indeed have misled a superficial observer; but it cannot have escaped Bacon's notice that the Queen never led "from hopes to hopes" her own people, who were usually delighted with her fooling of the rest. In practice, Bacon does not seem to have favored such measures even as an expedient. During the relatively critical period between 1607 and 1609 he was quite ready to deceive the people into a return to what he regarded as their proper devotion to the King; but it was on a profitable foreign war, not on empty promises, that he meditated.

That, whatever his private feelings, Bacon was no more favorable to tyranny than Machiavelli, is shown by his interpretation of the myth of Jove and Briareus, which perhaps had best be discussed here. In the essay *Of Seditions and Troubles,* he remarks that:[447]

The poets feign that the rest of the gods would have bound Jupiter; which he hearing of, by the counsel of Pallas, sent for Briareus, with his hundred hands, to come to his aid. An emblem, no doubt, to show how safe it is for monarchs to make sure of the good will of common people.

The precept contained in this passage is of frequent occurrence in Machiavelli's works [448] and may in a measure owe to their influence its presence here. As for its symbolism, I think it probable that Bacon is indebted for it to Boccaccio and to Comes. The former sees in the particular Jove of this myth an earthly king and, citing "Theodontius," explains the story thus:[449]

Jove, after his victory over the Titans, became insufferably arrogant; wherefore his wife, his brother, and some friends, having assembled near the island of Neritho and called others to them, conspired to drive him from his kingdom. The plot having been revealed to him by a sea-captain who discovered it, he called to his aid Briareus, one of the Titans who had

---

[446] III.
[447] XII. 129.
[448] *Discorsi*, II. 23; *Prince*, 9.
[449] *De gen. deor.*, IV.

remained alive and a most powerful man, and allying himself with him so punished the conspirators that they never again dared to attempt anything against him. Briareus was said to have a hundred hands because he was at the head of many men, the one being used to signify the many.

Natalis Comes, explaining the similar monster Geryon, says as follows: [450]

Others have believed that by Geryon, who had many arms, legs, and eyes, governed by one will, it was intended to signify the union and concord of citizens, who are unconquerable so long as all stand together loyally, as indeed Plutarch declares in his *Politics*.

Plutarch, in his *Political Precepts,* has reference not to the people but to the statesmen of a city. Comes's " concordiam civium " therefore illustrates the mental process by which Bacon probably arrived at his " common people," though of course it is possible that the figure of Briareus, often used figuratively, was familiar to him in some closer source.

The Sister of The Giants,[451] *The Crown of Nemesis*,[452] *and The Preference of Ulysses.*[453]

Bacon disliked the multitude both as a statesman and as a scientist; for he knew it to be intolerant and envious of authority, indifferent and often hostile to learning. Perhaps he was lacking in broad human sympathy, and indeed was somewhat critical and warped in regard to the common interests of life; yet it must be confessed that his experiences were hardly of a nature to make him passionately democratic. For years he struggled with singularly arrogant and stupid parliaments, he was robbed by his servants, he was dragged from power with a vicious ruthlessness largely born of envy, and the splendid eloquence with which he preached his great dream fell on deaf ears so far as practical assistance was concerned. And if he found the multitude slow to take up valuable ideas he discovered it to be ever eager for worthless or harmful rumors, ever quick to disseminate them and to distort them into something worse than they were before. He saw public opinion become rebellious in favor of an insolent and seditious favorite; he had to write in defence of the Queen's memory. Such

---

[450] VII. 1. 468.
[451] XIII. 107.
[452] XIII. 135.
[453] VI. 170.

experiences as these are doubtless reflected in his essay on the sister of the giants and in the passages which I have called the Crown of Nemesis and the Preference of Ulysses.

Bacon's essay on the sister of the giants is so short that I will quote it entire. It goes thus:

> The poets tell us that the Giants, being brought forth by Earth, made war upon Jupiter and the gods, and were routed and vanquished with thunderbolts, whereupon Earth, in rage at the wrath of the gods, to revenge her sons brought forth Fame, youngest sister of the Giants.
>
> The meaning of the fable appears to be this: by Earth is meant the nature of the common people; always swelling with malice towards their rulers, and hatching revolutions. This upon occasion given brings forth rebels and seditious persons, who with wicked audacity endeavour the overthrow of princes. And when these are suppressed, the same nature of the common people, still leaning to the worse party and impatient of tranquillity, gives birth to rumours and malignant whispers, and querulous fames, and defamatory libels, and the like, tending to bring envy upon the authorities of the land: so that seditious fames differ from acts of rebellion not in race and parentage, but only in sex: the one being feminine and the other masculine.

One might suppose that the expression of animus in this essay was artfully intended for the eyes of kings; but the essays on Metis and the Cyclops were open to royal perusal also. As we shall see, Machiavelli was equally aware of the dangerous nature of popular murmurings. It is characteristic of the difference between the two men that the Italian betrays none of Bacon's harassed irritation.

That Bacon regarded seditious rumor as not only hateful but dangerous is seen by his essay *Of Seditions and Troubles:*

> Libels and licentious discourses against the state, when they are frequent and open; and in like sort, false news often running up and down to the disadvantage of the state, and hastily embraced, are amongst the signs of troubles. Virgil giving the pedigree of Fame, saith she was sister to the Giants:
>
> > Illam Terra parens, ira irritata Deorum,
> > Extremam (ut perhibent) Cœo Enceladoque sororem
> > Progenuit.
>
> As if fame were the relics of seditions past; but they are no less indeed the preludes of seditions to come. Howsoever he noteth it right, that seditious tumults and seditious fames differ no more but as brother and sister, masculine and feminine; especially if it come to that, that the best actions of a state, and the most plausible, and which ought to give greatest contentment, are taken in ill sense, and traduced: for that shews the envy

great, as Tacitus saith, "conflata magna invidia, seu bene seu male gesta premunt." Neither doth it follow, that because these fames are a sign of troubles that the suppressing of them with too much severity should be a remedy of troubles.

To the warning with which this passage closes, Bacon returns later in the essay:[454]

To give moderate liberty for griefs and discontentments to evaporate (so it be without too great insolency or bravery), is a safe way. For he that turneth the humours back, and maketh the wound bleed inwards, endangereth malign ulcers and pernicious imposthumations.

Here we catch an echo of Machiavelli's words:[455]

... for when these humors can find no ordinary vent through which to discharge themselves, they seek those extraordinary ones which are the ruin of a state.

Bacon's interest in the subject of rumors was not merely an involuntary and angry one. He saw in the dissemination of reports a valuable political instrument deserving of the careful attention of statesmen, and he began what was intended to be an extensive study of its peculiarities and possible uses:[456]

The poets make Fame a monster. They describe her in part finely and elegantly; and in part gravely and sententiously. They say, look how many feathers she hath, so many eyes she hath underneath; so many tongues; so many voices; she pricks up so many ears.

This is a flourish. There follow excellent parables; as that she gathereth strength in going: that she goeth upon the ground, and yet hideth her head in the clouds: that in the day-time she sitteth in a watch tower, and flieth most by night: that she mingleth things done with things not done: and that she is a terror to great cities. But that which passeth all the rest is, they do recount that the Earth, mother of the Giants that made war against Jupiter and were by him destroyed, thereupon in an anger brought forth Fame; for certain it is that rebels, figured by the Giants, and seditious fames and libels, are but brothers and sisters; masculine and feminine. But now, if a man can tame this monster, and bring her to feed at the hand, and govern her, and with her fly other ravening fowl and kill them, it is somewhat worth. But we are infected with the style of the poets. To speak now in a sad and a serious manner. There is not in all the politics a place less handled, and more worthy to be handled than this of fame.

---

[454] XII. 129. See also XI. 231.   [455] *Discorsi*, I. 7.
[456] XII. 283.

The description of Rumor in the passage quoted above is an accurate paraphrase of that in the fourth book of the *Æneid;* and it was probably to Virgil, and also to Ovid, that Bacon owed his interpretation of the myth. The giants were a conventional symbol of rebellion, which in Bacon's times could no longer assume the dignity of a war of the barons. The interpretation of Fama as the seditious murmurings of the multitude was therefore a natural one. Virgil actually adopts it when he tells how " the fiendlike goddess spreads from tongue to tongue " that Queen Dido and her lover are spending their time in luxurious ease, forgetful of their dignity and their high ambitions, " enthralled by unworthy passion." Ovid's description of Rumor's dwelling is equally to the point: [457]

Here is Credulity, here is heedless Error, unfounded Joy and panic Fear; here sudden Sedition and unauthentic Whisperings.

It is perhaps worth adding that Boccaccio also understood Earth's vengeance as that of the weak upon the strong. Explaining the fact that Rumor was intended to shame the gods, he says: [458]

This I judge to mean nothing more than that the humble, being unable to strive on equal terms with the might of the great, try to avenge themselves by making them infamous with their words.

So much for the sister of the giants. Bacon devotes an essay to another harsh goddess, Nemesis, whom he interprets as the spirit of precariousness, of lurking reverses and misfortunes. He explains her being crowned thus:

Nemesis is distinguished also with a crown; in allusion to the envious and malignant nature of the vulgar; for when the fortunate and the powerful fall, the people commonly exult and set a crown upon the head of Nemesis.

That Bacon spoke feelingly, almost with a premonition of his own case, would appear from a passage in the essay *Of Envy:*

This public envy seemeth to beat chiefly upon principal officers or ministers, rather than upon kings and estates themselves.

It will not do, however, to go too far with this conjecture. His remark in the same essay that " when envy is gotten once into a state, it traduceth even the best actions thereof " is practically a trans-

---

[457] *Metam.*, XII. 59-61.   [458] *De gen. deor.*, I.

lation from Tacitus;[459] and Juvenal's tenth satire with its bitter "crown your doors with bays!" may have contributed towards suggesting the crowning of Nemesis. Furthermore the man of power whose downfall Bacon probably had in mind was Adrastus, king of Argos, the only one of the famous Seven to escape from the attack upon Thebes. The Thebans, as Bacon might read in Comes,[460] built a temple to Nemesis in commemoration of Adrastus's ruinous defeat, and their ferocity and vindictiveness in the war are of course notorious.

He who seeks to overturn accepted ideas is rarely applauded; if he is not stoned as an iconoclast, he is laughed at as a dreamer. Now in a measure Bacon actually was a dreamer, and was therefore regarded with suspicion even by his fellow scientists. One of his editors, commenting on the lack of a certain matter-of-fact acumen which appears in him, is probably right when he says:[461]

It supplies also a natural explanation of another singular fact; namely, the little communication which he seems to have had with the scientific men of his own time and the solitude in which (as he himself complained) he was compelled to prosecute his enterprise. For we know of no man of any scientific eminence who was either a fellow-labourer or a disciple.

Truly inspired as he was, Bacon interpreted this general aloofness as a sign of sheer grossness and materialism, and it is probable that he included the majority indeed in his conception of the populace. Certain it is that the first book of the *Advancement of Learning* closes as follows:[462]

Nevertheless I do not pretend, and I know it will be impossible for me by any pleading of mine, to reverse the judgment, either of Æsop's cock, that preferred the barleycorn before the gem; or of Midas that being chosen judge between Apollo president of the Muses, and Pan god of the flocks, judged for plenty; or of Paris, that judged for beauty and love against wisdom and power; or of Agrippina, "let him kill his mother so he be emperor," that preferred empire with condition never so detestable; or of Ulysses, "that preferred an old woman to an immortality," being a figure of those which prefer custom and habit before all excellency, or of a number of the like popular judgments. For these things continue as they have been: but so will that also continue whereupon learning hath ever relied, and which faileth not: "wisdom is justified of her children."

Of the volley of metaphors quoted above, those of Æsop's cock

---

[459] *Historia*, I. 7.
[460] IX. 18. 668. [461] VI. 443. [462] VI. 170.

and of Paris were conventional; that of Midas was not improbably suggested by Comes,[463] who explains the king's ears as symbolical of his mercenary administration of justice, money and material considerations alone having weight with him in all disputes;[464] but the allusion to Ulysses is something of a puzzle. I suspect it to be derived from some distorted echo of a passage in Cicero's *De Oratore*,[465] in which Antony, the conservative, arguing that plain, homely culture is enough for any lawyer, says as follows:

> Though all the world exclaim against me, I will say what I think: that single little book of the Twelve Tables, if anyone look to the fountains and sources of laws, seems to me, assuredly, to surpass the libraries of all the philosophers, both in weight of authority and in plenitude of utility. And if our country has our love, as it ought to have in the highest degree —our country, I say, of which the force and natural attraction is so strong that one of the wisest of mankind preferred his Ithaca, fixed, like a little nest, among the roughest of rocks, to immortality itself—with what affection ought we to be warmed towards such a country as ours, which pre-eminently above all other countries is the seat of virtue, empire, and dignity?

Here we have Ulysses brought in to defend an unenlightened conservatism: the application fits like a glove. Bacon, however, does not talk of Ithaca; and what Ulysses actually says in the *Odyssey*[466] is that he had rather have his own wife than immortality and Calypso. I should suspect Bacon of having made an intentional substitution; but he seems to quote: "qui vetulam prætulit immortalitati." The truth may be, after all, that somebody before him drew upon both passages and left him an emblem or an allegory ready to his hand.

Juno's Suitor,[467] *Endymion,*[468] *Narcissus,*[469] *and Styx.*[470]

Bacon's opinion of kings and aristocrats would necessarily be expressed with caution; yet I fancy that it may be read between the lines in some of his essays, and notably in those entitled *Juno's Suitor, Endymion, Narcissus,* and *Styx*. By 1609, when *De*

---

[463] IX. 15. 662.

[464] It will be remembered that Midas was punished with the affliction of ass's ears because he pronounced an unreasonable judgment.

[465] I. 44.
[466] V. 151-158.
[467] XIII. 121.
[468] XIII. 106.
[469] XIII. 88.
[470] XIII. 90.

sapientia veterum first appeared, Bacon had learned a good deal about the mighty, not without hard experiences. As early as 1593 Elizabeth had taught him that an inferior may not offer cooperation, nor hope to be pardoned for the offence till he has humbled himself or has been humbled; and there is a painful difference between the fearlessness for which he was then punished and the pitiful intention, confided to his diary five or six years later, to so deport himself toward the Earl of Suffolk as to " make him think how he should be reverenced by a Lord Chancellor, if I were." He had learned much about favorites, too, though he was to know more and worse of them later; and he had conversed with young hopes of great name, and with exquisites like Sir Pearcy Shafton. In a word, when in 1609 he published *The Wisdom of The Ancients,* Bacon had seen all the sights of the Court.

The essay entitled *Juno's Suitor* is, I think, largely original in conception, and there is no mistaking its tone. It goes as follows:

> The poets tell us that Jupiter in pursuit of his loves assumed many different shapes,—a bull, an eagle, a swan, a shower of gold: but that when he courted Juno, he turned himself into the ignoblest shape that could be, a very object of contempt and ridicule; that of a wretched cuckoo, drenched with rain and tempest, amazed, trembling and half dead.
>
> It is a wise fable derived from the depths of moral science. The meaning is that men are not to flatter themselves that an exhibition of their virtue and worth will win them estimation and favour with everybody. For that depends upon the nature and character of those to whom they apply themselves. If these be persons of no gifts or ornaments of their own, but only a proud and malignant disposition (the character represented by Juno), then they should know that they must put off everything about them that has the least show of honour or dignity, and that it is mere folly in them to proceed in any other way; nay that it is not enough to descend to the baseness of flattery, unless they put on the outward show and character of abjectness and degeneracy.

Natalis Comes, interpreting Jove's amorous metamorphoses,[471] sees in the king of the gods an earthly monarch and in these myths the symbol of his contemptibleness when he abandoned himself to unworthy passions; but when he passes to the episode of the cuckoo, it is the lawlessness of that bird that he asks us to remember. I think it probable that Bacon, doubtless remembering Jupiter as a hen-pecked husband, but even more recalling his own mortifying

---

[471] II. 1. 74.

experiences with the mighty, was less impressed with the god's lawlessness than with his abject creeping into favor. It is not impossible, too, that he put his own construction upon the following tale, published in 1600 in Francis Thynne's *Emblemes and Epigrames*:

> The morall Seneca [472] whose penn intreating matters grave,
> I finde amongst his learned workes this worthie tale to have:
> There was a kinge of high renowne which iustice did upholde.
> To him three sonns did nature give, of courage feirce and bold.
> To eche the choice of birdes hee gave, wherbye that hee might learne
> The severall humors of their minde and manners to discerne.
> The eldest, of his haughtie harte, the Eagle proud did chuse.
> The second, of feirs disposition the Hawke would not refuse.
> The youngest, of a myleder minde, the vulgar Thrushe did take,
> On whome the kinge bestowed his crowne and him his heire did make.
> Iudge what the kinge ment by this guifte, for I may not disclose it.
> And thow perhapps maie be deceived in thinkinge for to glose it.

The somewhat cryptic tone of the last lines might suggest something deeper than the obvious moral, and it would have been like Bacon to seize upon the fact and to attribute a "haughtie harte" to the king as well as to his son.

Bacon's interpretation of the myth of Endymion might lead one to suspect that he knew Lyly's secret, for his Endymion is the type of the royal favorite. More probably, however, his source is the myth itself, which after all tells us plainly enough that high-placed Diana was smitten with a humble youth whom she visited in secret and who profited materially by the connection. Certainly Juvenal is following Bacon's line of thought when to the parent of a handsome boy he says: [473]

Well, your Endymion will become the paramour of some married lady he loves, but before long—when a Servilia offers him money—of one whom he hates. Her he will strip bare of all her finery; for what is there that any of them, be she an Oppia or a Catulla, will deny to her passions?

Bacon sees the matter less coarsely, or perhaps he seeks to avoid "generalities and vulgar observations":

---

[472] If Thynne really found this tale in Seneca he was more fortunate than I have been.

[473] *Satires*, X. 316 seq.

The fable relates, as I take it, to the dispositions and manners of princes. For princes being full of thoughts and prone to suspicions, do not easily admit to familiar intercourse men that are perspicacious and curious, whose minds are always on the watch and never sleep; but choose rather such as are of a quiet and complying disposition, and submit to their will without inquiring further, and show like persons ignorant and unobserving, and as if asleep; displaying simple obedience rather than fine observation. With men of this kind princes have always been glad to descend from their greatness, as the moon from heaven; and to lay aside their mask, the continual wearing of which becomes a kind of burden. . . . And it is true that favourites of this class are commonly prosperous in their private fortunes; for princes though they may not raise them to honours, yet since their favor springs from true affection and not from considerations of utility, they generally enrich them with their bounty.

In *De augmentis*,[474] Bacon gives a different but very interesting explanation of the myth of Endymion. Discussing Pan, he says:

The story that Pan once drew the Moon apart into deep woods, seems to have reference to the intercourse of sense with heavenly or divine things. For the case of Endymion is different from that of Pan. To Endymion the Moon descended of her own accord as he slept; for divine influences sometimes steal spontaneously into the understanding when at rest, and withdrawn from the senses; but if they are invoked and solicited by the sense, as by Pan, then they afford no other light but that,

> As by the wayward moon's inconstant light
> A path through woods.

One is tempted, here, to brush aside investigation, so transparent and beautiful is the symbolism. Yet inquiry repays the effort; for while we immediately feel that Bacon is touching upon the ultimate nature of spiritual inspiration and religious certitude, we are not at once clear as to the details of his thought or the sources of his medium of expression, and both are more complex than would at first appear.

In the passage quoted above, Bacon asserts what he has already implied in connection with Jupiter's golden chain: all questions concerning ultimate spiritual matters must be left to religion which, in turn, may answer only as divine revelation shall dictate. In the *Advancement of Learning* [475] he discusses one of these questions at length:

For Human Knowledge which concerns the Mind, hath two parts; the one

---

[474] VIII. 456. [475] VI. 254.

that inquireth of the substance or nature of the soul or mind, the other that enquireth of the faculties or functions thereof. Unto the first of these, the considerations of the original of the soul, whether it be native or adventive, and how far it is exempted from laws of matter, and of the immortality thereof, and many other points do appertain: which have been not more laboriously enquired than variously reported; so as the travail therein taken seemeth to have been rather in a maze than in a way. But although I am of the opinion that this knowledge may be more really and soundly enquired even in nature, than it hath been; yet I hold that in the end it must be bounded by religion, or else it will be subject to deceit and delusion; for as the substance of the soul in the creation was not extracted out of the mass of heaven and earth by the benediction of a producat, but was immediately inspired from God; so it is not possible that it should be (otherwise than by accident) subject to the laws of heaven and earth, which are the subject of philosophy; and therefore the true knowledge of the nature and state of the soul, must come by the same inspiration that gave the substance. Unto this part of knowledge touching the soul there be two appendices; which, as they have been handled, have rather vapoured forth fables than kindled truth; Divination and Fascination.

Bacon's precise meaning as to the investigation of the faculties by science has been explained elsewhere,[476] but his views on the means whereby we may approach loftier mysteries require some discussion. What he says about Endymion would seem to assert that dreams have, at least occasionally, the authority of divinely inspired visions, and that such occurrences are made possible by the release of the mind from the body in sleep. Practically the same doctrine was professed by the Neo-Platonists, and I think it probable that Bacon was acquainted with it not only in the works of those philosophers but also in Boccaccio who, discussing the Virgilian episode of the two gates, says as follows: [477]

Porphyry understands these lines to mean that all dreams are genuine visions; for he believes that when the body is asleep, the soul, released in a measure from bondage, strives to assume its full divinity, and though still enfolded in earthly garments yearns upward, and sees certain things with the eyes of the spirit. Most of these things it sees imperfectly, however, or fails to understand. Therefore it is said that those things which it perceives without obstruction from its mortal veil come forth by the transparent gate of horn, and those which it perceives less clearly emerge from the gate of ivory.

---

[476] I. 102 seq.; VI. 254, note; etc.
[477] *De gen. deor.*, I, sub *De somno*.

Symbols of Worldly Wisdom 183

Bacon is far from accepting the Neo-Platonic doctrine in its entirety. In the essay *Of Prophecies* he clearly includes dreams when he says,[478] " My judgment is, that they ought all to be despised," and elsewhere he speaks of them as revealing nothing more than the state of the body.[479] His discussion [480] of " Divination," too, which was largely based on dreams, is as sceptical as his initial comment. As a matter of fact he does not mention dreams in his interpretation of Endymion, and I question whether he means more than he actually says,[481] or more, indeed, than we feel him to imply. Left to its inner consciousness, the mind may have intimations that can dispense with argument.

To return from a rather long digression to Bacon's worldly symbolism, his interpretation of Narcissus (the " intolerably proud, fastidious, and disdainful " young man who was punished as we all know) is a striking little study of such as withdraw the hem of their garment from life:

In this fable are represented the dispositions, and the fortunes too, of those persons who from consciousness either of beauty or some other gift with which nature unaided by any industry of their own has graced them, fall in love as it were with themselves. For with this state of mind there is commonly joined an indisposition to appear much in public or engage in business; because business would expose them to any neglects and scorns, by which their minds would be dejected and troubled. Therefore they commonly live a solitary, private, and shadowed life; with a small circle of chosen companions, all devoted admirers, who assent like an echo to everything they say, and entertain them with mouth-homage; till being by such habits gradually depraved and puffed up, and besotted at last with self-admiration, they fall into such a sloth and listlessness that they grow utterly stupid, and lose all vigour and alacrity. And it was a beautiful thought to choose the flower of spring as an emblem of characters like this: characters which in the opening of their career flourish and are talked of, but disappoint in maturity the promise of their youth. The fact too that this flower is sacred to the infernal deities contains an allusion to the same thing. For men of this disposition turn out utterly useless and good for nothing whatever; and anything that yields no fruit, but like the way of a ship in the sea passes and leaves no trace, was by the ancients held sacred to the shades and infernal gods.

In a general way, the type which Bacon embodies in Narcissus is familiar enough; yet not all can afford to have no business, and he

---

[478] XII. 205.   [479] IX. 20.   [480] VI. 256.
[481] Giordano Bruno says the same in closely similar terms but with no reference to dreams.

who is permanently surrounded by a little court of sycophants is usually wealthy, or powerful, or both. In what class of people did our author observe such youths? The portrait seems familiar: a young man of handsome appearance, but intolerably proud, fastidious and disdainful, who lives apart, surrounded by an obsequious coterie, enjoying what he does not owe to any industry of his own; a young man at once haughty and weak, but not without gifts and graces, who as he grows older becomes heavy and stupid, and who finally dies without an achievement to his credit. Does one not seem to see certain portraits with titled names inscribed under them, in a gallery? I do not think it fanciful to believe that Bacon had in mind the originals of some of those portraits. In the essay *Of Friendship* there occurs the following passage: [482]

It is a strange thing to behold what gross errors and extreme absurdities many (especially of the greater sort) do commit, for want of a friend to tell them of them; to the great damage both of their fame and fortune: for as St. James saith,[483] they are as men that look sometimes into a glass, and presently forget their own shape and favour.

There is enough, I think, in Boccaccio and in Comes to have suggested Bacon's interpretation. Certainly what the two say frequently recalls it. Boccaccio interprets Echo as fame, and continues thus: [484]

Fame flies from many who care little about it and who, seeing in water (that is, in unsubstantial worldly pleasures) themselves (that is, all their ambition), disdain renown, and presently pass away as if they had never been, leaving behind them names not unlike the flower, which in the morning is purple and fresh but in the evening drooping and faded; and even if such men seemed to shine with a certain splendor until they died, their reputations fade away like mist as soon as the grave closes over them.

Natalis Comes gives two interpretations of Narcissus. In the first he declares [485] that dissolute men are slowly but surely punished by the beauty they love so grossly; in the second he says as follows: [486]

God does not always punish sin at once, but His hand falls the more heavily on the sinner when the hour comes; and this is clearly shown by the fable of Narcissus. He who is unduly puffed up with his beauty, or the greatness of his achievements, or the nobility of his blood, and forgets that he owes these things to the charitable goodness of God: he, I

---

[482] XIII. 172.
[483] *James*, I. 23.
[484] *De gen. deor.* VII.
[485] IX. 16. 663.
[486] X. sub *De Narcisso*.

say, turns these very things into misfortunes, even as a sick stomach turns to poison the most excellent foods.

Again, interpreting the myth of Medusa,[487] Comes says something which Bacon may have remembered and applied to Narcissus:

> Others have explained the deadly power of Medusa as pride and arrogance; for two things are told about the monster: that she polluted Minerva's temple, and that she contended with the goddess as to the beauty of her hair. Now those who are puffed up with pride and petulance respect neither gods nor men; and being of no use to others and even of less use to themselves, may be said to have been changed into stones.

"Put not your faith in princes!" If the essay on Narcissus recalls Pepys, that on Styx brings to mind poor Strafford, for it deals with the treachery of monarchs. It does not, however, accuse them of bad faith toward their ministers (which, perhaps, had been too dangerous a liberty to take) but toward each other, and in that matter of treaties to which the accepted laws of statesmanship practically denied the guarantee of honor. One thing only, he tells us, insures observance even despite self-interest. That thing is necessity, whether imposed by inability to act or by fear of the consequences. For a symbol Bacon chooses the myth of Styx, according to which the faithfulness of the gods to what they swore by that infernal river reflected their fear of the penalty in case of failure,—exclusion from the banquets of their fellow gods:

> The fable seems to have been invented in allusion to treaties and compacts of princes: in respect of which it is but too true that whatever be the solemnity and sanctity of the oath they are confirmed with, yet they are little to be depended on; insomuch that they are used in fact rather with an eye to reputation and fame and ceremony, than for confidence and security and effect. . . . There is adopted therefore but one true and proper pledge of faith; and it is not any celestial divinity. This is Necessity (the great god of the powerful), and peril of state, and communion of interest. Now Necessity is elegantly represented under the figure of Styx: the fatal river across which no man can return. . . . And so it is that if the means of hurting be taken away, or if a breach of the treaty would endanger the existence or the integrity of the state and revenue,—then the treaty may be considered to be ratified and sanctioned and confirmed as by the oath of Styx: for then it is upon peril of being interdicted from the banquets of the gods; which was the ancient expression for the rights and prerogatives of empire, and wealth, and felicity.

---

[487] VII. 11. 492.

The conditions codified in the famous eighteenth book of the *Prince* were not of recent origin when Machiavelli wrote, nor were they near to their end. Bacon was justified by history and by contemporary practice in imputing treachery to the diplomacy of princes. As for his symbolism, his interpretation of Styx as necessity [488] or, better, as compulsion, is probably a felicitous application of a passage in the *Æneid*: [489]

> The next place is of woeful ones, who reckless, with their hands
> Compassed their death, and weary-sick of light, without avail
> Cast life away; but now how fain to bear the poor man's bale
> Beneath the heaven, the uttermost of weary toil to bear!
> But law forbiddeth: the sad wave of that unlovely mere
> Is changeless bond; and ninefold Styx compelleth to abide.

Here are men who may not withdraw their hands from what they have put them to. As a symbol of fear, the Styx is to be found in Servius's famous commentaries,[490] and it is specifically associated with fear of the consequences by Natalis Comes who explains Acheron as fear and Styx as the hatred of sin that comes of penitence, and adds: [491]

Therefore souls are said to cross the Stygian marsh, which flows out of Acheron.

Again, discussing the infernal streams in general, he says: [492]

What indeed can deter men from wickedness more than the knowledge that one day they will be called upon to account for their past actions, and that on that day lying and excuses will be of no avail, but rather their sins will stand out as boils upon a body?

In regard to the interpretation of the banquets of the gods, Lactantius [493] explains these last as human kings who at an early date divided the earth among them; but as far as I know, Bacon had no ground for regarding *convivium deorum* as a frequently used metaphor. He doubtless had in mind some individual instance of its use in this sense, but I am not acquainted with it.

---

[488] "It is the argument of tyrants," said Pitt, "it is the creed of slaves."
[489] VI. 435-441.
[490] *Æn.* VI. 324.
[491] III. 2. 129.
[492] III., proem.
[493] *De Div. Inst.*, I. 11. 14. 15.

Symbols of Worldly Wisdom 187

Actæon[494] *and Pentheus, Midas,*[495] *Iambe,*[496] *and Cassandra.*[497]

The world reflected in the *Prince* was no place for an ingenuous man. It is perhaps significant, however, that the precepts laid down symbolically by Bacon are entirely conventional, and more than once are taken over from Comes together with their medium of expression. One must not be too curious about the doings of princes or the dogmas of the church; one must not chatter; one must beware of giving unrequested or ungracious advice. Milton was to be told the same things in fewer words: an open face and a shut mouth.

Bacon symbolizes the dangers of knowing too much about princes in the myth of Actæon, and those of being too curious about the mysteries of faith in that of Pentheus, who having climbed a tree to spy upon the Bacchanalia, saw double for the rest of his life:

> The first of these fables seems to relate to the secrets of princes, the other to the secrets of divinity. For whoever becomes acquainted with a prince's secrets without leave and against his will, is sure to incur his hatred; and then, knowing that he is marked and occasions are sought against him, he lives the life of a stag; a life full of fears and suspicions. Often too it happens that his own servants and domestics, to curry favour with the prince, accuse and overthrow him. For when the displeasure of the prince is manifest, a man shall scarcely have a servant but will betray him; and so he may expect the fate of Actæon.
>
> The calamity of Pentheus is of a different kind. For the punishment assigned to those who with rash audacity, forgetting their mortal condition, aspire by the heights of nature and philosophy, as by climbing a tree, to penetrate the divine mysteries, is perpetual inconstancy, and a judgment vacillating and perplexed. For since the light of nature is one thing and the light of divinity another, they are as men that see two suns.

Natalis Comes not only associates the dangers discussed above, but symbolizes all in the one myth of Actæon:[498]

> We are admonished above all by this fable not to be too curious about matters which do not concern us; for it has been disastrous to many to know the secrets of others, whether princes, great men, communities, or, above all, gods; for the least suspicion that a man is cognizant of their secrets may lead to his destruction.

And again, in the synoptical index:[499]

---

[494] XIII. 108.
[495] V. 452.
[496] XIII. 101.
[497] XIII. 83.
[498] VI. 24. 442.
[499] X. sub *De Acteone*.

The meaning is that all impertinent curiosity should be avoided; for a knowledge of the secret counsels of princes has been disastrous to many.

Here, then, we have the general idea. As for the details in the first case, Bacon's knowledge of life might very well have supplied them;[500] but it is also possible that they were partly suggested to him by Alciati. In his very popular emblem-book entitled *Emblematum Flumen,* that author interprets the myth of Actœon as a warning to those who employ rogues, probably taking his cue from Fulgentius and Boccaccio, whose explanation is that a hunter's dogs often devour his substance. As for the details in the case of Pentheus they are probably original with Bacon who, as we have seen, frequently repeats that the means of science are not those of faith, and that the use of them in matters of belief leads to a twofold confusion.

In *De augmentis Scientiarum,*[501] Bacon gives an entirely different interpretation of the myths of Orpheus and Pentheus.

And that circumstance of the tearing to pieces of Pentheus and Orpheus amid the orgies of Bacchus, has an evident allegorical meaning; for every ruling passion is extremely hostile and inveterate against two things; whereof one is curious inquisition; the other, free and wholesome advice. Nor does it make any difference if that inquisition were merely for the sake of looking on, as from a tree, without any ill-feeling; nor again if the advice be tendered ever so sweetly and skilfully; for the orgies cannot upon any conditions endure either Pentheus or Orpheus.

Bacon's exegesis here is not so much an appropriation from any single author as a synthesis of hints to be found in several. Thus the impression that Orpheus and Pentheus were martyred by the dissolute might easily be gathered from a reading of Comes and Boccaccio. The latter makes Eurydice represent carnal desire and Orpheus moral persuasion.[502]

When natural desire has plunged into hell, that is into a worldly life, the prudent man with his eloquence (that is, with his sincere persuasion) strives to lead it up again; or in other words, to lead it back to virtue.

Orpheus tries to put an end to undesirable practices by establishing a periodic celebration of the Bacchanalia during which the

---

[500] Cf. old Fidus's long admonition to the heroes of *Euphues and His England,* which probably expresses the general opinion.

[501] VIII. 468.

[502] *De gen. deor.* V, sub *De Orphæo.*

Symbols of Worldly Wisdom 189

celebrants are withdrawn from the community; but the women tear him to pieces, conceiving that he has devised the rites "in order to make known to men their shames and their filthiness." In Natalis Comes [503] the women kill Orpheus "because he is drawing the men away from them"; and they murder Pentheus [504] because:

> ... in truth much immorality took place under cover of the Orgies and Bacchanalia, wherefore Pentheus, King of the Thebans, thought to stop all this wickedness by force. But it is not safe for kings to attempt to end in one day deeply rooted habits of lust and intemperance.

It is not only the vulgar who object to having their doings observed and published. Bacon knew right well that kings are not to be trifled with in this matter and that he is indeed a foolish minister who chatters. We have his views on the subject in a fragment of his *Cogitationes de Scientia Humana:* [505]

> The fable of Midas's servant may be seen to have a bearing on widespread libels. In fact, it is related that Midas's chamber-servant, having discovered his master to have ass's ears, did not dare to tell anybody, and yet, in his inborn stupidity, could not keep it to himself. Therefore, putting his mouth to a hole in the ground, he told what he had seen; and the reeds thus informed of the matter, rustling in the wind repeated it. The meaning is: when the defects and vices of kings and nobles are discovered by their servants, these, moved by their vanity as courtiers and confidants, prove impatient of the restraints of discretion and fail to keep the matter to themselves. For even though perchance they abstain from actually telling yet they allow other indications of what they know to escape; and such indications soon find their way to that dangerous reed the pen of the libeller, who, especially in times inclined to excitement and disorder (in times like restless winds as it were), spreads these rumors among the people in his seditious and slandering libels.

Bacon's little sketch of Grub Street pens whispering in a malignant breeze of scandal is not much less original, I suppose, than Pope's immortal picture of the divers; yet that mention of a seditious wind leads one curiously back to Virgil by way of the essay *Of Seditions and Troubles:*

> Shepherds of people had need know the calendars of tempests in state; which are commonly greatest when things grow to equality; as natural tempests are greatest about the Equinoctia. And as there are certain hollow blasts of wind and secret swellings of seas before a tempest, so are there in states:

---

[503] VII. 14. 504.   [504] V. 13. 330.   [505] V. 452.

Ille etiam cœcum instare tumultus
Sæpe monet, fraudesque et operta tumescere bella.

It was natural that Bacon should find volubility not only dangerous but also silly. As a minister he had to listen to Parliament; as a scientist, to the Schoolmen. It is in this last capacity that he turns impatiently upon babblers. He is commenting on Pan:[506]

As for that little woman, Pan's putative daughter, it is an addition to the fable, with a great deal of wisdom in it: for by her are represented those vain babbling doctrines about the nature of things, which wander abroad in all times and fill the world,—doctrines barren in fact, counterfeit in breed, but by reason of their garrulity sometimes entertaining; and sometimes again troublesome and annoying.

"That little woman" is Iambe. Apollodorus, relating the sad quest of Demeter for her daughter Persephone, says:[507]

Some women were in the house, and when they bid her sit down beside them, a certain old crone, Iambe, joked the goddess and made her smile.

And in the Homeric hymn to Demeter we find the following:[508]

Careful Iambe, who pleased her moods in aftertime also, moved the holy lady with many a quip and jest to smile and laugh.

It may seem far-fetched to make Iambe the type of the uncomprehending babbler; yet what else is she, in her attempt to cheer with quips and jests the grief of a bereaved goddess?

Bacon was familiar not only with the loquacity of the vain gossip and of the pedantic philosopher but also with that of the rhetorician. Despite Erasmus, Latin eloquence was still tinged with the Ciceronianism of the early humanists; and English prose continued to labor under similar influences. In this matter as in others, Bacon was in advance of his times, and yet less so than he conceived himself to be. Compared with the stark directness of a Locke his symbolism is Euphuistic; but as we have seen it is no mere mannerism. He shows unmistakable pleasure in it, and well he may; but it is justified in his eyes not only because he is inclined to regard the myths as genuine symbols, but also because he is conscious of the advantages of using a language popular with

---

[506] XIII. 101.
[507] *Library*, I. 5. 1.
[508] *Hymn to Demeter*, 200-210.

his readers. Of art for art's sake, even though it be real art, he has little good to say: [509]

Here therefore is the first distemper of learning when men study words and not matter: whereof though I have represented an example of late times, yet it hath been and will be secundum maius et minus in all time. And how is it possible but this should have an operation to discredit learning, even with vulgar capacities, when they see learned men's works like the first letter of a patent or limned book; which though it hath large flourishes, yet it is but a letter? It seems to me that Pygmalion's frenzy is a good emblem or portraiture of this vanity: for words are but the images of matter; and except they have life of reason and invention, to fall in love with them is all one as to fall in love with a picture.

I believe that the simile in this passage was suggested by the myth itself, especially as told by Ovid, in whose version of it [510] one reads: "And with his own work he falls in love"; and again: "Pygmalion looks in admiration and is inflamed with love for this semblance of a form."

However harmful they may sometimes be, the babbler and the wind-bag are ultimately ridiculous; but there is another who belongs to their ineffectual brotherhood, and he is entirely tragic. He is the man who with sound and weighty things to say yet goes through life disregarded because he does not know when and how to speak. The very evidence of what he sees so clearly is his stumbling-block and his torment. The exasperation of failure only spurs him to a more tactless vehemence, and his vehemence only provokes more impatient shrugs. He is the general who gruffly preaches preparedness to those thriving in peace; he is the prophet without honor in his own country; he is Cassandra, warning in fierce anguish against the admission of Helen into Troy. According to the classical poets, it was Apollo who condemned Cassandra to speak in vain, and the boon she had received from him was made ineffectual not by her inability to use it but by her virtue in refusing to pay for it. Yet in the *Heroides* [511] she speaks roughly to Ænone:

What art thou doing, Ænone? Why art thou committing the seed to the sand? Thou art ploughing the sea-shore with oxen to no purpose. The Grecian heifer is coming to ruin thee, and thy country, and thy home.

Chaucer, too, like Boccaccio before him, conceives of her as a

---

[509] VI. 120.   [510] *Metam.*, X. 251-253.   [511] *Heroides*, V.

harsh adviser, who says bitter exasperating things to abandoned Troilus:[512]

> Weep if thou wolt, or leef; for, out of doute,
> This Diomede is inne and thou art oute

Did Bacon take his cue from such passages as those quoted above? Certain it is that he chooses Cassandra as the symbol of unfortunate plain speaking:

> This fable seems to have been devised in reproof of unreasonable and unprofitable liberty in giving advice and admonition. For they that are of a froward and rough disposition and will not submit to learn of Apollo, the god of harmony, how to observe time and measure in affairs, flats and sharps (so to speak) in discourse, the differences between the learned and the vulgar ear, and the times when to speak and when to be silent; such persons, though they be wise and free, and their counsels sound and wholesome, yet with all their efforts to persuade they scarcely can do any good; on the contrary, they rather hasten the destruction of those upon whom they press their advice; and it is not till the evils they predicted have come to pass that they are celebrated as prophets and men of far foresight.

The essay closes with illustrations from Roman history, such as that of Cato of Utica, which not impossibly contributed to Bacon's interpretation of the myth.

Tithonus,[513] *Memnon,*[514] *Silenus,*[515] *and The Satyrs.*

That there should be but little romance in the rules of conduct which Bacon had to offer at forty-eight is not, perhaps, surprising; but that the author of *The New Atlantis* should have regarded youth and age as equally ridiculous, love as childish, and an early death as an escape from satiety, disappointing performance, and ultimate misfortune is remarkable. Nevertheless, such is the burden of his essays on Tithonus and Memnon, of a passage on Silenus and the satyrs, and of much else besides. I am inclined to believe that these sentiments were largely genuine, and to regard them as reflecting the same limitations which prevented Bacon from seeing things just as they were in the field of science; yet it must not be forgotten that he had a certain mediæval tendency to accept views already formulated by others.

---

[512] *Troilus and Criseyde,* V. 217-223.
[513] XIII. 120.   [514] XIII. 119.   [515] XIII. 99.

The essay on Tithonus is one of those neat philosophical miniatures which Bacon knew so well how to paint. I will indulge my inclination to quote it entire.

> It is an elegant fable they relate of Tithonus; that Aurora was in love with him, and desiring to enjoy his company forever, begged of Jupiter that he might never die; but forgot, with a woman's thoughtlessness, to add to her petition that neither might he suffer the infirmities of age. So he was exempted from the condition of dying; but there came upon him a strange and miserable old age, such as he must needs undergo to whom death is denied, while the burden of years continues to grow heavier and heavier; so that Jupiter, pitying such a condition, changed him at last into a grasshopper.
>
> This fable seems to be an ingenious picture and description of pleasure; which in its beginning, or morning-time, is so agreeable that men are fain to pray that such delights may last and be their own forever; forgetting that satiety and loathing of the same will come upon them, like old age, before they are aware. So that at last when men have become incapable of the acts of pleasure and yet retain the desire and appetite, they fall to talking and telling stories about the pleasures of their youth, and find their delight in that: as we see in lewd persons who are always harping upon indecent stories, and in soldiers that are forever recounting their deeds; like grasshoppers, whose vigour is only in their voice.

There is an extraordinary non sequitur in this essay, which infers as the consequences of satiety the manifestations of regretful impotence. It is not, perhaps, without significance as a confusion of thought, and I believe it to be a fairly trustworthy clue to Bacon's sources.

One of the sources I have alluded to above is already present, probably, to the reader's mind: Cicero's *De senectute*. It will be recalled that Tithonus is mentioned in that essay as the spokesman for an earlier writer on old age, and it will also be remembered that Tully deprecates the desire for an indefinite prolongation of life on the score that it would be a dragging out of satiety:

> Undoubtedly, as it seems to me at least, satiety of all pursuits causes satiety of life. Boyhood has certain pursuits: does youth yearn for them? Early youth has its pursuits: does the matured or so-called middle stage of life need them? Maturity, too, has such as are not even sought in old age, and finally, there are those suitable to old age. Therefore as the pleasures and pursuits of the earlier periods of life fall away, so also do those of old age; and when that happens man has his fill of life and the time is ripe for him to go.[516]

---

[516] XX. 76.

Here, then, we have it laid down that all pleasure ends in satiety; and presently the same opinion is even more explicitly set forth:

> For what advantage has life,—or, rather, what trouble does it not have? But even grant that it has great advantage, yet undoubtedly, it has either satiety or an end.[517]

From these premises Cicero of course passes to the position that old age has no unhappy hankerings; but at this point Bacon turns from *De senectute* to the *Mythologiæ*, where he finds the following:

> What else does his having been turned into a grasshopper mean but the garrulity and loquacity of old age? For indeed, even as old men are peevish so also they are boastful and great praisers of past times.[518]

Comes does not account for the behavior he describes, and the added touch in our essay is probably original. Indeed I think it likely that Bacon meant to say about pleasure something similar to what Tully said about life: that it led to satiety or came to a physical end.

If the essay on Tithonus pictures old age as impotent desire, that on Memnon even less cheerfully portrays youth as unintelligent daring and merely apparent worth. It goes as follows:

> Memnon, according to the poets, was the son of Aurora. Conspicuous for the beauty of his arms, and great in popular reputation, he came to the Trojan war; where rushing with breathless haste and headlong courage at the highest mark, he engaged Achilles, the bravest of all the Greeks, in single fight; and fell by his hand. In pity of his fate Jupiter sent birds to grace his funeral that kept up a continual cry of grief and lamentation. His statue also, as often as the rays of the rising sun touched it, is said to have uttered a mournful sound.
>
> The fable seems to apply to the unfortunate deaths of young men of high promise. For such are as it were the sons of the morning, and it commonly happens that, being puffed up with empty and outward advantages they venture upon enterprises that are beyond their strength, provoke and challenge to combat the bravest heroes, and falling in the unequal conflict are extinguished. But the death of such persons is wont to be followed by infinite commiseration; for of all mortal accidents there is none so lamentable, none so powerful to move pity, as this cropping of the flower of virtue before its time: the rather because their life has been too short to give occasion of satiety or of envy, which might otherwise mitigate sorrow at their death and temper compassion. And not only do lamentations and wailings hover like those mourner birds about the

---

[517] XXIII. 84.

[518] VI. 4. It is possible that Comes was influenced by *Iliad*, III. 173-177, and Bacon was doubtless familiar with the passage too.

funeral pile; but the same feeling of pity lasts long after: and more especially upon all fresh accidents and new movements and beginnings of great events, as by the touch of sunrise, the regret for them is stirred up again and renewed.

Little indeed is to be found in Bacon's usual source-books to account for the interpretation quoted above; little more than Boccaccio's surmise [519] that the birds are symbols of Memnon's fame, and the following in Servius: [520]

He was held in such honor by his comrades that these bewailed his loss so bitterly as to move to compassion the gods, who turned them into birds.

One more source, however, is suggested by the epithet of " sons of the morning " which is applied to Memnon and his like. Bacon can hardly have used the expression without recalling Isaiah: [521]

> How art thou fallen from heaven,
> Oh Lucifer, son of the morning!
> How art thou cut down to the ground,
> Which didst weaken the nations!

He doubtless attached to the lines the meaning which Milton was so magnificently to express, and therefore saw in the son of the morning one who indeed was full of promise, but dared with mad presumption, and fell, and was extinguished. It may be that Satan was suggested to him not only by the son of Aurora but also by the " young men of high promise " he had in mind. For these cannot have been such as are distinguished by personal qualities only; not for such is infinite mourning that lasts long after and is renewed " upon all fresh accidents." Princes are mourned thus. It is princes and aristocrats that are " puffed up with empty and outward advantages." Bacon professes to speak of all young men of high promise, but I suspect that Memnon is the dashing brother of Narcissus; the one who does not live long enough to disappoint expectation. All this may be fanciful on my part; yet I am hardly inclined to think it so. In his *Memorial of Henry Prince of Wales* he says: [522]

He died to the great grief and regret of the whole kingdom, as being a youth who had neither offended men's minds nor satiated them. The goodness of his disposition had awakened manifold hopes among numbers of all ranks, nor had he lived long enough to disappoint them.

---

[519] VI.

[520] *Æn.* I. 751.

[521] *Isa.*, 14. 12.

[522] XII. 19.

If I am right in the supposition I have ventured to express above, Bacon's interpretation of Memnon is not so cheerless after all. His comments on Icarus come to mind, and his essay *Of Goodness and Goodness of Nature*. Bacon was not a misanthrope. Yet in that very essay, which asserts that "the inclination to goodness is imprinted deeply in the nature of man," we presently read: "For divinity maketh the love of ourselves the pattern; the love of our neighbours but the portraiture." Both statements are true; yet, somehow, he who makes them lacks the sympathetic insight to see both those conditions of the soul together, in tragic union. The essay *Of Love* reveals the man, I think. For him, love is "this weak passion." That one phrase measures the absurdity of those who attribute *Romeo and Juliet* to him. The interpretation which made the judgment of Paris a symbol of the folly of love was conventional in Bacon's day,[523] but he gives it his full approval:[524]

As for the other losses, the poet's relation doth well figure them; that he that preferred Helena, quitted the gifts of Juno and Pallas. For whosoever esteemeth too much of amorous affection quitteth both riches and wisdom.

It was neither ambition nor greed of wealth that separated Bacon from his fellows; it was the walls of that palace which was in Atlantis for him and in Xanadu for Coleridge. There is another passage in the essay *Of Love* which should have laughed Mrs. Gallup to scorn:

It is a poor saying of Epicurus, "Satis magnum alter alteri theatrum sumus": as if a man, made for the contemplation of heaven and all noble objects, should do nothing but kneel before a little idol.

Because he saw mankind as from the windows of his palace, he interpreted the satyrs and Sileni thus:[525]

And in their company[526] are ever found the Satyrs and Sileni; that is old age and youth; for all things have their merry and dancing time, and likewise their heavy and tippling time. And yet to one who truly considers them, the pursuits of either age appear perhaps, as they did to Democritus, ridiculous and deformed,—like to a Satyr or Silenus.

The Sirens,[527] *Dionysus,*[528] *and Nemesis.*[529]

Bacon's views on youth, age, and love, even though they be

---

[523] Cf. Alciati, Thynne, Boccaccio, etc.
[524] XII. 111.
[527] XIII. 169.

largely adopted views, are not cheerful. His opinion of pleasure, and indeed of all pursuits and even of life itself, is no less bleak. It is set forth at length in the essays on the Sirens, Dionysus, and Nemesis. For these as for the others it is possible to find sources, but sources elaborated with what seems to me an unmistakable emphasis on the gray side of the picture.

"As for the song of the Sirens," says Bacon, "its fatal effect and various artifice, it is everybody's theme, and therefore needs no interpreter." The song of the Sirens is indeed a hard-worked symbol of the allurements of pleasure; but Bacon by no means stops at the simpler and more general meaning attributed to the myth, which last, therefore, he relates in detail:

> The Sirens were daughters (we are told) of Achelous and of Terpsichore, one of the Muses. Originally they had wings; but being beaten in a contest with the Muses which they had rashly challenged, their wings were plucked off, and turned by the Muses into crowns for themselves, who thenceforward all wore wings on their heads, except only the mother of the Sirens. These Sirens had their dwelling in certain pleasant islands, whence they kept watch for ships; and when they saw any approaching they began to sing; which made the voyagers first stay to listen, then gradually draw near, and at last land; when they took and killed them. Their song was not all in one strain; but they varied their measures according to the nature of the listener, and took each captive with those which best suited him. So destructive the plague was, that the islands of the Sirens were seen afar off white with the bones of unburied carcasses. For this evil two different remedies were found; one by Ulysses, the other by Orpheus. Ulysses caused the ears of his crew to be stopped with wax; and himself (wishing to make trial of the thing without incurring the danger) to be bound to the mast; at the same time forbidding any one at his peril to loose him even at his own request. Orpheus not caring to be bound, raised his voice on high, and singing to his lyre the praises of the Gods, drowned the voices of the Sirens, and so passed clear of all danger.

Bacon's interpretation of the myth of the Sirens is curious and minute. For the most part, however, it is not original, as the following table will, I think, show:

Bacon's Interpretation	*Parallels in Other Writers*
Pleasures spring from the union of abundance and affluence with hilarity and exultation of mind.	That they (the Sirens) were the companions of Proserpine was feigned, I believe, because by Proserpine was understood the abundance of Sicily in all things; to which abundance are due rich foods

And formerly they carried men away at once, as if with wings, by the first view of their charms.

For a mischief so fraught with cunning and violence alike, there are proposed three remedies: two from philosophy, the third from religion. The first method of escape is to resist the beginnings, and sedulously to avoid all occasions which may tempt and solict the mind. This is the waxing up of the ears, and for minds of ordinary and plebeian cast—such as the crew of Ulysses—is the only remedy. But minds of a loftier order, if they fortify themselves with constancy of resolution, can venture into the midst of pleasures; nay and they take delight in thus putting their virtue to a more exquisite proof; besides gaining thereby a more thorough insight — as lookers on rather than followers—into the foolishness and madness of pleasures.

Heroes of this order may therefore stand unshaken admidst the greatest temptations, and refrain themselves even in the steep-down paths of pleasures; provided only that they follow the example of Ulysses, and forbid the pernicious counsels and flatteries of their own followers, which are of all things most powerful to unsettle and unnerve the mind.

But of the three remedies, far the

and the libidinous actions often provoked by them (Boccaccio).[530]

They are called in Greek draggers. . . . One is dragged away by the following three allurements of love. . . . The Sirens are called winged because they penetrate so quickly into the minds of lovers (Fulgentius).[531]

Why, amid the sweet songs of the Sirens, was it necessary either to stop up ones ears or to have oneself tied to the mast? Because when one faces the allurements of illicit pleasure one must either turn a deaf ear to them or submit to the strictest control of one's reason (Natalis Comes).[532]

Those things which his comrades passed by after their ears had been waxed Ulysses, though in truth tied to the mast, passed by anyhow. These Sirens (that is the allurements of pleasure) he heard and saw—knew, in other words, and judged of—but he passed them by just the same (Fulgentius).[533]

Others have interpreted the Sirens as the voices of flatterers, the eloquence of whom, being pleasant to the hearer, has caused the Sirens to be called daughters of the Muses. However, such voices drag the hearer down to ruin. (Natalis Comes).[534]

Whoever, then, would avoid calam-

---

[530] *De gen. deor.* VII.
[531] *Mythologicon*, II, 11.
[532] IX. 1. 622.
[533] *Mythologicon*, II, 11.
[534] VII. 13. 501.

Symbols of Worldly Wisdom

best in every way is that of Orpheus; who by singing and sounding forth the praises of the gods confounded the voices of the Sirens and put them aside: for meditations upon things divine excel the pleasures of the sense, not in power only, but also in sweetness.	ities and hardships, must either follow the example of Ulysses and close his ears to the dishonest promptings of life or he must listen to the admonitions of Orpheus and other wise men and hear them alone. . . . It is necessary, then, that Orpheus or some other friendly and wise man should drown the voices of the Sirens with sagacious and devoted advice. (Natalis Comes).[535]

Bacon's interpretation of the episode of Orpheus, quoted in the preceding paragraph, seems to be his own, and I do not know of any immediate sources for the symbolism of the passage following that in which the wings of the Sirens are explained:

But doctrine and instruction have succeeded in teaching the mind, if not to refrain altogether, yet to pause and consider consequences; and so have stripped the Pleasures of their wings. And this redounded greatly to the honour of the Muses—for as soon as it appeared by some examples that Philosophy could induce a contempt of Pleasures, it was at once regarded as a sublime thing, which could so lift the soul from earth, and make the cogitations of man (which live in his head) winged and ethereal. Only the mother of the Sirens still goes on foot and has no wings; and by her no doubt are meant those lighter kinds of learning which are invented and applied only for amusement; such as those were which Petronius held in estimation, he who being condemned to die, sought in the very waiting-room of death for matter to amuse him, and when he turned to books among other things for consolation, would read (says Tacitus) none of those which teach constancy of mind, but only light verses. Of this kind is that of Catullus:

> Let's live and love, love, while we may;
> And for all the old men say
> Just one penny let us care;

and that other,—

> Of Rights and Wrongs let old men prate, and learn
> By scrupulous weighing in fine scales of law
> What is allowed to do and what forbid.

For doctrines like these seem to aim at taking the wings away from the Muses' crowns and giving them back to the Sirens.

The application of what Bacon says about the Muses to the

---

[535] VII. 13. 500.

Sirens is in a measure original but on the other hand it is closely reminiscent of what Boccaccio has to say in defense of poetry. In the eighteenth chapter of the fourteenth book of *De genealogiis deorum* Boccaccio, fighting valiantly under the banner of Petrarch, turns upon those who attack poetry in the name of "that most famous and holy man, Boethius." It will be remembered that when Philosophy appears to the imprisoned statesman she at once drives away the Muses who are trying to comfort him:[536]

> Beholding the Muses, the inspirers of song, standing round my bed, and lending words to my grief, she was displeased; and looking upon them with a stern and threatening aspect, "Who gives permission," says she, "to these soul-enervating daughters of the theatre to approach this disconsolate person? So far are they from remedying his woes by any art of theirs, that they nourish them by their soft and enfeebling poisons. It is they who teach their votaries to choke and destroy, by the pernicious brambles of the passions, the most abundant and useful crops of reason. ... Be gone, ye baneful Sirens, with your strains that enchant to destruction! Be gone; leave him to me. It is only my sober muse that can effectuate his cure."

Here indeed is a weapon in the hands of prejudiced austerity; but the fiery and skillful Florentine fairly breaks it in two:

> Behold, oh most sagacious King,[537] to what the crafty arguments of these rascals tend! But the plain truth shall suffice to confound them. I have already shown who the Muses were, and what their honorable titles, and how great the obligations of illustrious men towards them. Still the iniquitous voices raised against them are not silent. Forward, then; I must press on further. It must be evident from what has already been said that there are two classes of poets: the one praiseworthy, venerable, and ever dear to pious men; the other base, shameful, wicked, and indeed deserving, as I have said, not merely of being banished from cities but of being driven from the world. The same may be said of the Muses, which are of one genus but two species—The one kind, which deserve all praise, dwell in groves of bay-trees, near the Castalian spring, and are adorned with garlands, and noted for the sweetness of their song; the others, who are led by the comic poets, dwell in theaters, on the stage, amid garish shows, and bestow their favors for gold on the base multitude. ... The enemies of poetry have perhaps understood, now, that when Boethius cries that the Muses are courtezans he has reference to that trivial kind of Muses; and in fact he says "theatrical courtezans." This the enemies of the poets would know if they had read what Philosophy says next. She says: "Leave him to be cared for and healed by my Muses." And in

---

[536] *De consolatione philosophiæ*, I, prose 1.

[537] Hugo IV of Cyprus to whom the book is dedicated.

order to make it even clearer that he blames only those others, Philosophy repeatedly comforts Boethius with verses and poetic fancies. If Philosophy calls the Muses to the aid of her doctrine, evidently they cannot be dishonest or wicked!

The illustrious men whom Boccaccio names as indebted to poetry are such as Job and Jerome, and he cites Josephus and Origen to the effect that the Book of Job is written in hexameters and the Psalms in various classic meters. In other words he follows Petrarch in proclaiming the *poeta theologus* and thus giving the early Renaissance a battle-cry which, as we have seen, Bacon echoes when he speaks of " Parables, which are a divine poesy." The later Renaissance, turning from the Bible to Plato and Horace, proclaimed the *poeta philosophus*—the instrument of moral enlightenment rather than of religious inspiration—and this is the kind of thing Bacon has in mind in the essay on the Sirens. The conception was generally accepted and even the pious Comes stood up for the Muses:[538]

> These goddesses are of great comfort in adversity and of no small encouragement to splendid deeds; even as, on the other hand, they restrain us from indulging in illegitimate pleasures. As Theocritus says in the *Cyclops*:
>
> > Nicias there is no cure to make one well of love.
> > To abate the torments of its burning fever fire
> > Useless are all things, balms and enchanted potions,
> > Save only one: the pure charms of the Muses.
>
> It was in their gift to inflame the souls of warriors to valor in war; in their gift to console the afflicted; in theirs to immortalize noble deeds: and indeed many men have been inspired to the achievement of virtue by the examples placed before them by the Muses, as appears in Plutarch's little book on music. Homer also judged it undeniable that heroes fired by austere and lofty songs which reminded them of great deeds once accomplished, were presently filled with a new might when they faced the enemy. Indeed, such were the purposes of the ancient poets and singers that they professed themselves to be not only the moderators of the souls of men but masters of conduct. In the Greek cities the rudiments of poetry were taught to the young; nor were the Muses stripped of all sensual attractiveness, but rather they appeared modest and chaste. Thus it was that the musicians who taught the measures of song, of the lyre, and of the pipes were able to call themselves the reformers and masters of morals, as did Pythagoras and the Pythagorians after him. It was for this reason that Homer called bards correctors of manners, as when he

---

[538] VII. 15. 507.

wrote in the third book of the *Odyssey* that Agamemnon left a bard as the protector and monitor of Clytemnestra.

It is unnecessary to follow Comes further in his confused and yet explicit defense of the Muses. Enough has been said to show that Bacon's views on poetry were those of his times.

There is a tang of almost mediæval asceticism about Bacon's view of pleasure as something to be held at arm's length. Pleasure is a snare. The necessary ethical complement follows in the essay on Dionysus: all objects of eager pursuit are vanity. It will be recalled that Dionysus was the son of Semele by Jupiter. She having been burned to death by the godhead she demanded to behold in her lover, Jove received their unborn child into his thigh, whence it came forth a girl-faced boy destined to conquer the world. Dionysus was educated by Proserpine and himself became an educator as well as a conqueror, teaching men how to cultivate vineyards and make wine:

. . . whereby becoming famous and illustrious, he subjugated the whole world and advanced to the furthest limits of India. He was borne in a chariot drawn by tigers; about him tripped certain deformed demons called Cobali,—Acratus and others. The Muses also joined his train. He took to wife Ariadne, whom Theseus had abandoned and deserted. His sacred tree was the Ivy. He was accounted likewise the inventor and founder of sacred rites and ceremonies; yet such as were fanatical and full of corruption, and cruel besides. He had power to excite phrensy. At least it was by women excited to phrensy in his orgies that two illustrious persons, Pentheus and Orpheus, are said to have been torn to pieces; the one having climbed a tree to see what they were doing; the other in the act of striking his lyre. Moreover, the actions of this god are often confounded with those of Jupiter.

Dionysus, it is said, did indeed reveal his god-like nature by arising from the grave shortly after his burial.

Bacon sees in Dionysus the symbol of all overmastering desires— love, greed of gold, ambition, and the rest—and reads this meaning into the details of the myth with what appears to be inspired felicity. If I am not mistaken, the symbolism of the essay on Dionysus is, in fact, rather an original development of hints than anything approaching a mosaic of appropriations. To such hints Bacon's conception of his subject is abundantly open, for it emphasizes eager desire as mental orgasm to the point of making him say that: "Under the person of Bacchus is described the nature of Desire, or passion and perturbation." Now one of the earliest and most frequently repeated interpretations of the myth of Dionysus is that it stands for drunkenness, as well as for the life-story of the vine. The Greeks themselves worshipped the god as an embodiment of the reproductive forces of nature, and Comes repeats this explanation as well as the others. For the Neo-Platonists Bacchus's mirror was the lure and Bacchus's cup the draught of worldly preoccupations by which the soul was partly chained to earth. For Lactantius, finally, Bacchus was the insolent leader of a dissolute rout. Material, then, was not lacking. Nevertheless it did not furnish Bacon with the details of his symbolism,—that is to say, not directly. When he tells us that human passions, like Dionysus, die only to spring up again, he is, by an independent act of his imagination, transferring Come's symbolism from the vine to man's impulses.

Bacon interprets the parentage of Dionysus and the circumstances attending his birth as follows:

Under the person of Bacchus is described the nature of desire or passion and perturbation. For the mother of all desire, even the most noxious, is nothing else than the appetite and aspiration for apparent good: and the conception of it is always in some unlawful wish, rashly granted before it has been understood and weighed. But as the passion warms, its mother (that is the nature of good), not able to endure the heat of it, is destroyed and perishes in the flame.

I think I am safe in asserting that in this passage we have the confirmation of what I have said elsewhere concerning the episode of Mordant and Amavia in *Faerie Queene*, II. 1. There also those who mistake apparent for real good drink the loss of what they seek in the draught of Bacchus. The cup is Circe's; but in the *Philebus* it is Bacchus who mingles earthly joy and grief in the bowl of the spirit,[539] and in Macrobius it is Bacchus's cup that destroys in the soul descending earthward to embodiment the knowledge of heavenly things:[540]

As the soul is drawn down to the body it begins to experience a confusion like the confused murmuring of a forest in the wind. This is what Plato means in the *Phædo* when he says that the soul is drawn into the body in a state of intoxication. By the strange drink he means us to understand the influx of matter which burdens the soul and drags it down. The

---

[539] Jowett's Plato, IV. 637.   [540] *Comm. in somn. Scip.* I. 12.

visible sign of this mystery is the Cup of Bacchus,—that starry cup situated between Cancer and Leo. The intoxication which comes over the descending soul at this point manifests itself as the confused sound of wind in the forest. And with intoxication comes its companion forgetfulness, already beginning to creep into the mind; for if the souls of men brought with them to their bodies a clear memory of heavenly things as they knew them above, there would be no question as to the divinity of mankind.

The Cup of Bacchus becomes also the Mirror of Bacchus,[541] and dazzles as well as intoxicates with earthly preoccupations. Nor is it merely in heaven, a snare to approaching souls only. It offers still deeper oblivion and still more hopeless exile to the lips of mortals.[542] It is the pool that chains Narcissus flat to earth.[543] Yet only the lower part of the soul may be thus enslaved. Says Plotinos:[544]

Not the whole soul enters into the body. By her higher part, she ever remains united to the intelligible world; as, by her lower part, she remains united to the sense-world. If this lower part dominates or rather, if it be dominated (by sensation) and troubled, it hinders us from being conscious of what the higher part of the soul contemplates. . . . Every soul has a lower part turned towards the body, and a higher part turned towards divine Intelligence.

Bacon, having given an account of the parentage and conception, so to speak, of passion, speaks of its period of gestation in the soul as follows:

Itself while still in embryo remains in the human soul (which is its father and represented by Jupiter), especially in the lower part of the soul, as in the thigh; where it is both nourished and hidden; and where it causes such prickings, pains, and depressions in the mind, that its resolutions and actions labour and limp with it.

In his conception of the duality of the soul, Bacon was doubtless influenced by Telesio. This passage, however, is concerned not with the related souls of Telesian philosophy but with the parts of the same soul, and I believe that we have here one more indication of Bacon's familiarity with the Neo-Platonists.

---

[541] Stewart, *The Myths of Plato*, 239; Plotinos, *Fourth Ennead*, Book 3, Section 12.

[542] Plotinos, *Enneads*, I. 6. 8; Porphyry, *De Ant. Nymph*, cap. 34.

[543] Plotinos, *loc. cit.;* Ficino, *In Plat Sympos*, cap. 17; Stewart, 240.

[544] *Enneads*, IV. 8. 8.

Earthly desires are insidious and persistent, Bacon tells us.[545] Ivy was rightly consecrated to Bacchus, for "the master passion spreads itself like ivy about all human actions and resolutions, forcing itself in and mixing itself up with them"; and it was aptly said that the god came to life again after death:

For the passions seem sometimes to be laid asleep and extinguished; but no trust can be placed in them, no, not though they be buried; for give them matter and occasion, they rise up again.

Spenser clearly understood the symbolism of ivy, as the "lascivious armes" of that plant in *F. Q.* II. 12. 61 convincingly prove; and I do not doubt that Bacon understood it also. It is quite possible, however, that Dickens was not the first to observe "the ivy green," and that the insidious inroads of the Biblical tares in the wheat (or indeed of weeds in the philosopher's own flower-beds) had their influence. In the essay *Of Nature in Men* it is remarked that:

A man's nature runs either to herbs or weeds; therefore let him seasonably water the one, and destroy the other.

As for the symbolism of Bacchus's resurrection, it may well be, as I have already suggested, a transposition of the interpretation to be found in the *Mythologiæ*:[546]

That Dionysus was torn to pieces and buried, and that he rose from the grave: all this concerns nothing more than the cultivation of the vine. For from shoots cut off and partially buried, sound and fertile vines spring up. That he slept three years with Proserpine also refers to the vine which, during its unproductive period, is said to sleep with the goddess; for vines grow largely in their roots.

It should be noticed, however, that Macrobius applies this part of the myth directly to the human soul. Explaining individual souls Neo-Platonically as emanations which come from and return to the One, he symbolizes the seeming breaking up of the cosmic spirit thus:[547]

Indeed, the Orphics conjectured that Dionysus himself was to be understood as νοῦν ὄλιχον who came from the one but divided himself into the many. Therefore in their sacred legends it is related that Dionysus was torn to pieces but rose up whole from his buried fragments; for νοῦς, which we have said to mean the soul, emerging from the one into the many, and

---

[545] XIII. 40, 141.   [546] V. 13. 234.
[547] *Comm. in somn. Scip.*, I. 12. 12.

returning from plurality to oneness, fulfills its earthly functions and yet does not abandon its mysterious nature.

Bacon raises his voice in warning. To become obsessed with earthly pursuits is to commit oneself to a course of action that is often weak or ridiculous; sometimes cruel; always, from a philosophical point of view, unprofitable and vain:

Most true also it is that every passion of the more vehement kind is as it were of doubtful sex, for it has at once the force of the man and the weakness of the woman.

And again:

Tigers also are kept in its stalls and yoked to its chariot; for as soon as Passion ceases to go on foot and comes to ride in its chariot, as in celebration of its victory and triumph over reason, then is it cruel, savage, and pitiless towards everything that stands in its way. Again, there is humour in making those ridiculous demons dance about the chariot: for every passion produces motions in the eyes, and indeed in the whole countenance and gesture, which are uncomely, unsettled, skipping, and deformed; insomuch that when a man under the influence of any passion, as anger, scorn, love, or the like seems most grand and imposing in his own eyes, to the lookers on he appears unseemly and ridiculous.

And still more impressively:

And again that part of the allegory is especially noble which represents Bacchus as lavishing his love upon one whom another man had cast off. For most certain it is that passion ever seeks and aspires after that which experience has rejected. And let all men who in the heat of pursuit and indulgence are ready to give any price for the fruition of their passion, know this—that whatever be the object of their pursuit, be it honour or fortune or love or glory or knowledge, or what it will, they are paying court to things cast off—things which many men in all times have tried, and upon trial rejected with disgust.

I think it safe to believe that the first two passages quoted above are generalizations of what Comes has to say about drunkenness as symbolized by the myth of Bacchus; and it seems to me at least possible that the third passage is an expansion of a certain tirade of Lactantius's against the god. The *Mythologiæ* says as follows: [548]

The god also symbolizes the nature of drunkards of whom some are made bold by wine, others as timid and talkative as women. Therefore the god was believed to be both male and female. . . . He was accompanied by wicked and harmful demons called Cobali, among which Acratus held the

---

[548] V. 13. 333.

principal place; for many are the evil consequences of drunkenness and immoderate drinking: talkativeness, boldness, waste, shamelessness, anger, and many other similar ills; and also clamor and uproar; all of which the ancients called bad spirits. . . . Indeed, because of the ways of drunkards the ancients taught that lynxes, tigers, panthers and leopards followed Dionysus and drew his chariot: for intemperate drinking stamps men's souls with the natures of these beasts and makes them furious.

To be intoxicated with an obsession is still to be intoxicated. Drunkenness may well be regarded as the type of all violent disorders of the spirit; and Bacon furthermore regards it as the strongest incentive to all such disorders:

It is a wise parable, too, that of the invention of the vine; for every passion is ingenious and sagacious in finding out its own stimulants. And there is nothing we know of so potent and effective as wine, in exciting and inflaming perturbations of every kind, being a kind of common fuel to them all.

As for the episode of Ariadne, one seems to see the shake of the head and to hear the grave comment when one reads in Lactantius:[549]

But this invincible master of India basely yielded to love and lust. Having come to Crete with his half-human companions he met a shameless woman on the shore. Doubtless he played the man with all the self-confidence given him by his victories! Doubtless no sign of weakness was seen in him! Yes indeed! This betrayer of her country, this murderer of her brother, this woman abandoned and rejected by another, he set free, and married, and lifted up to heaven with him!

So much for the myth of Dionysus. The grim tone which distinguishes Bacon's interpretation is not, as we have seen, wholly spontaneous; yet it is far from perfunctory, and it occurs again with even more unmistakable sincerity in the essay on Nemesis. For the ancients, Nemesis was the humbler of arrogance. Natalis Comes probably suggested Bacon's interpretation in the main. He too explains the goddess as mutability, which " can shake not only men but also things," [550] and he explains her parentage and her wings much as Bacon does. Yet the two pieces are strikingly different in tone. The Italian's Nemesis is much like Dante's Fortune: heaven-appointed to superintend equable distribution, to impose moderation, to enforce law. How different is Bacon's:

---

[549] *Div. Institutionum*, I. 10.   [550] IX. 19.

> ... it was the office and function of this goddess to interrupt the felicity of fortunate persons, and let no man be constantly and perpetually happy, but step in like a tribune of the people with her veto; and not to chastise insolence only, but to see also that prosperity however innocent and moderately borne had its turn of adversity; as if no one of human race could be admitted to the banquets of the gods except in derision.

And she is crowned because the malignant envy of the people crowns her when a great man falls; and she rides a stag (a long-lived animal) because whoever does not die young and so elude her, has her, so to speak, on his back. Who can doubt that there is bitterness here? For Comes she is the child of night because men are blind to God's justice; for Bacon because, "the human not agreeing with the divine judgment," men cannot see why good Ripheus should fall.

The long and curious emblem-book of Bacon's mythological symbols is now ended; before leaving it, I will pause a moment to draw from it certain general conclusions. The most comprehensive of these, which may be inferred from the popularity of *De sapientia veterum,* has already been touched upon. Bacon was by no means singular in actually giving credence to such interpretations as those in his book. Sandys's translation of Ovid, equipped with a complete commentary of this kind, appeared between 1621 and 1626; a handsome English translation of Ripa's *Iconologia* (which on the Continent had gone through seven editions between 1593 and 1630) was published in 1709. About this matter, however, I do not suppose that there has been much doubt. There has been uncertainty, instead—or perhaps, indeed, mistaken confidence—in regard to other questions: the originality of Bacon's symbolism and the sources of his thought. On these points I venture to believe that the present investigation has cast fresh light.

In his preface to *De sapientia veterum,* Mr. Spedding says:

> The object of the work was probably to obtain a more favourable hearing for certain philosophical doctrines of Bacon's own; for it seems certain that the fables themselves could never have suggested the ideas, however a man to whom the ideas had suggested themselves might find or fancy he found them in the fables.

And again:

> The interpretation of each fable is in fact an "essay or counsel", civil, moral, or philosophical; embodying the results of Bacon's own thoughts and

observation upon the nature of men and things, and replete with good sense of the best quality.

These views, which have been more or less generally accepted, can no longer be held, I think, as they stand. It is doubtless true that Bacon sought to make his book attractive; but we have little reason to believe that he intended to appeal only to the fancy of the public, and none at all to regard the essays as nothing more than the play of his own fancy upon the myths they explain. The very fact that he conceived of classical mythology as probably allegorical should put us on our guard against such an opinion. It was not by discarding the wisdom of learned divines that men sought to understand the mysteries of the Scriptures. But the evidence accumulated in the preceding pages may dispense, I think, with *a priori* arguments. If the twenty odd parallels in Spenser's case [551] can hardly be accounted for as a matter of coincidence, the more than forty in Bacon's leave still less room for such an explanation. Here too we have not merely general resemblances but correspondences of detail, quirks of expression; here too Comes and Boccaccio make clear what would otherwise be ambiguous or incomprehensible.

The author of a brilliant work on the Renaissance in Italy utters an often-forgotten truth when he says: [552]

Au fond, changeant d'école, les humanistes n'ont fait que changer de maître. Leur pensée demeure en tutelle. Leur raison garde des béquilles. Ce n'est pas du jour au lendemain que l'esprit peut devenir adulte et se risquer à marcher seul. Les anciens ont remplacé les Pères de l'Eglise; le laurier du poète a supplanté le bonnet du docteur; Cicéron a détrôné saint Thomas; mais c'est tout.

This is said about the fifteenth century. By the sixteenth Machiavelli was placing considerable faith in his own experience; and yet he spoke in the name of antiquity and was very much more indebted to Livy, Cicero, Aristotle, Polybius, and others besides than is popularly supposed. In the seventeenth century came Galileo; but let us remember that Galileo was crushed by the defenders of authority. Bacon's England had no Inquisition to fear, however little her Puritans lacked the good will; but Bacon himself testifies that it was almost dangerous there to meddle with author-

---

[551] Cf. Lemmi, *The Symbolism of The Classical Episodes in The Faerie Queene*, P. Q. VIII, 1929.

[552] P. Monnier, *Le Quattrocento*, I. 260.

ity, and the *Anatomy of Melancholy* is a monument built of ancient opinions and hoary beliefs. Bacon's intuitions were in advance of all this, but his habits of mind were not. He had flung off not only St. Thomas but also Aristotle; yet his ideas were heavily indebted to Empedocles, Plato, Cicero. He had formulated inductive logic; yet his desire to induce from the facts was more than equaled by his impulse to deduce from authority. He had a vision of scientific reform; but the germ of it was in the Italian reformers, in the alchemists, in Tully. He proposes to " hold firm to the works of God, and to the sense," and to conduct a rigidly experimental investigation: [553]

> wherein it will be like that labour of Hercules in purging the stables of Augeas, to separate from superstitious and magical arts and observations, anything that is clean and pure natural, and not to be either contemned or condemned.

Aye, but what do we presently find in his notes? This, for example: [554]

> It is an ancient tradition that blear-eyes infect sound eyes; and that a menstruous woman looking upon a glass, doth rust it: nay, they have an opinion that seemeth fabulous; that menstruous women going over a field or garden, do corn and herbs good by killing the worms.

If we regard as contrary to fact and probability the originality of Bacon's symbolism, we shall the more readily understand the sources and nature of his philosophical thought. In the essay on Cœlum, in that on Pan, and in others besides, we have seen Bacon appropriate from Comes not only symbolical externals but doctrines too. We have noted his indebtedness to Empedocles also, and to Plato, to Lucretius, to Scripture, probably to the Neo-Platonists. Under the circumstances, it is certainly rash to make much of his indebtedness to Democritus and Telesio. The Renaissance was philosophically eclectic,—or perhaps I should say eclectically tentative. Spenser, in the episodes of the Garden of Adonis and of the Judgment of Nature, is at least hospitable to the views of Plato, Pythagoras, Aristotle, Lucretius, and Alanus de Insulis. Telesius doubtless did exert some influence on Bacon's conception of the soul; but, in my opinion, so did the Neo-Platonists. He probably did contribute to Bacon's theory of " spirits ", and the

---

[553] V. 118.   [554] V. 129.

early Greeks did too; but the fact remains that Bacon persistently uses the language of the alchemists and obviously has them in mind almost as often as he talks of experimental science. Indeed his indebtedness to the Hermetic philosophers is characteristic. Renaissance England did not change *ab ovo*; but Bacon's mental habits were rooted exceptionally deep in the past. One is tempted to call him a mediæval philosopher haunted by a modern dream.

The dream never ceased to beckon; but what about real life? If Bacon is not a misanthrope, neither, assuredly, is he an optimist. Often he breaks with his usual sources in putting a pessimistic construction upon his myths. For Comes the satyrs are the shepherds of God's forest-bound sheep, and Nemesis is the minister of His justice. For Virgil it is the good (not the as yet untempted) that die young;[555] and Erasmus associates the poet's words with Memnon by setting them over against the myth of Tithonus.[556] Lactantius, too, would perhaps have been startled by what appears to be Bacon's comment on his words. He would not have been puzzled, however. Surely he would have nodded a " Res ita est ut dixit: omnia vanitas!" Would he have done so rightly? Is Bacon's pessimism mediæval? Not more so, I think, than the stern ethics of his mother. Bacon may have been a Lord Chancellor, but he was curiously unlike a lord and still less like an aristocrat. His meticulous piety, his shocked dislike of the nobility, his disapproval of Pygmalion: these are the solid virtues of the middle class. His animadversions on the multitude are no argument against me: Charles II would never have spoken of the good people of England as Bacon did. Bacon's natural bent was not that of the monk but of the scholar, and indeed I think the fact explains much. English scholarship was sedate enough, and Bacon's copious allusions to Cicero and Seneca do not reflect his own predilections alone. I question whether the austerity of his views is not more stoic than ascetic; whether, indeed, it is not, though unintentionally, more academic than sincere. In a measure it is neither religious nor philosophical, but personal and bitter. If Bacon was a precursor he was also a misfit, nursing an uncomprehended dream. He wore the robes of a Lord Chancellor; but the face that looks out at us from his portrait is the anxious face of the servant of the king.

I have said that Bacon was not singular in his times for his

---

[555] *Georgics*, III. 65 seq.   [556] *Adagiorum*, III. 9. 43.

belief in mythological symbolism; but he certainly was so for the astonishingly copious use which he made of it in his prose works. As I have shown elsewhere, the only one who approaches him as a symbolist is a poet, Spenser. The fact is not without significance. Much has been said about Bacon's indifference to literature as such, and his own utterances on the subject might seem decisive. So might those of Petrarch on the subject of his Italian poetry. I have said that Bacon's symbolism is not original. But what is mere lath and plaster in the *Mythologiæ* is a thing of life in the *Wisdom of The Ancients*. Surely it is not difficult to recognize the hand of an artist in this transformation. The interpretation is touched up, completed, fitted nicely to the myth, which acquires a new vividness as form and content blend in vital unity. The whole conception is made loftier, more spacious, more beautiful; and the simple beauty of word and cadence harmonizes with it perfectly. An artist is at work here; an artist who at times might be compared with Spenser. How extraordinary it would be if this man had possessed the unimaginative accuracy of the scientist. Photography is the negation of good painting. Spenser had a vision of moral law which uninspired persons have tried to reduce to a treatise on ethics; Bacon had a vision of scientific enlightenment. The beginner in painting is told to look through half-closed eyes, that he may grasp values and ignore commonplace details. The born painter is naturally unconscious of such details, to the exasperation of others and sometimes to the ruin of himself. I do not mean to define Bacon as solely a man of letters; a certain duality of nature urged him on in the path which his father had traced for him. Yet, though a painstaking counselor, he made his mark as an orator. And one senses the brilliant artist rather than the shrewd pleader in Johnson's famous tribute. It may be doubted whether Choate, for instance, would have felt elated if the jury he addressed had become absorbed in his eloquence.

Spenser is frequently declared to stand on the threshold of the Renaissance: looking forward, yet half-turning to listen to the voice of the mediæval past. Bacon stands beside him, and one reason for his wealth of picturesque symbolism is that he also has his ear turned to the past. At most he is a short step in advance. His symbolism is self-explanatory, while Spenser's is mediævally cryptic. His, concerns itself with the welfare of men; Spenser's, more exclusively with the welfare of souls. His, theorizes about experimentation; Spenser's, is purely speculative. There, however, I think the difference ends. Beside the picturesque confusion of mediæval romance you may see the perverse ingeniousnss of scholastic classification; beside mysticism, mysticism; beside deep piety, deep piety; beside a vision, a vision. Such is the backward-looking aspect which the minds of both men have in common. The other aspect shows Bacon and Spenser to us as equally children of the sixteenth century. Not for them the cool precision of a Copernicus, a Kepler, a Galileo. Bacon stands in a little group of theorists and dreamers, with Telesio, Campanella, Giordano Bruno. The poet and the essayist both breathe the spirit of a great enthusiasm; both speak a gorgeous language, rich with images and melodies, that the age of disenchantment was not to know. *The Wisdom of The Ancients* is not the *Faerie Queene,* but we shall not understand it if we think of it as something very different.

BIBLIOGRAPHY

In the following bibliography are listed the books mentioned in this monograph, and also some of the others I had in mind when I wrote the Introduction.

Adamson, J. W., *Pioneers of Modern Education*. Cambridge, Univ. Press, 1905.

Alanus de Insulis, *De planctu Naturæ*. See Migne's *Patrol. s. Lat.*, vol. 210. Paris, 1855.

Alciati, A., *Emblematum flumen*. Photo-lith facsimile by Holbein Society. Manchester, 1871.

Apollonius, *Argonauticorum libri quatuor*. Edited by J. Shaw. Oxford, 1779.

Apuleius, *Opera omnia*, vols. 1 and 2. In Valpy's *Script. Lat.* London, 1825.

Aristotle, *Aristotelis Stagiritæ Opera*. Lugduni, apud Antonium Vincentium, 1561.

———, *The Works of Aristotle Translated Into English*. Oxford, Clarendon Press, 1928.

Ascensius, J. B., *Opera Vergiliana docte et familiariter exposita*. Lugduni, 1517.

Ashmole, E., *Theatrum chemicum Britannicum*. London, Grismond, 1652.

Augustinus, *De civitate Dei*. See Migne's *Patrol. s. Lat.*, vol. 7. Paris, 1861-65.

Aurner, N. S., *Caxton: A Mirror of Fifteenth Century Letters*. Boston, Houghton Mifflin, 1926.

Ayala, B., *De iure et officiis bellicis*. Antwerp, 1597.

Bacon, F., *The Works of Francis Bacon*. Edited by J. Spedding, R. Ellis, and D. Heath. Boston, Houghton, Mifflin & Co.

Beckmann, J., *A History of Inventions, Discoveries, and Origins*. Translated by W. Johnston. London, 1846.

Belloni, A., *Il poema epico e mitologico*. Milan, Vallardi, 1928.

Benedictus Figulus, *A Golden and Blessed Casket of Nature's Marvels*. Translated by A. E. Waite. London, Elliott, 1893.

Berdan, J., *Early Tudor Poetry*. New York, Macmillan, 1920.

Berthelot, M. P., *Introduction à l'étude de la chimie*. Paris, Steinheil, 1889.

Bianchini, G. M., *Il pensiero filosofico di Torquato Tasso*. Padua, Drucker, 1897.

Bigg, G., *Christian Platonists of Alexandria*. Oxford, Clarendon Press, 1913.

Blount, T., *Glossographia*. London, Newcomb, 1670.

Boccaccio, G., *De genealogiis deorum gentilium*. Venice, A. De Zannis, 1511.

Baccaccio, G., *La genealogia degli dei de'gentili.* Translated by G. Betussi. Venice, Sansovino, 1569.

Boethius, *Opera omnia,* vol. 2. Paris, 1860.

Boissier, G., *La religion romaine d'Auguste aux Antonins.* Paris, 1874.

Bolton, H. C., *The Follies of Science at The Court of Rudolph II.* Milwaukee, Pharm. Rev. Pub. Co., 1904.

Browne, T., *Pseudodoxia Epidemica.* See *Works,* ed. by S. Wilkin, London, 1852, vols. 1, 2.

Bruno, G., *Le opere italiane di Giordano Bruno.* Edited by P. de Lagarde. Gottingen, 1888.

———, *Scripta.* Edited by A. Gfrorer. Stuttgart, 1836.

Burckhardt, J., *The Civilisation of The Renaissance in Italy.* Translated by S. G. Middlemore. New York, Macmillan, 1921.

Burton, R., *The Anatomy of Melancholy.* Edited by A. R. Shilleto. London, Bell, 1912.

Bush, D., *Mythology and The Renaissance Tradition in English Poetry.* London, Milford, 1932.

Cambridge History of English Literature.

Cambridge Modern History.

Capella, M., *De nuptiis philologiæ et Mercurii.* Edited by U. F. Kopp. Frankfort, Varrentrapp, 1836.

Cartari, V., *Vere e nove imagini degli dei degli antichi.* Padua, 1615.

Celler, L. (Leclercq), *Origines de l'Opera.* Paris, Didier, 1868.

Cicero, *Opera omnia,* vols. 2, 6, 7, 8. Edited by Baiter and Kayser. Leipzig, 1860.

Clemens of Alexandria, *Stromata.* See Migne's *Patrol. s. Gr.,* vols. 8 and 9.

Comes, Natalis, *Mythologiæ, sive explicationum fabularum.* Venice, 1581.

———, *Mythologiæ, sive explicationum fabularum.* Padua, 1616.

Comparetti, D., *Vergil in The Middle Ages.* Translated by E. Benecke. New York, Macmillan, 1895.

Cornutus, L. A., *Phurnuti liber de natura deorum.* See *Opuscula mythologica,* edited by J. Gale, Amsterdam, 1688.

Courthope, W. J., *A History of English Poetry.* London, Macmillan, 1910.

Decharme, P., *La critique des traditions religieuses chez les Grecs.* Paris, Picard, 1904.

De Wulf, M., *History of Mediæval Philosophy.* Translated by P. Coffey. London, 1909.

Diodorus Siculus, *Bibliotheca.* Paris, Mueller, 1855.

Dionysius the Areopagite, *Opera omnia.* See Migne's *Patrol. s. Gr.,* vols. 3 and 4.

Du Bartas, *Sepmaine on création du monde.* Paris, 1588.

Duff, J. W., *A Literary History of Rome in The Silver Age.* London, Unwin, 1927.

Dunbar, H. F., *Symbolism in Medieval Thought.* Yale University Press, 1929.

Erasmus, D., *Opera omnia,* vol. 1. Lyons, 1703.

Eusebius, *Preparatio Evangelica.* See Migne's *Patrol. s. Gr.,* vols. 19-24.

Evans, E. P., *Animal Symbolism in Ecclesiastical Architecture.* New

Ficino, M., *Sopra lo Amore*. Edited by G. Rensi. Lanciano, Carabba, 1914.

Flamini, F., *I significati reconditi della Commedia di Dante*. Livorno, Giusti, 1903.

Frazer, J. G., *The Golden Bough*. London, Macmillan, 1911.

Frezzi, F., *Il Quadriregio*. Edited by Artiziani and Pagliarini. Foligno, Campana, 1725.

Froude, J. A., *History of England from The Fall of Wolsey to The Death of Elizabeth*. New York, Scribner, 1875.

Fulgentius, *Opera omnia*. See Staveren, *Auctores mythographi Latini*. Lyons, 1742.

Gardiner, *History of England from The Accession of James I to The Disgrace of Chief-Justice Coke*. London, Hurst and Blackett, 1863.

Gesta Romanorum. Translated by C. Swan. London, 1824.

Gibbon, E., *The Decline and Fall of The Roman Empire* (See especially Chapter XVI). New York, Macmillan, 1914.

Giraldi, L. G., *De deis gentium Syntagmata XVII*. Lugduni, apud hœredes Jacobi Iunctæ, 1565.

Glover, T. R., *Virgil*. New York, Macmillan, 1912.

Golding, A., *The XV Bookes entitled Metamorphosis translated out of Latin into English meter*. London, 1593.

Gomperz, T., *Greek Thinkers*. Translated by Magnus and Berry. London, Murray, 1912.

Gosson, S., *The Schoole of Abuse*. Shakespeare Society Publications. London, 1841.

Graf, A., *Miti, leggende e superstizioni del Medio Evo*. Turin, Loescher, 1892.

———, *Roma nella memoria e nelle immaginazioni del Medio Evo*. Turin, Loescher, 1882.

Green, H., *Shakespeare and The Emblem-Writers*. London, 1870.

Greene, R., *Conny-Catching Tracts*. See *Life and Complete Works*, ed. by A. B. Grosart, London, 1881, vol. 10.

Greener, W. W., *The Gun and Its Development*. London, 1881.

Grote, G., *History of Greece* (Especially I. 16.). London, Murray, 1854.

Guy, H., *Histoire de la poesie française au XVI siècle*. Paris, Champion, 1910.

Gwatkin, *Early Church History*. London, Macmillan, 1909.

Haight, E. H., *Apuleius and His Influence*. New York, Longmans, 1927.

Halle, J., *Historiall Expostulation In Percy Society Publications*, XI.

Harington, J., *Apologie of Poetrie*. Introduction to translation of *Orlando Furioso*. London, 1634.

Heraclitus, *Heraclidis Pontici Allegoriæ Homeri*. See *Opuscula mythologica*, ed. J. Gale, Amsterdam, 1688.

Hersman, A. B., *Studies in Greek Allegorical Interpretation*. Univ. of Chicago Press, 1910.

Hesiod, *Theogony*, etc. Translated by T. Cooke. London, 1856.

Hoffding, *A History of Modern Philosophy*. Translated by E. Meyer. London, Macmillan, 1900.

Holy Bible.

Homer, *Opera omnia*. Translated by George Chapman. New York, Scribner's Sons.

Horatius Flaccus, *Opera omnia*. Edited by G. Long. London, 1874.

Hortis, A., *Studi sulle opere latine del Boccaccio*. Trieste, 1879.

Hughes, M. Y., *Virgilian Allegory in The Faerie Queene*. In P. M. L. A., Sept., 1929.

Hulme, F. E., *Natural History Lore and Legend*. London, Quaritch, 1895.

———, *Symbolism in Christian Art*. New York, Macmillan, 1899.

Hyginus, *Poeticon astronomicon*. See Staveren, *Auctores mythographi Latini*. Lyons, 1742.

Inge, W. R., *The Philosophy of Plotinus* (Especially I. 30, 78, 110). New York, Longmans, 1918.

Irenæus, *Contra hæreses*. See Migne's *Patrol. s. Gr.*, vol. 7.; or *Ante-Nicene Christ. Libr.*, vols. 5, 9.

Irving, D., *The History of Scotish Poetry*. Edinburgh, Edmonston, 1861.

Isidore of Seville, *Etymologiæ*. Edited by F. W. Otto. Leipzig, 1833.

Janus Lacinius, *The New Pearl of Great Price*. Translated by A. E. Waite. London, Elliott, 1894.

Julian, *Works*, vol. 2. Translated with notes from Petau, etc. London, 1798.

Justin Martyr, See Migne's *Patrol. s. Gr.*, vol. 6; or translation by Dods in *Ante-Nicene Christ. Libr.*

Juvenal, *Satiræ*. Edited by A. Macleane. London, 1857.

Kopp, H., *Die Alchemy in Alterer und Neuer Zeit*. Heidelberg, Winter, 1886.

Lactantius, L. C., *Divinarum institutionum*. See Migne's *Patrol. s. Lat.*, vols. 6 and 7; or *Ante Nicene Christ. Libr.*, vols. 21, 22.

Lactantius, P., *Commentarii in Thebaida*. See Bode, *Scriptores rerum mythicarum Latini*, Cellis, 1834.

Landino, C., *Comento sopra la Comedia di Dante*. Florence, 1507.

Legouais, C., *Ovide moralisé*. Edited by De Boer. Amsterdam, Muller, 1915.

Lemmi, C., *The Symbolism of The Classical Episodes in The Faerie Queene*. In *Philological Quarterly* VIII. 3, 1929.

Lodge, T., *Defence of Poetry, Music and Stage Plays*. Shakespeare Society Publications. London, 1853.

———, *A Learned Summarie upon The Famous Poeme of William of Salust Lord of Bartas*. London, Nevill, 1638.

Lobeck, *Aglaophamus*. Leipzig, 1829.

G. de Lorris and J. de Meun, *Le roman de la rose*. Edited by Marteau. Paris, 1878.

Lucian, *Works*. Translated by W. Tooke. London, 1820.

Lucretius, *De rerum natura*. Edited by G. Wakefield. London, 1823.

———, *De rerum natura*. Edited by G. Wakefield, translated by J. Munro. Cambridge, 1866.

Lydgate, *The Fall of Princes*. Edited by H. Bergen. Oxford Univ. Press, 1924.

Lydgate, *The Assembly of Gods*. Edited by O. L. Triggs. Chicago, Univ. of Chicago Press, 1895.

Lyly, J., *Euphues and His England*. Edited by E. Arber. London, 1868.

Macaulay, T. B., *Lord Bacon*.

Machiavelli, N., *Discorsi sopra la prima Deca di Tito Livio*. Milan, Sonzogno, 1930.

———, *Il Principe*. Edited by M. Scherillo. Milan, Hoepli, 1924.

———, *Dell'arte della guerra*. Milan, Sonzogno, 1930.

McIntyre, J., *Giordano Bruno*. London, Macmillan, 1903.

Macrobius, *Opera omnia*. Edited by F. Eyssenhardt. Leipzig, 1868.

Maier, M., *Atalanta fugiens*. Oppenheim, Galler, 1618.

Maurus, R., *De universo:* See Migne's *Patrol. s. Lat.*, vols. 107-112.

Maximus Tyrius, *Dissertationes*. Edited by Reiske. Leipzig, 1774.

Mela, P., *De situ orbis*. Edited by Barbari. Leipzig, 1806.

Meyer, E. S., *History of Chemistry*. Translated by G. M'Gowan. New York, Macmillan, 1891.

Michel, A., *Histoire de l'art* (Especially I. 1. 17). Paris, Colin, 1905.

Monnier, P., *Le Quattrocento*. Paris, Perrin, 1912.

Montaigne, M., *Les essais de Montaigne*. Paris, Lemerre, 1872.

Morley, H., *English Writers*. London, Cassell, 1887-1895.

Mott, L. F., *The System of Courtly Love*. Boston, Ginn, 1896.

Nitchie, E., *Vergil and The English Poets*. New York, Columbia Univ. Press, 1919.

Onosander, *De imperatoris officio*. Edited by A. Koechly. Leipzig, 1860.

Origen, *Contra Celsum*. See Migne's *Patrol. s. Gr.*, vols. 11-17; or *Ante-Nicene Christ. Libr.*, vols. 10, 23.

Orosius, *Historia adversus paganos*. See Migne's *Patrol. s. Lat.*, vol. 31.

Orphic Hymns. Translated by T. Taylor. Chiswick, 1824.

Osgood, C. G., *Boccaccio on Poetry*. Princeton Univ. Press, 1930.

Ovidius Naso, *Carmina*. Edited by A. Riese. Leipzig, 1871.

Palæphatus, *De incredibilibus historiis*. See *Opuscula mythologica*, ed. by J. Gale, Amsterdam, Wetsten, 1688.

Paracelsus, *Opera omnia*. Geneva, 1658.

Pausanias, *Description of Greece*. Translated by T. Taylor. London, 1824.

Pernety, A. J., *Dictionnaire Mytho-Hermetique*. Paris, 1787.

Petit de Julleville, L., *Histoire de la Langue et de la littérature française*. Paris, Colin, 1896.

Petrarch, F., *Canzoniere*. Edited by Carducci and Ferrari. Florence, Sansoni, 1928.

———, *Letters*. Translated by G. Fracassetti. Florence, 1863-70.

Physiologus. Translated by J. Carlill. New York, Dutton, 1924.

Plato, *The Dialogues of Plato*. Translated by B. Jowett. Oxford Univ. Press, 1924.

Plinius Secundus, *Naturalis historiæ*. Edited by Hardouin. Paris, Lemaire, 1827.

Plotinos, *Complete Works*. Translated by K. S. Guthrie. Alpine, Platonist Press, 1918.

Plutarch, *Opera omnia*. Paris, 1624.

Polybius, *History*. Translated by J. Hampton. Oxford, 1823.
Pontano, G., *Opera*. Venice, 1513.
Porphyry, *De antro nympharum*. Translated by T. Taylor. London, 1823.
Post, C. R., *Mediæval Spanish Allegory*. Cambridge, Harvard Univ. Press, 1915.
Proclus, *Commentary on Plato*. See Plato, *Works*, tr. by Sydenham and Taylor, London, 1804, vol. 1.
Propertius, *Carmina*. Edited by A. Paley. London, 1872.
Pugin, A. W., *Glossary of Ecclesiastical Ornament*. London, 1868.
Rabelais, F., *Les Œuvres de François Rabelais*. Edited by Lefranc. Paris, Champion, 1912.
Rajna, P., *Le fonti dell'Orlando Furioso*. Florence, Sansoni, 1900.
Redgrove, H. S., *Alchemy Ancient and Modern*. London, Rider, 1911.
Ronsard, P., *Œuvres complètes*. Edited by P. Blanchemain. Paris, 1857.
Roscher, W. H., *Lexikon der griechischen Mythologie*. Leipzig, 1884.
Rutherford, J., *The Troubadours*. London, Smith, Elder & Co., 1873.
Sabinus (G. Schuler), *Fabularum Ovidii interpretatio*. Leipzig, 1559.
Saintsbury, G. E., *The Flourishing of Romance and The Rise of Allegory*. New York, Scribner's Sons, 1897.
Sandys, G., *Ovid's Metamorphoses, Englished, Mythologiz'd, and Represented in Figures*. London, 1640.
Sandys, J. E., *A History of Classical Scholarship*. Cambridge, Univ. Press, 1903.
Scaliger, J. C., *Poetices*. Editio quarta. In bibliopolio commeliniano, 1607.
Schevill, R., *Ovid and The Renascence in Spain*. Univ. of California Press, 1913.
Schofield, W., *English Literature from The Norman Conquest to Chaucer*. New York, Macmillan.
Seneca, *Opera*, vols. 2 and 3. Edited by C. Fickert. Leipzig, 1842.
Seneca, L. A., *Workes, both morrall and naturall*. Translated by T. Lodge. London, 1614.
Servius, H. M., *Commentarii in Virgilium*. Edited by H. A. Lion. Gottingen, 1826.
Schoell, F. L., *Mythologistes italiens et poètes elisabethains*. In *Rev. de lit. comp.*, I. 1924.
Sidney, P., *A Defence of Poesy*. Cambridge, 1831.
Spedding, J., *Francis Bacon and His Times*. Boston, Houghton Mifflin & Co.
Spingarn, J. E., *A History of Literary Criticism in The Renaissance*. New York, Columbia Univ. Press, 1912.
Stewart, J. A., *The Myths of Plato*. New York, Macmillan, 1905.
Strabo, *Geography*. New York, Putnam Sons, 1917.
Sudre, L., *Publii Ovidii Nasonis Metamorphoseon libros*. Thèse, Faculté des lettres de Paris, 1893.
Symonds, J. A., *The Renaissance in Italy*. New York, Holt, 1888.
Tacitus, *Opera*. Edited by F. Haase. Leipzig, Tauchnitz, 1855.
Tasso, T., *Il messaggiero*. Venice, Giunti, 1582.

Thorndike, L., *A History of Magic and Experimental Science*. London, Macmillan, 1923.

Thucydides, *History of The Peloponnesian War* (Especially II. 15). Translated by H. Dale. New York, Harper, 1860.

Thynne, F., *Emblems and Epigrams*. Publications of Early English Text Society, no. 64.

Ticknor, G., *History of Spanish Literature*. Boston, Houghton Mifflin, 1891.

Timbs, J., *Curiosities of Science*. London, Lockwood, 1865.

———, *Stories of Inventors and Discoverers*. London, Lockwood, 1863.

Tiraboschi, A., *Storia della letteratura italiana*. Milan, 1822.

Toffanin, G., *Il Cinquecento*. Milan, Vallardi, 1929.

Trabalza, C., *La critica letteraria*. Milan, Vallardi, 1915.

Trivet, N., *Nicolai Triveti in Ovidii Metamorphoses Commentarii*. Mod. Lang. Assoc. of Am., col. of facsimiles, no. 50, 1926.

Upham, A. H., *The French Influence in English Literature*. New York, Columbia Univ. Press, 1911.

Valeriano, J. P., *Hieroglyphica*. Francofurti ad Moenum, Kempferr, 1614.

Vatican Mythographers. See *Scriptores rerum mythicarum Latini*, edited by G. Bode Cellis, 1834.

Villari, P., *Niccolò Machiavelli*. London, Paul & Co., 1878.

Vergilius Maro, *Opera omnia*. Edited by T. L. Papillon. Oxford, Clarendon Press, 1892.

Vives, J. L., *Opera*. Basileæ, 1555.

Voigt, G., *Petrarque, Boccace, et les Débuts de l'Humanisme*. Translated by Le Monnier. Paris, Welter, 1894.

Warton, T., *History of English Poetry*. London, 1840.

Watson, F., *The Ante-Nicene Apologies*. Cambridge, Johnson, 1870.

Whittaker, T., *The Neo-Platonists*. Cambridge, Univ. Press, 1928.

———, *Macrobius*. Cambridge, Univ. Press, 1923.

Wilkins, E. A., *The Chicago MS. of The Genealogia Deorum*. Chicago, Chicago Univ. Press, 1927.

Wilson, T., *The Arte of Rhetorique*. Edited by G. H. Mair. Oxford, Clarendon Press, 1909.

Withington, R., *English Pageantry*. Cambridge, Harvard Univ. Press, 1918.

Zeller, E., *Stoics, Epicureans, and Sceptics*. Translated by Reichel. London, Longmans, 1892.

———, *A Historical Outline of Greek Philosophy*. Translated by S. F. Alleyne. New York, Holt, 1890.

INDEX

Achelous, 159-161.
Acteon, 187.
Adonis, 13, 34.
Æneid, 9, 19, 20.
Æsculapius, 34, 39, 118-122.
Alchemy, 13, 14, 42, 77-120, 147-149, 155.
Alciati, 21, 143, 188.
Anaxagoras, 133.
Apollo, 17, 21, 33, 37.
Apuleius, 10, 29.
Areopagite, 16, 72.
Aristotle, 8, 15, 18, 27, 50, 125, 127.
Atalanta, 104-109.
Atlas, 36, 122.
Augustine, 11, 19.

Bacchus, 21, 31, 47, 202-207.
Bartas, 20-25.
Bercuire, 9.
Bible, 8, 19, 73, 97, 140, 145, 195.
Boccaccio, 1, 9-12, 21, 48, 65, 66, 119, 128, 129, 152, 158, 164, 172, 176, 182, 184, 188, 195, 197, 210.
Boethius, 10, 21.
Briareus, 172.
Browne, 41.
Bruno, 7, 24.

Capella, 1.
Cartari, 1, 21.
Cassandra, 191.
Centaurs, 20.
Ceres, 38, 47.
Chaucer, 191.
Chrysippus, 41.
Cicero, 8, 10, 21, 22, 26, 27, 41, 92, 178, 193.
Coelum, 20, 49-55.
Comes, 1, 2-7, 21, 27, 44, 45, 51, 58, 59, 63, 67, 70, 90, 91, 97, 102, 104, 116, 122, 130-133, 137, 142, 152, 159, 162, 164, 165, 168, 173, 178, 179, 184, 186, 187, 189, 194, 198, 201, 205, 206, 207.
Cornutus, 6, 29, 165.
Cupid, 5, 39, 55-61.
Cyclops, 167-169.

Daedalus, 37, 47, 109.
Democritus, 25, 50.
Deucalion, 98-101.
Diana, 17, 24.
Diodorus, 21, 26, 28, 115.

Diomedes, 161.

Empedocles, 27, 29, 50, 133.
Endymion, 180-183.
Eolus, 124-127.
Erasmus, 21.
Erichthonius, 103.
Euhemerus, 11.
Eusebius, 11.

Fathers, 10, 11, 21, 26, 28.
Ficino, 6, 15-19, 21, 26.
Fulgentius, 9, 10, 21, 26, 124, 128, 155, 157, 164, 188, 198.

Giraldi, 1, 21, 26.
Graces, 19.
Griffin, 22.

Hades, 35.
Heraclitus, 28.
Hercules, 31, 34, 38, 48.
Herodotus, 21, 28.
Hesiod, 55.
Higinus, 26.
Homer, 19, 27.
Horace, 10, 26, 152.
Hydra, 47.
Hylas, 127.

Iambe, 190.
Icarus, 109-117.
Isidore, 9, 10, 21.
Ixion, 20, 34, 101-103.

Julian, 32, 40, 43.
Juno, 3, 10, 13, 17, 24, 28, 29.
Jupiter, 3, 4, 10, 17, 20, 28, 29, 34, 38, 47, 179.
Juvenal, 177, 180.

Lactantius, 4, 10, 152, 186, 206, 207.
Landino, 19.
Legouais, 9, 42.
Lethe, 47.
Lucian, 26, 28, 117.
Lucretius, 21, 27, 55, 61, 76, 84, 85, 135, 153.

Machiavelli, 159, 160, 163, 166, 167, 172, 175.
Macrobius, 1, 6, 10, 21, 26, 33-35, 53, 57, 62, 63, 64, 203, 205.
Maier, 143.

Mantuan, 27.
Mars, 14, 17, 29.
Maximus Tyrius, 29, 43.
Medusa, 20, 37, 39.
Memnon, 194-196.
Mercury, 13, 17, 29, 34, 47.
Mermaids, 24.
Metis, 164-167.
Midas, 189.
Minerva, 17, 28, 34, 47.
Montaigne, 7.
Muses, 17, 18, 48, 199.
Mythra, 31, 32.

Narcissus, 20, 183-185.
Nemesis, 176-177, 207.
Neo-Platonists, 10, 14-20, 182, 203, 204.
Neptune, 3, 10, 11.

Onosander, 159.
Orpheus, 12, 27, 55, 61, 152-156.
Ovid, 76, 145, 176, 191.

Palæphatus, 26, 28.
Pan, 10, 13, 29, 38, 47, 61-74, 126, 169.
Pandora, 30, 170, 171.
Paracelsus, 76.
Paris, 47, 196.
Pausanias, 1, 6, 21, 26, 38.
Pentheus, 188.
Perseus, 156-159.
Petrarch, 9, 16, 21, 42.
Phaeton, 47.
Plato, 8, 14, 21, 25, 27, 70, 72, 74, 134, 139, 152, 154, 156, 169, 203.
Pliny, 6, 10, 21, 22, 26.
Plotinos, 21, 30-32, 139.
Plutarch, 1, 6, 21, 22, 26, 29, 160.
Pluto, 4, 19.
Polybius, 28.
Porphyry, 31, 40, 43.

Posidonius, 154.
Proclus, 30, 40.
Prometheus, 47, 128-141, 169.
Proserpine, 74-91.
Proteus, 28, 91-98.
Pygmalion, 191.

Rabelais, 9.
Sabinus, 27, 39.
Sandys, 12, 25-27, 161.
Saturn, 4, 14, 20, 29, 49.
Satyrs, 39, 196.
Scaliger, 27.
Scylla, 36, 48, 117, 123.
Seneca, 22, 27, 154.
Servius, 1, 10, 21, 27, 35-38, 62, 125, 128, 152, 164, 186, 195.
Sirens, 22, 36, 196.
Sister of Giants, 173-176.
Sphinx, 142-145.
Strabo, 4, 21, 26, 28, 161.
Styx, 185-187.
Sybils, 12.

Tacitus, 177.
Tantalus, 35, 48.
Tasso, 6, 21.
Telesio, 204.
Thomas Aquinas, 72.
Thucydides, 28.
Thynne, 48, 180.
Tithonus, 192-194.
Trivet, 9.
Troubadours, 9.
Typhon, 126, 162-164.

Ulysses, 29, 31, 178.

Valeriano, 1, 21, 22, 27.
Venus, 5, 14, 17, 20, 29, 34.
Virgil, 73, 119, 145, 176, 186, 189.
Vives, 21, 27, 43.
Vulcan, 17, 47.

Printed in the United States
99730LV00005B/9/A